FEARLESS
MEDIA

FEARLESS MEDIA

Survival of the Fittest
in Today's Media 2.0 World

PETER CSATHY

Chairman, CREATV Media

www.creatv.media

Published by CREATV Media
www.creatv.media
peter@creatv.media

ISBN 978-0-9980132-2-0

Contents

Preface ix

Introduction 1

I Media 2.0 (18) Year in Review 7

1 2018's Media 2.0 Headline Stories (A Year of M&A, #METOO, Fake News & Fear ... Lots of Fear) 9

2 2018's "Fearless Five" Media 2.0 Companies 15

II How Did We Get Here? 23

3 History Repeats? 25

4 The Day the Music (Business) Died – A Cautionary Tale ("Bye, Bye, Music Revenue Pie") 27

5 Google's Shot Seen Around the World (YouTube's "Lazy Sunday") 33

6 Netflix Seized the Day (The Rise of Premium OTT Video) 37

7 Apple Strikes Again! (The iPhone's Mobile-Driven, Short-Form Video Revolution) 43

8 Facebook – The Original Social Animal (& The Rise of Social Media) 47

**III And So, Here We Are
– The State of Media 2.0 in 2019
(Cross-Platform, Crowded & Confusing)** 51

Part III, Section 1 Setting the Stage 53

9 Welcome to Hollywood's New "Golden Age" (It's the Content, Stupid!) 55

Part III, Section 2 Today's Multi-Platform Video World   **61**

10   Netflix and Other Premium OTT Players (Or Wannabes) ("The New Faces of the Content Industry")   63

11   Disney v. Netflix – What it Means (And is the Threat Real?)   107

12   HBO Now, ESPN+ & The Unbundled Stand-Alone OTT Video Players (Less Taste, More (Ful)Filling?)   115

13   Digital-First, Millennial-Focused Video Companies (The Artists Formerly Known as "MCNs")   127

14   All Media is Social (Or is it the Other Way Around?)   161

15   Don't Forget About the Brands! (Or, "And Now a Word … I Mean, Video … From Our Sponsors")   171

16   The Mainstreaming of Live Video Streaming   175

Part III, Section 3 Today's Streaming-First Music World   **181**

17   The Rise & Dominance of Music Streaming   183

18   The Music Industry's YouTube "Problem"   187

19   Music's Streaming Wars (Can Any Pure-Play Win Against the Behemoths?)   193

20   A Special Word to Music Artists ("Don't Fear the Streaming Reaper")   209

Part III, Section 4 Our Immersive New Media 2.0 World of XR – VR, AR & MR   **213**

21   The XR Market – An Overview   215

22   VR – The Virtual Gets Very Real   219

23   AR – Significantly Augmenting its Early Success   229

24   VR, AR & The Great Unknown   239

Part III, Section 5 Games & Esports   **245**

25   Esports & E-Thletes   247

PART III, SECTION 6 OFFLINE, LIVE REAL WORLD EXPERIENCES   **253**

26   LIVE EXPERIENCES – THE OFT-FORGOTTEN MULTI-PLATFORM
PLANK (& THE ONLINE/OFFLINE VIRTUOUS CYCLE)   255

27   INNOVATORS IN IMMERSIVE LIVE EXPERIENCES ("THERE'S NO
PLACE LIKE DOME")   263

PART III, SECTION 7 SOCIAL IMPACT – THE STEALTH PLANK, RISING ... **269**

28   MEDIA 2.0'S UNPRECEDENTED POWER TO MOBILIZE & DO
"GOOD"   271

**IV   2019 & BEYOND
– WHERE MEDIA 2.0 IS GOING**   **275**

29   MY TOP 10 MEDIA 2.0 PREDICTIONS FOR 2019   277

30   VC PREDICTIONS – FOLLOW THE MONEY (WHERE MEDIA &
TECH INVESTORS ARE PLACING THEIR BETS)   291

**V   HOW TO ACT FEARLESSLY IN 2019
AND BEYOND**   **303**

31   MEDIA 2.0'S TOP 10 LESSONS & STRATEGIES   305

EPILOGUE A PERSONAL NOTE FOR OUR INCREASINGLY DIGITAL, VIR-
TUAL AGE   315

APPENDIX MEDIA 2.0 LAW SCHOOL (NEWS YOU CAN USE)   319

APPENDIX 1 CREATORS – "MUST KNOW" LEGAL ISSUES WHEN USING
MUSIC BY JORDAN BROMLEY, PARTNER, MANATT PHELPS &
PHILLIPS   321

APPENDIX 2 MEDIA 2.0 INVESTMENT AND M&A (KEY ISSUES TO CON-
SIDER FROM BOTH SIDES OF THE TABLE) BY GREG AKSELRUD,
PARTNER, STUBBS ALDERTON & MARKILES AND SAM CREATV
VENTURES   327

Preface

ERE I am, nearly 30 years into the long and winding road of my ca-reer in media, entertainment and technology – a "curiosity-driven career" that I certainly didn't map out. But, precisely because I didn't map it out, I have had a front row seat to a broad swath of technology's ongoing and increasingly relentless transformation of the media and en-tertainment business.

My wife and I frequently joke that I am a bit like Jerry Maguire, but in the new tech-transformed media and entertainment world. Remember that great Cameron Crowe movie of the same name? Jerry was the sports agent who was always there at the right time – in great moments of sig-nificance – but not quite in the center of the picture *(like the scene where Jerry's body is cut off and only slightly visible in a picture standing next to quarterback Drew Bledsoe during the NFL draft)*. That's me. I was there at the beginning of mass online, social community – just about to be hired by my former Universal Studios colleague Steve Hansen who had become the #2 at web-based community builder GeoCities. But, Yahoo!'s acqui-sition got in the way *(while Hansen made a cool $40 million with one year of service ... sorry Steve, but that news is public!)*. Here was one of my very first business lessons. Timing. It may not be "everything," but it certainly is a lot of things. I had missed that one by only a matter of a days *(should have taken Steve's call a couple weeks earlier!)*.

Then, I was on the front lines of the Napster-driven *(the illegal one)* dig-ital transformation of the music industry, serving as president and COO of music pioneer Musicmatch, which was ultimately acquired by Yahoo!

for $160 million *(the late David Goldberg, then at Yahoo!, was a key driver of that deal)*. I led a business development team that invented the legitimate on-demand music streaming world that we all know and love today. We were amongst the first (if not *the* first) to negotiate those on-demand music licensing deals. We believed in an on-demand anytime, anywhere world 15 years before where we are today with Spotify, Apple Music and others – and when virtually no one (certainly not many in the music business) believed in what they then called the "rental" model, as opposed to "owning" the music. We asked them at the time whether there really is any difference if your music is available to you on demand anytime? We certainly didn't think so – and apparently we were right, given streaming's overwhelming dominance today.

After Musicmatch, a brilliant young mind approached me to partner with him to create a new kind of media company – a company fueled by user-generated content. Kind of like YouTube … very much like YouTube … in fact, it *was* YouTube *before* YouTube … or anything like it. We called our company TV Drive, and the visionary behind it was Dmitry Shapiro. Dmitry and I pitched several venture capitalists (VCs), including *the* VC (blue chip Sequoia) that instead funded a small little company called YouTube just a few months later *(hmmm, did we give them the idea?)*. No one (other than Sequoia) "got it." None of the VCs understood how democratized user-generated content (UGC) could amount to anything. So, we didn't get the funding. YouTube did.

And, Dmitry? He ultimately continued to drive his vision – eventually got the funding – but got there second. It didn't matter that TV Drive (which ultimately became Veoh) eventually built a massive audience of its own. All that mattered was that Veoh wasn't first. And that it was alone in the world, with no Google-like sugar daddy behind it. As a result of that fortuity (or lack thereof), YouTube won, while Veoh was Veoh*(ver)*. Again, timing in action – this time, as a result of VC and strategic in-action. *(In* *an interesting twist, Dmitry subsequently spent several years at Google and is now pioneering again as a startup entrepreneur for his company Metaverse, which I discuss later in Chapter 23).*

Next stop, CEO of SightSpeed. Right. You never heard of it, but we were pioneers again. We were Skype video and Apple FaceTime before those existed, and before anyone believed that consumer live social video chat would amount to anything, or that enough of us would feel comfortable doing it. Well, I believed – and we ultimately sold the company to Logitech with an unheard of 3X investor return during the worldwide financial market meltdown of 2008 *(am proud of that … no, not the world collapsing, but our result in spite of it).* Chalk that one up to our VC's unwavering belief in the power of our team and technology *(thanks Roger Strauch and Dan Miller of Roda Group!)* and my team's relentless tenacity *(something that virtually all successful entrepreneurs have).*

And now, we can't even imagine a world without personal, social live video streaming playing a crucial role in our overall communications arsenal. Certainly our kids can't *(what would they do with all their time?).* Roger and Dan were right. And, patient – something all too rare in the world of venture capital. And, it paid off. Other VCs would have pulled the plug on SightSpeed too early and missed out on a big win.

Ahh yes. Timing. And, the occasional need for patience. There's another lesson for you ….

Then, Sorenson Media, where I served as president & CEO for nearly 4 years. It is Sorenson Media technology that enabled mass market premium online video in the first place. We were pioneers. Innovators.

For the past five years, I dropped the operator role (a decade of that does that to you). I took all these disparate and diverse threads from my own personal business "story" and weaved them together to form **CREATV**

Media, a media, entertainment and technology-focused business development, advisory and investment firm. My business is essentially comprised of three parts: (1) working closely with a handful of the best and most innovative media and tech entrepreneurs and companies as a board member or advisor to accelerate growth, optimize results, and maximize impact; (2) identifying and developing new strategic business opportunities and facilitating game-changing transactions and M&A; and (3) making direct venture investments. Writing, speaking, mentoring, working with incredible talent (artists, creators, athletes) to help them tell their stories, and supporting causes that generate positive impact and change, are all "extra credit."

As a result of my somewhat unique palette, I am fortunate to always be meeting the innovators and influencers in media, entertainment and technology. Listening to their stories. Telling their stories to others. Connecting the dots. Respecting those who are passionate and fearless about the opportunities. Helping those who are bold and confident enough to acknowledge that they can use the help. Out of strength. Not weakness. And, I engage with them daily, so I find myself smack dab in the midst of those on the bleeding edge. Keeps me fresh.

I also engage regularly with the press and other influencers who see many things and offer their own perspectives. That keeps me even fresher. The common thread for me is innovation, positivity and passion. I work with those who prioritize these traits (and want to have some fun in the process). All of them want to change the world for the better. Innovative media and tech are the means to that end.

All along the way, I have also been a writer. I have published two Amazon bestselling books – *Media 2.0(17)* and *Media 2.0(18)*. Contributed regularly to leading media, entertainment and tech publications, including *Variety*, *TechCrunch*, and *Billboard*. And, have blogged since 2006, with nearly 1,800 posts under my belt on my own *Digital Media Update*. I have collected stories, lots of them, as a result of my somewhat unique broad-based old media/new media window on the world and the disruptive forces transforming it, and my direct access to key stakeholders and influencers behind them. I have invested countless hours in trying to make sense of it all *(drinking gallons of coffee and waking up far too early in the process ... although I find myself reaching more and more for green tea)*.

After writing my last book, I swore I wouldn't do it again. Yet, here I am for round 3. Clearly, a glutton for punishment. This time, I've completely reimagined and significantly expanded my earlier writings. I've also added several entirely new, "evergreen" chapters that should stand the test of time. So, even if you read *Media 2.0 (17)* and *Media 2.0 (18)*, this is very much a new book that is deserving of a new title. The earlier title simply no longer "fit" *(besides, my wife never liked it anyway and that's reason enough!)*. This book, unlike the ones before it, is fundamentally a call to action. Its underlying, core theme is the need to take bold and audacious action in our brave new tech-driven media and entertainment world (what I call "**Media 2.0**"). In other words, the need to be *fearless*!

That's why I call it ***FEARLESS MEDIA***.

Here's how I lay it out.

Part I brings the past year forward – front and center – and recaps the big media and tech stories of 2018, giving critical context to the rest of the book. I also christen my "**Fearless Five**" – the five Media 2.0 companies that, in my view, made the boldest and most audacious moves of the past year. Amazon topped my list in 2017. Who tops my third class for 2018? Read on ....

But, how did we get there? What led us to 2018's Media 2.0 realities (including its leaders and innovators)? Part II takes you on a journey through the ghosts of "traditional" Media 1.0 past. It is a tale of action and inaction. Of fearlessness and fear. Of winners and losers. It sets the stage for everything else.

In Part III, I discuss Media 2.0's current state of play that resulted from the forces that drove our journey in Part II – and offer a *snapshot* of what it looked like as 2018 ended and 2019 began. Because I can't cover it all, I focus my discussion on the worlds of video, music, new immersive technologies (virtual reality, augmented reality, mixed reality), games and eSports – without forgetting that live "offline" events and experiences are fundamental elements of any true multi-platform story. I identify today's innovators and leaders and discuss both how they broke out of the pack, yet remain vulnerable due to Media 2.0's accelerating rate of change. Remember, no one has it all figured out. Even today's winners must continuously innovate, and their actions and experiments offer clues to where the world of technology-infused media and entertainment is going.

In Part IV, I look forward to 2019 and beyond and offer my annual Media 2.0 predictions. I also present the thoughts of leading VCs. Last year, I specifically predicted that SiriusXM would buy Pandora. And, voila, it did. Was happy with that one.

Part V ties it all together. Here I discuss lessons learned and identify concrete strategies and actions that flow from the book's earlier pages, so that you can become a Media 2.0 superhero (perhaps inspired by comics genius Stan Lee, a creative visionary we lost as 2018 ended).

By the time you finish this book, you will be a Media 2.0 maven. That's my promise to you. *Bold and audacious?* Well, you gotta be in Media 2.0 land.

Three important things to keep in mind as you read this book.

First, remember that it is intended to be a *snapshot*, the details of which will blur by the day due to the frenetic pace of these digital times. I take my snapshot here as of late November 2018 due to publishing realities, which means that several elements of my discussion may have changed by the time you read this. As one glaring example, in last year's *Media 2.0 (18)* book, I praised Kevin Spacey for his innovative spirit and laid out his thoughts about OTT video in connection with his pioneering role in Netflix's *House of Cards*. Well, what a difference a year makes. Soon after I published, he fell from grace (to put it mildly). Suffice it to say that this, right here, is the only reference to Spacey now (apart from mentioning him one more time in my 2018 year in review chapter, for all the wrong reasons).

But, Spacey's screeching 180-degree change in industry fortunes in 2018 underscores the need for and utility of a book like this. Yes, it is a bit anachronistic to write a fixed book about an industry that frequently changes significantly (and sometimes even radically) on a weekly, if not daily, basis. At the same time, many of its lessons are universal, timeless, and never lose relevance. At a minimum, it serves as an industry time capsule and guidebook.

Second, let me be clear. I identify companies that *I believe* are leading players and bold innovators in our new Media 2.0 world, based on my own analyses and conversations with industry insiders and influencers. That means that subjectivity permeates these pages. Some of you will agree with my perspectives and certain names and companies I include in (or omit from) this book. But others won't. That's all part of the fun, though. Stirs up some great debates. And, great debates lead to new perspectives. New perspectives lead to new ideas. New ideas lead to innovation. And, innovation leads to transformation. That's ultimately what this book is all about – transformation of the world of media and entertainment at the hands of evolving technology fueled by bold action.

Finally, solid, credible sources support every factoid. Sometimes I identify them, but many times I do not. Not necessarily conventional, I know. But, this is intended to be a relatively informal and entertaining "read," so rest assured those sources exist. If you have any doubts about any of them, just reach out to me.

So, with those three things out of the way – and in the illustrious words of CNN's resident "everyman" Chris Cuomo – *"Let's get after it!"*

INTRODUCTION

WE live in a brave new digital world – where technology drives new transformational ways to connect, communicate, share, sell, entertain, influence and impact. Disruptive new ways to tell stories, find an audience for those stories, and enable that audience to engage with those stories (and with each other).

Just look around you. Everyone you see right now is likely online, looking down, desperately clutching his or her mobile phone – and holding it virtually every waking hour (and increasingly while falling asleep). Just think about it. 93% of millennials use their phones in bed. Why? To share their deepest, most personal thoughts, "connect" (albeit, virtually), and consume ever-increasing volumes of content. Some of that content is social. Some educational. Some is motivational and inspirational. Others, purely commercial. Much of it is entertainment, and much of it is increasingly entertaining.

All of that content – no matter how good, bad, commercial, and impactful (or not) – is media that now, for the first time, has the opportunity to reach virtually anyone, anytime, anywhere on the planet over the Internet and through that mobile device. Through that extension of the self. Our lifeline in this borderless world. After all, we now live in a world with more mobile devices (7 billion) than people on our planet. Just think about that reach.

I call this technology-infused content revolution "**Media 2.0**" – and its accelerated pace over just the past few years has been astounding. Media 2.0 impacts us all. In ways we realize, but many (*most?*) we don't, and won't until we look back years from now. It's up to content creators and the ecosystem that supports them – including business executives, marketers, distributors, investors, technology enablers, students – to seize that opportunity and make content that is impactful, effective, engaging. And, if creators successfully accomplish those goals, then here's the most exciting part – those creators will not be alone in getting the message out. Now, invisible armies of messengers will do that for them. I like what I see, hear or read, and I tell two friends … and so on … and so on. I, on the receiving end, become the rebroadcaster.

Here's just one example of that power. We share a clever little video en masse – which then goes viral – and transform a tiny upstart e-commerce company into quasi-men's lifestyle media company Dollar Shave Club that Unilever acquired in 2016 for $1 billion. Or, together we transformed a lonely kid in Sweden into social media superstar PewDiePie with 50 million subscribers around the planet and a payday of well over $15 million in 2016. And then, in 2017, we transformed him right out of our collective psyches as a result of his subsequent anti-Semitic and racist rants. Yes, the gods giveth, and the gods taketh away! (a highly valuable lesson for all of our kids in our unforgiving *"what happens online, stays online"* Media 2.0 world).

Of course, as with any tectonic *("tech-tonic"?)* shift, potential seismic downsides exist. After all, technology – which enabled creation of the mass media and entertainment business in the first place – has threatened it ever since. Evolving technology, by its very nature, disrupts the order of things. Established rules of the game. Lucrative, long-standing business models.

Consider this fun fact (which ain't so fun for the traditional media business). The Boston Consulting Group forecasts that $30 billion in profits will shift away from the traditional TV world over the next four years, with most of that wealth transferring to the new tech-driven media giants like Netflix. To add insult to injury, in a late summer 2017 letter to "The Donald's" top trade official at the White House, new Media 2.0 behemoths Google, Netflix and Amazon coldly rubbed it in and boldly anointed themselves *the new faces of the American content industry, winning Emmys and Oscars.*"

Media veteran and IAC Chairman Barry Diller sounded the alarm in 2018. Those tech giants won't just buy traditional media companies, "*I think they'll actually supersede them,*" he decried. Now *that's* a statement. And, by year-end, the media and entertainment landscape had, in fact, fundamentally changed as a result of one of its headline stories – mega Media 2.0-fueled M&A. AT&T/Time Warner. Disney/Fox. Comcast/Sky. If that wasn't a Media 2.0 wake-up call, then I don't know what is.

Traditional global advertising agencies certainly aren't immune either. Google and Facebook now own essentially 2/3 of the increasingly cannibalizing global digital ad market. Facebook (which includes Instagram, of course) alone controls 87% of U.S. social video ad spending, a figure that translates into $6.81 billion for 2018. And, for the first time, digital advertising surpassed $100 billion in the U.S. and accounted for more than 50% of total U.S. advertising dollars.

Amidst this crazy pace and these daunting realities, fear and loathing understandably permeate the ranks of those in power in "traditional" media and entertainment. The immediate instinct by many in periods of disruption is to either ignore that technology or lash out against it. But, you know what? In all of these cases – including our current Media 2.0 digitally-driven revolution – technological advancements and transformation ultimately led to more overall media and entertainment content consumption and industry success, not less. Technology expanded the overall pie. Massively.

Take these tech-driven examples. Live entertainment expanded into movies, movies led to television, television to ... well, what exactly is "television" these days? In any event, Deloitte Digital reports that American adults set new records for content consumption in 2016 by engaging in 10 hours and 39 minutes of media daily. Just chew on that factoid a bit. That's a lot of hunger for compelling content. And, that means a lot of opportunity for creators (and all those in the overall creator eco-system).

That doesn't mean that there is no pain, of course. There always is in periods of disruption, and there certainly is significant pain now *(which undoubtedly leads to significantly more Xanax prescriptions in Hollywood)*. I am not minimizing that.

The king of traditional media himself – Steven Spielberg – struck a sobering note in 2017 at the opening of USC's new School of Cinematic Arts. Spielberg predicted a massive *"implosion"* and *"paradigm shift"* relating to long-established business models in the overall film industry at the hands of new digitally-driven realities. Perhaps not necessarily what the crowd on hand wanted to hear as they pondered their future media and entertainment careers, but they needed to hear it *(that goes for my daughter and her fellow students who study the music industry's new realities at USC's Thornton School of Music across the street)*. The simple truth is that many leading players today will, in fact, disappear tomorrow *(Blockbuster anyone?)*. Even Amazon's CEO Jeff Bezos – seemingly immune from competitive forces (and the world's richest man because of it) – famously told his troops as 2018 ended, *"I predict one day Amazon will fail."*

But, you know what? The overall market and monetization opportunity has always gone in one direction – up and to the right. New multi-billion dollar media and entertainment companies emerge in record time to transform our content choices and experiences. Take Bezos's Amazon, for example. Amazon today is very much a Media 2.0 company. It is an outright leader, in fact, with its Amazon Prime Video and Amazon Music Unlimited services. Amazon jousts with another great tech-driven media company that starts with an "A" – Apple – to take the crown for being the most valuable company on the planet. Both crossed the $1 trillion mark in rapid succession mid-2018. Make no mistake. Content was a significant value driver for both companies.

In any event, new business models ultimately emerge and settle in based on new rules of the game established by those industry players who take action. Who are *fearless!* That's the opportunity here.

So, I am optimistic that our current digital revolution ultimately will do the same for the world of media and entertainment. After all, although the forces behind it can be terribly unsettling, frequently daunting, and even downright scary, they also offer never-before-possible game-changing opportunities. More stories to tell, and more ways to tell them. More audiences to find, and more ways to reach them. More opportunities to monetize, and more ways to fuel even more innovation and creation.

And, here's the exciting part. If creators and those supporting them do their jobs right, Media 2.0 also gives consumers a windfall. More high quality content that speaks uniquely to them as individuals. More compelling stories – from more voices – offering more perspectives. More content consumers will "play forward" to their own networks. Everyone wins, or at least has a shot of winning, *so long as they take action.*

And that's Media 2.0's punch-line – its fundamental lesson and universal truth. *You can't harness Media 2.0's power and potential to thrive (let alone survive) if you aren't in the game in the first place. Passivity holds no role in our Media 2.0 world. It is a time for action, not reaction!*

Why did the television industry settle on the twenty-two minute sitcom format with eight minutes of commercials to round out the half hour?

Why did the movie business settle on specific fixed release windows? Why does terrestrial radio pay no licensing royalties to music labels and artists when online radio does? Certainly these realities weren't preordained by some higher power. And, they aren't just historical anomalies. Those forward-looking executives who took action at the time defined those realities. Boldly. And those and other rules of the game still hold true today – decades later – and have for years defined the allocation of hundreds of billions of dollars to players in the media and entertainment business. Shouldn't those rules be reimagined now amidst new multi-platform realities? And, if so, is it better to be the reimaginer or reimaginee? *(Yes, that's a rhetorical question)*.

So, act upon the need to "act." Start some fires internally. Hire the best teams you can, and strip out layers of bureaucracy to empower them. *Don't just say that, do it!* Invest significantly in understanding Media 2.0. Get out there – out of your offices – and into the "field" where innovation is happening. Be part of the conversation. Indeed, immerse yourself in it. Attend both formal and informal gatherings of the new Media 2.0 tribe. Experiment – even if you don't have "it" figured out (like a convincing traditional business model). Take solace in the fact that no one does. Things move too fast and the old rules simply do not apply.

Rapidly iterate. Create, but fail fast – destroying what doesn't work and then starting anew. Be tenacious. Relentless. Otherwise, the competition – indeed your entire business – may pass you by.

Significant, potentially transformational opportunities await. But, only for those who actively immerse themselves into the world of Media 2.0. Act boldly. Take chances. Are *fearless*.

I call this mindset, and the bold, audacious actions that flow from it, *"FEARLESS MEDIA."*

So, let's get fearless!

PART I

MEDIA 2.0 (18) YEAR IN REVIEW

"*Don't bury the lead!*" That's what editors always teach reporters – and, to a certain extent, I am one of them. So, I won't this year. I'll start with a brief foundational summary of 2018's Media 2.0 headline stories. After all, as 2018 ends, so begins the media and entertainment world of 2019 – tech-transformed and significantly different from the one before it.

And, oh, what a fascinating year it was ….

1

2018's MEDIA 2.0 HEADLINE STORIES

(A YEAR OF M&A, #METOO, FAKE NEWS & FEAR ...
LOTS OF FEAR)

WE live in a new "Golden Age" of media and entertainment where Netflix alone spent a reported $13 billion in 2018 to exclusively showcase 700 television programs and 80+ feature films *(I discuss that more in Chapter 10)*. That's the exciting part. At the same time, however – and at the risk of being a downer – 2018 was a year perhaps most characterized by fear. Fear in both the ranks of traditional Media 1.0 land ... and in the world itself.

While our tech-transformed world of media and entertainment evermore frequently came together quite literally via game-changing M&A, much of the U.S. and global political and social fabric seemingly tore apart right before our eyes. Both, driven by fear. In Hollywood, the new digitally-driven world order disrupted long-established business models, which caused slow-moving former "winners" to either relent and be swallowed up by new Media 2.0 champions, or slowly wither away a la the ghosts of Blockbuster Video past. The smart ones chose the former path.

As I predicted last year, a steady stream of epic M&A drove one of 2018's Media 2.0 headline stories. AT&T finally closed its acquisition of storied, yet perhaps overly traditional, Time Warner ($85 billion) and later grabbed full control of new media pioneer Otter Media ($1 billion). Disney beat back Comcast in its battle for Fox's prized entertainment assets to drive its new subscription streaming video ambitions ($71.3 billion). But then, the Comcast empire struck back, outbidding Rupert Murdoch's Disney-fied 21st Century Fox to acquire control of U.K. media giant Sky ($39 billion).

Meanwhile, on the music front, Spotify's long-anticipated massive IPO led the way in terms of headlines. But, the pace of M&A accelerated here too. As I predicted last year, ubiquitous Pandora was swallowed up whole by 19% shareholder SiriusXM ($3.5 billion), Sony acquired near 100% control of mega-music publishing house EMI ($2 billion), and Warner Music Group picked up youth-focused new media company Uproxx (unreported sum, but likely for a song).

Just wait. For reasons discussed throughout this book, more major M&A is coming.

"Fake News!" became a dominant downward-spiraling content story of 2018. This was not at all surprising, given November's critical mid-term elections and "The Donald's" disturbing and dangerous persistent refrain to anyone who would listen that the media (arch-nemesis CNN, in particular) is *the enemy of the people.* First Amendment? What First Amendment? Pipe bombs to media outlets be damned! Our fear*ful* "leaders" gave disturbing new Orwellian meaning to their oath "to protect and defend our Constitution." Our not-so-benevolent dictator used that mantra – and his most uttered words of the year *("Witch Hunt!")* – to deflect potential *(likely?)* crimes and misdemeanors of his own doing. The positive spin on all this was that, by year-end, many of us felt that we had reached bottom amidst a new wave of awareness and activism, culminating in a somewhat cleansing mid-term election that restored at least some semblance of optimism and balance of power.

"Fake News"-driven fortunes *(or, should I say, misfortunes?)* changed radically for Facebook in 2018, one of the previous year's Media 2.0 darlings. Facebook – central to too many of our own social media-obsessed lives at this point – found itself in the center of that storm. In just one day, Facebook stock plunged 20%, wiping out $125 billion in market value in the single biggest loss in stock market history. And, as year-end approached, Facebook suffered a major security breach that compromised the privacy of 90 million user accounts. Even the Zuck himself wasn't immune from that one, and somewhat scarily conceded, *"We do not yet know whether any private information was accessed."* Yes, it was that kind of year. And, as a result, more than a quarter of U.S. Facebook users reported that they had deleted the app (although Facebook's active user base in the U.S. and Canada remained fairly steady at 185 million).

Amidst it all, brand safety became a critical central topic for previously immune Media 2.0 players. Those justifiable concerns deeply and adversely impacted the heavily ad-dependent video ecosystem. Many formerly "hot" young new media companies saw themselves decimated as a result. Whereas Vice Media previously could do no wrong, it had become a shell of its former self by year's end. Disney, which had previously invested $400 million in Vice, wrote off 40% of its investment as the holidays approached *(not exactly a holly, jolly Christmas)*. Things got even worse for long-time new media darling Defy Media. It shut down completely in November as a result of overspending and overdependence upon Facebook's ever-changing ad algorithms. Whereas it was the best of times for these and other new media companies just a couple years back, 2018 was decidedly the worst.

Frequently faceless Media 2.0 forces like Facebook (and those dependent upon it) weren't alone in seeing their fortunes and reputations change radically in 2018. Some of the industry's most powerful, very public faces faced the music as well. 2018 was a year when the media and entertainment industry finally confronted and exorcised its own more personal demons, banishing some of its leading players who for years had acted with impunity. Longtime mogul Harvey Weinstein became the poster child of the #MeToo Movement (in all the worst possible ways), but a seemingly endless parade of horribles followed in rapid succession. In addition to Weinstein, #MeToo purged Kevin Spacey, Matt Lauer, Charlie Rose, and Les Moonves – and a seemingly endless list of others from Media 2.0 – led by victims who could stay quiet no more. Will this lead to permanent change in the worlds of old and new media? One thing is certain, #MeToo has already changed the face (and faces) of Media 2.0. Quite literally.

Amidst all of this tumult, if ever there were a need for quality, binge-worthy escapist entertainment, this was that year. And, thankfully, we had a lot of great content with which to hunker down amidst an election year where "Trump did Trump" – attacking and ranting against social media and its evils as he himself trolled the world via Twitter. Talk about biting the much larger hands that feed. As the nation's soul burned, Media 2.0 entertainment and news sources prospered. Yes, divided we fall *(and we certainly began 2019 as a nation divided like never before, at least for decades)*. But, united we stood (or rather sat) in our respective escape pod living rooms, binging on Netflix (or Amazon Prime Video or Hulu) and purging (as we read the tweets of a certain someone). Election 2018 couldn't come soon enough, the results of which were heralded in via our AI-driven voice assistants who spoke to nearly 50% of us on smart speakers.

Perhaps HBO's and Netflix's epic battle for the 2018 Emmy crown represented the year's ongoing epic battle between so-called "traditional" versus "new" media more than anything else. "Television" (whatever that means anymore) is now solidly our go-to premium entertainment source.

And, while the most revered and awarded shows like *Game of Thrones* and *The Crown* could equally live on HBO and Netflix, how they got to their respective homes is very different. Literally, via very different rules of the game.

HBO still mostly does it the old-fashioned way, driven by Hollywood creative execs and their more subjective judgments and instincts (although that is sure to change over time under its new AT&T ownership). The result is "the few, the proud" shows on HBO. Netflix, on the other hand, extensively mines and leverages its deep pools of data to determine what kinds of stories and programming will resonate with its increasingly massive subscriber base. The result is a bountiful harvest of "good and plenty" content, much to the chagrin of most other players who wonder how they can compete against Netflix's $13 billion content "budget." In a notorious statement by Randall Stephenson, CEO of HBO's new owner AT&T, HBO represents the Tiffany of the Media 2.0 video world, whereas Netflix represents its Walmart *(meanwhile, Wall Street immediately pointed out to Stephenson that Walmart's revenues topped HBO's by 100X in 2017)*. And so it went, the battle of old Hollywood versus new Hollywood.

Mark my words. We will look back, scratch our heads at all of these forces, and wonder, *"What the hell happened in 2018, and how did we get to this point?"* As many asked, *"What side of history do you want to be on?"*, 2018's mid-term elections offered some clues – and, perhaps most importantly, hope. Something we all desperately needed as the year came to a close. It was time to close the books on a too-frequently fear-filled 2018, and start anew. Fearlessly. It was time to reshape the order of things.

So now, let's begin down that path. Let's first discuss the bold creators, innovators and leaders in Media 2.0 who will show us the way (or at least inspire us). First stop, 2018's "Fearless Five Media 2.0 Companies." The ones that boldly went where too few were willing to go ....

2

2018's "Fearless Five" Media 2.0 Companies

N OT all Media 2.0 players acted out of fear in 2018. In fact, in Media 2.0's game of "survival of the fittest," the new mega-players – virtually all driven by technology and very different DNA – made us marvel. And, remember, if nothing else, my goal with this book is to emphasize Media 2.0's possibilities – and the urgency to take bold action to seize transformational opportunities and reach new heights of creativity, impact, and overall "success" *(however you define it)*.

With that in mind, welcome to my third **"Fearless Five"** – the five companies that I believe made the boldest and most audacious Media 2.0 moves of the year. That doesn't mean that these companies ultimately will be the most successful. But, it does mean that they were the most fearless and placed the biggest Media 2.0 bets in 2018. Each can be defined by its own signature *Wow!* Moment. I name them in order of "audacity."

#1 Most Fearless – MoviePass

No company shook things up and frightened the entertainment establishment more than MoviePass in 2018. Talk about audacious, *"Damn the torpedoes"* was its mantra. Nevermind the naysayers. Nevermind the powers that be. Analytics firm Helios and Matheson bought MoviePass. Laid its life on the line for it. Bet the company. Crashed and burned with it toward the end of July, when cash had exited the building and the MoviePass service itself literally crashed. But, just like Jason Vorhees in the *Friday the 13th* movies, MoviePass kept getting up. A new plan here. A new plan there. *How did it work again?* Who knows? But, somehow, through it all, MoviePass just kept on, keeping on. And, millions of frequently confused, yet intrigued, customers signed up.

Listen people. Being "fearless" doesn't mean that you'll always be successful. "Fearless" means that you act boldly, audaciously and go for it. MoviePass did that in spades, and the media and entertainment business will never be the same again because of it. Make no mistake. MoviePass may be gone (or certainly close to it), but it certainly will not be forgotten. Movie theater subscriptions are here to stay. *(One early prediction – within 12-18 months, Amazon will offer a theater subscription service of its own as yet another incentive to sign up for Prime).*

2018 "Wow!" Moment – Helios and Matheson bets the company on MoviePass to disrupt the movie theater industry's fundamental business model (and ends up disrupting itself, alternatively crashing and burning throughout the year).

#2 MOST FEARLESS – AMAZON

Speaking of Amazon, this Sasquatch from the great Northwest thrashed its way to become my #1 most fearless company last year – and dropped one spot this year only because only MoviePass matched its audacity, and had more to lose (its life itself). Amazon's #2 position is quite a feat amidst the cacophony, change and competing forces vying for victory. As of year-end, Amazon is no longer an under-the-radar mega-force in the world of media and entertainment. Amazon has absolutely arrived, placing content (premium video, music, live streaming, and books of course) front and center in its quest to open up its virtual mega-mall to all of us (and keep us there). It rivals even mighty Netflix in terms of its willingness to spend billions on original video programming and global expansion to inject meaningful fear into the market leader.

Amazon's treasure trove of data about each of us is disturbingly deep, directly tied to every single detail of every single product search and purchase we make. An invaluable, rich record of our shopping habits and desires, reflecting how willing we are to part with our cash (and for what). Then, there's Amazon's massively successful consumer electronics business – the Echo and Alexa's now-ubiquitous soothing voice, not to mention the Kindle that started it all. And, of course, most of us have by now experienced Amazon's virtually impossible-to-duplicate and audacious multi-platform moves in the "offline" physical world. This giant now releases its feature films in our movie theaters, relentlessly builds brick and mortar stores in our shopping malls, and operates Whole Foods (its most mind-boggling offline move to date). Intimidating to all other players indeed (even almighty Apple).

2018 "Wow!" Moment – Amazon reportedly plans to build up to 3,000 physical retail locations over the next few years to expand its multi-platform media and brand engagement strategy.

#3 MOST FEARLESS – NETFLIX

After dropping one notch to #4 last year, behemoth premium OTT video leader Netflix returns to the same #3 position that it held two years back – which is absolutely intended to signify a real strategic shift for its overall place in the Media 2.0 world (and in my own thinking about the company) as 2018 ends. Netflix is justifiably paranoid, because all other global be-hemoths are absolutely out to get it. Some, like Amazon and Apple, carry weapons and boast resources that Netflix can't match. Nonetheless, with characteristic bravado, Netflix continues to stave them off and surprise in terms of building its overall dominance of, and dominion in, our lives.

Netflix continues to fearlessly march forward and dole out billions and bil-lions on its originals content strategy. It is reported to have spent an eye-popping (or more like heart-stopping) $13 billion to exclusively showcase 700 television shows and 80 original feature films in 2018. And it does so unapologetically. CEO Reed Hastings continues to stoically tell investors that Netflix will continue to burn boatloads of cash for years and years to come in pursuit of those ends and to beat back the proliferating global competition. That's the very definition of "fearless." Not easy for the oth-ers (even the behemoths) to compete anywhere close to its scale. And, that's the point. Netflix buys it all, so others can't.

2018 "Wow!" Moment – Netflix spends $13 billion to fund its content and exclusively feature more than 700 television series and 80 films.

#4 MOST FEARLESS – WNDRCO/QUIBI

Jeffrey Katzenberg's new company WndrCo raised $1 billion this past year to launch premium mobile-first SVOD service Quibi (as in "*Quick Bites*") and go where others – including the ghosts of Verizon (go90) and Com-cast (Watchable) – had failed. Is that fearless? Or is it just good? WndrCo's counterintuitive approach has people scratching their heads. Does Quibi (previously known as NewTV) have a chance, or doesn't it? Ahh, yes, it's Katzenberg, so it must. While other mobile-first new video compa-nies struggled greatly in 2018 to find new cash to fund operations, Wn-drCo bucked the trend. Massively. Its forthcoming mobile-first Netflix-ian vision of video will launch late 2019, following a script that no others have dared to produce (or, even had an opportunity to dare). Quibi will feature expensive Hollywood-style productions for a heads down mobile-first millennial audience. Think *Game of Thrones*, but in bite-sized, mostly vertical format under the Quibi banner.

Will Quibi ultimately succeed? Fail? No one knows, of course. Not even Katzenberg and crew *(they freely admit that)*, because no one has ever tried this before. But, all the major studios are certainly behind it. Literally, every single major studio helped finance Quibi. So, quality content is not the question. Instead, the fundamental question is whether a viable opportunity exists for a mobile-first version of Netflix. The answer may surprise us all, since none of the major subscription video players out there today – Netflix, Amazon, Hulu, DirecTV Now – place any real focus on mobile-driven content at this point. That's a blind spot that Quibi hopes to exploit. And, with all that cash, it certainly may.

2018 "Wow!" Moment – Quibi raises $1 billion (and looks to raise $1 billion more) to become the first mobile-first, Netflix-like subscription video service and beat that giant and others to the punch.

#5 MOST FEARLESS – MSG (THE MADISON SQUARE GARDEN COMPANY)

Here's one that is completely different than anything that has ever made it before to my "Fearless Five." MSG. It's not your father's (or mother's) Madison Square Garden group anymore. Yes, it still owns that storied venue, and some not-so-storied sports teams that play in them (the New York Knicks, New York Rangers). But, that's so yesterday. MSG's "tomorrow" throws out the venue playbook of old, and commits itself – in true audacious fashion – to completely reinventing the live event and venue experience with its MSG Sphere projects in Las Vegas and London (and other parts of the global sphere thereafter). The MSG Sphere is a fully-immersive 15,000-20,000 seat venue covered from top to bottom (both interior and exterior) in ultra-high resolution LED lights to give guests a truly immersive experience, one that doesn't require any headset or other wearable. The MSG Sphere hopes to blow our minds and overload our senses at a price tag of $350 million each. Will MSG's economics ever pencil out? Who knows! But, you gotta love the imagination and audacity of it all. I certainly do.

2018 "Wow!" Moment – MSG announces plans to spend $350 million for each new 360-degree mega-dome to reinvent venues and live entertainment experiences, immersively.

So, there it is. Like my list last year, many "honorable mentions" almost made the cut, most notably China media-tech giant **Tencent** that, among other things, owns a majority stake in **Tencent Music**, which I discuss later in Chapter 19. Suffice it to say, Tencent Music was bold and brash (and kicking a**) in 2018. While pure-play music service Spotify grabbed all the attention with its IPO, Tencent Music quietly plotted its own massive $2 billion IPO in the U.S. markets, using its significantly profitable business model (something Spotify never had) as its currency.

Other honorable mentions include **Apple** and **AT&T** (last year's #5). I discuss Apple at length throughout this book, including Apple's long-anticipated upcoming premium OTT video service (not to mention being the first U.S. company to hit the $1 trillion market milestone). Meanwhile, on the AT&T front, this giant finally closed its $85 billion take-over of Time Warner (rechristened WarnerMedia) in 2018 and acquired full control of Otter Media and its multiple digital-first media companies. AT&T continues to fearlessly build its Media 2.0 case as it bulldozes ahead in wireless, wired, pay TV, premium OTT, and now also in WarnerMedia-driven content production and immersive media. AT&T is now essentially everywhere it wants to be.

Meanwhile **Alibaba** (last year's #3) dropped out of my Top 5 entirely this year, as did last year's #2, **Facebook**. As we saw in Chapter 1, Facebook became perhaps the #1 most fear*ful* Media 2.0 company in 2018. Attacks of "fake news," privacy and brand safety – sprinkled with a touch of arrogance and industry *schadenfreude* – will do that to you.

At any rate, no doubt many of you may think that one or more on my list aren't worthy, while others most definitely are. But hey, it's my book. These are *my* **Fearless Five** companies that I applaud most for pure cojones.

Who will make the cut next year? More international players? Less obvious players? Perhaps even some startups? Will be fun to watch, and perhaps even actively influence in 2019.

PART II

HOW DID WE GET HERE?

BUT, that was all so last year. Now what? Well, before we move forward to Media 2.0's current state of play in 2019, we must first remember the past to fully understand how we got here. To fully grasp its lessons. And, to recall the bold and audacious actions (and not-so-bold inactions) that led to today's Media 2.0 "winners."

3

History Repeats?

THE Victrola changed everything when it came to sound, much like Guttenberg's printing press did for the written word. With the placement of a needle on a flat disc, songs that had been largely confined to small audiences now could break free and be experienced by the masses. Movies did the same for visual storytelling that previously had been bound by physicality – taking plays with limited audiences to all of us on the silver screen.

So, technology enabled creation of the mass media and entertainment business.

And, technology has threatened it ever since ….

By that I mean that technology has always been "scary" to the business of media and entertainment. Just when new businesses and business models establish themselves and reach some kind of state of equilibrium, they are inevitably disrupted by it.

Most of us "in the business" know the recurring cycle of destruction and rebirth – but it is worth repeating. On the music side, vinyl threatened live performances (but live performances continued to thrive), cassettes and later CDs *(8 tracks?)* threatened vinyl (but recorded music thrived and vinyl is making a surprising come-back), digital downloads threatened CDs (although more recorded music was consumed than ever before), and now streaming threatens digital downloads (but the global music industry continues to experience its most significant growth in two decades because of it).

On the video side, movies threatened live performances (but live performances continued to thrive), television threatened the movies and radio (but both continued to thrive), the Betamax/VCR (and ultimately DVR) and cable threatened traditional television (but broadcast television still thrived), DVDs threatened videocassettes (but recorded video thrived), and now digital video transactions and streaming threaten DVDs and theaters (although, again, significantly more consumption of video exists than ever before, including a never-ending supply of new global distribution platforms that increasingly pay top dollar for content).

In all of these cases, technological advancements and transformation ultimately led to more overall media and entertainment content consumption and industry success, not less. Much more in fact. Technology expanded the overall pie. Massively. And now, for the first time, we have pervasive broadband and near ubiquitous smart phones that make the world borderless. Virtually everyone can join the party and consume. We are insatiable. Voracious consumers who devour and retell stories that speak to us. Media 2.0 enables what was previously impossible. Limitless 24/7 global customer engagement, and distribution-multiplying social sharing. That's a nice foundation on which to grow a business. Fearlessly.

That's the opportunity here.

With this newly-emboldened mindset, let's take a journey together and see how the digital revolution first transformed our traditional Media 1.0 landscape into our frequently-frenetic new Media 2.0 world. I'll first start with music, because that's where it all began.

4

The Day the Music (Business) Died – A Cautionary Tale

("Bye, Bye, Music Revenue Pie")

NAPSTER *(the original, scary one)* and Apple – the music industry's 1-2 gut punch. These companies changed everything, in very different ways. And now, the traditional music business – that had been grounded in passive, highly lucrative physical retail album sales for many players – is, as they say, history.

Let's start with Napster, which arrived on the scene in 1999 to an unwitting music industry that was wholly ignorant of the technological forces around them. Am not blaming the industry, virtually all of us were. This is simply the reality.

Napster, of course, developed and popularized an entirely new form of content distribution – so-called peer-to-peer technology where the content creator's works (in this case, music) didn't reach consumers via usual channels. Now, with Napster, individual consumers made their own content (music) available to others directly – no music industry player needed to be part of the equation. And, that meant that those industry players (artists, labels) could (and were) cut out of any monetization of that content. For a behemoth global music industry that approached $40 billion the year that Napster launched, Napster was an earthquake for which the music industry was wholly unprepared.

The music industry could react in two fundamental ways to Napster's disruptive and deeply destructive impact on its traditional business model – reactively/negatively or proactively/positively. In other words, frantically out of fear – or boldly, with acceptance and action. It chose the former, and perhaps more immediately satisfying, path and lost precious time in the process. Precious time from which the traditional music label world never recovered (*I saw much of this pain first-hand from my catbird seat as president & COO of online music pioneer Musicmatch*).

Let's be clear. Napster *encouraged* (not merely enabled) mass piracy. That can't be denied. But the music industry's fundamental reaction to this rampant theft was destined to fail. It was all defense. No offense. I remember attending an industry conference in New York in 2003 where the Recording Institute Association of America's (RIAA) then-Chairman, Hilary Rosen, addressed the crowd, reciting a litany of individual lawsuits – several of which targeted the "small guy" (including children, grandparents, and one highly notorious case against a single mother). Yes, the RIAA "successfully" litigated some of them.

But, those seeming victories did little (and likely nothing) to fight the real problem – this new form of piracy spawned by the inexorable march of technology. And so, for every single lawsuit that the RIAA won, 1,000 more pirates joined the mutiny in what many at the time called a "whack-a-mole" strategy. Just when the RIAA knocked down one pirate, another boatload would spring up in its place.

Even worse, the music industry's myopic focus on litigation did the exact opposite – it exacerbated the problem. The pirates pounced on those corner case litigations (the children, the single mother), seized the narrative, and somehow turned the tables. They made the labels – and even leading artists like Metallica – the bogeyman. They transformed *them* into the bad guys and thereby fueled even more piracy.

Lessons to be learned here? First, technology (in this case peer-to-peer) relentlessly marches on and can't be simply litigated away. Second, faced with that reality, media and entertainment's best defense is a good offense. Focus first on action and innovation. Leverage new technologies and new forms of engagement. Spot new world realities fast and act even faster. Am not saying to wholly abandon litigation. But, when transformational new technology hits, harness its power to reach an even wider audience with different, better experiences. Experiences that consumers can't get elsewhere. Consumers will be willing to pay for them – I am convinced of that. Not all of them. But, significant numbers of them.

If you don't believe me, believe Steve Jobs. That's exactly what he did. This is where Apple enters this story.

Amidst the music industry's failed "litigate first, ask questions later" strategy, Apple offered hope to a reeling music industry desperately in need of it. In just 4 years, global music revenues had dropped a panic-inducing 20% to $32 billion. Steve Jobs positioned himself as being the music industry's savior. He approached the labels with a vision that was one part new-fangled Sony Walkman, and one part legitimate online music service (a la Musicmatch). It was the Apple iPod/iTunes combo pack of course – an elegant, easy-to-use, fully-integrated hardware/software and services approach that became Apple's hallmark.

The only problem with Jobs' pitch was that Apple's business model didn't align with the music industry's business model (although industry execs didn't appreciate that at the time). High margin hardware sales (in this case iPods) – not the content driving those sales – have always driven

29

Apple's business model, pure and simple. That's all that matters. So to maximize its end goal of iPod sales, Apple happily stripped out singles from albums and sold them for $.99, even though the then-current music business was dependent upon its decades-old album-oriented cash cow. Music (the content itself) was the industry's sole business. But, for Apple, music was just marketing – a means to an end. Its Trojan Horse to draw us in.

And, wow, did those iPods sell! My company partnered with Apple *(we developed the iPod software that got it into the PC world)*, and even we had no idea how massive those iPods would become. Apple launched its first iPods in Q4 2001 and sold 125,000 units that quarter. Those numbers ballooned to 22 million units just six years later in Q4 2007 *(had we known that, then Musicmatch ultimately would have sold for a significant multiple north of its ultimate $160 million).*

Not too long after Apple seized the day with the iPod – and still to this day – many *(most?)* in the music industry view Apple's iTunes revolution as having directly driven a massive transfer of wealth from the content creators to the technology wonks (in this case, Apple). And, it is hard to blame them. The iPod/iTunes combo pack later led to the iPhone ... which led to the iPad ... and, voila, we now have a $1 trillion dollar plus company with a stockpile of hundreds of billions of dollars in cash. At the same time, the labels were decimated and are now a shell of their former selves.

The music business's bitterness carried over to the overall media and entertainment industry and holds significant ramifications to this day. Justifiable media paranoia in dealing with Apple is one key reason why Apple still had not launched its long-anticipated branded premium streaming video service as 2018 ended.

But, here's the thing. In the ever-changing world of Media 2.0, even Apple's decade-old digital dominance in music is now challenged. Streaming music by the likes of Spotify and Pandora took off significantly from their relatively humble beginnings to threaten iTunes' download-focused dominance. Streaming, by far, now accounts for the music industry's largest single revenue piece *(more on that in Chapter 17)*. Apple certainly didn't see that coming. In fact, Steve Jobs once (in)famously and somewhat arrogantly proclaimed, *"The subscription model of buying music is bankrupt"* and couldn't be saved even by *"the Second Coming."* Well, in the words of another very different kind of creative genius, Dr. Seuss, when debunking the words of Cupertino's Grinch, *"it came just the same."*

Facing that music, Apple tried to join the streaming party. But, Cupertino was late this time *(still kind of a head-scratcher)*, and its early streaming attempts achieved very un-Apple-like results. More like crickets. See, even (al)mighty Apple fell victim to years of Media 2.0 denial and inaction. What did Apple finally do to change course in its new, highly challenged (and somewhat hostile) environment? It bought its way into the game, spending a cool $3 billion to buy Beats and Beats Music in 2014, later rebranding the service Apple Music.

So, Apple is safe now in the music game, right?

Well, I'll ask it this way. Is anyone ever safe in the world of Media 2.0? Of course not! And Apple's biggest challengers are not even usual suspects like Spotify. They are other major tech-driven media conglomerates like YouTube and Amazon, the latter which joined Apple in the $1 trillion club in 2018. YouTube is the biggest single player in the music world, and Amazon is increasingly a real contender.

You'll see why in Chapters 18 and 19.

5

GOOGLE'S SHOT SEEN AROUND THE WORLD

(YOUTUBE'S "LAZY SUNDAY")

ND where was Internet-driven video during Apple's iPod salad days? It wasn't really *there* yet, due to fundamental technological challenges posed by fundamentally challenged Internet networks at the time. In the early 2000's, those Internet pipes were a fraction of the size of what they are today, and then-current 3G wireless networks were even more challenged. Yes, heavily compressed audio files managed to "fit," but much larger video files could not (at least not easily or with quality). Conditions weren't quite ripe yet for Internet-driven, so-called over-the-top (OTT) video services that streamed premium movie and television content.

But, the narrow pipes at the time were just fine (or good enough) for short-form user-generated video content (UGC) where pristine quality wasn't nearly as important. That's when YouTube *happened*. And changed the world.

YouTube launched in 2005, but didn't become the YouTube juggernaut alone of course. No mega-success ever does. Apart from finding perhaps the single most A-list venture capital firm and financing partner in Silicon

Valley (Sequoia), YouTube also had a good old dose of timing (launching first ahead of Dmitry Shapiro's Veoh, *discussed earlier in the Preface*) and fortuity (*Saturday Night Live*) – specifically, Andy Sandberg and Chris Parnell and their now-classic homage to gangsta rap, *Lazy Sunday*, which aired in December of that year.

Lazy Sunday was a game-changer. Yes, people loved YouTube's dancing cats. But, for the first time on a mass scale, premium video content (in this case, television) was at the center of the universe of cool for the kids in a FOMO moment in time. And all of us, including media execs, took notice. No longer were we confined to simple next-day water cooler talk after watching that *SNL* moment. Now, we could immediately watch and endlessly share it over the Internet. That changed everything, because now the audience itself became the rebroadcaster, blasting out *Lazy Sunday* en masse to family, friends, colleagues. And, just like the Grinch's heart grew 3 sizes that Christmas, YouTube's audience grew massively during that 2005 holiday season. It was at that point that YouTube grabbed an insurmountable lead – and never looked back.

SNL's owner NBC didn't know what hit them. They simply didn't have the right kind of DNA to evaluate that kind of question. Did YouTube help or hurt them? Should they hit back? Should they not? They could have immediately litigated, sure. But, looking back at the music industry's Napster-driven legal fiasco, they didn't. Meanwhile, YouTube's founders looked the other way. Copyright infringement? What copyright infringement? Things were simply moving too fast, so they drove full speed ahead. Copyrights be damned!

Yes, the traditional media industry smartly launched its own answer to YouTube – premium video content-focused Hulu – fairly quickly in 2007 (relatively speaking, compared to the music industry's response to Napster). But Hulu wasn't a particularly serious play at the time. More like a hedge than a real bet. Hulu's studio founding fathers didn't take this opportunity too seriously until several years later *(I'll discuss that more in Chapter 10)*. And, right then and there, with those decisions (or non-decisions, take your pick) – and the *Lazy Sundays* that followed – Hollywood enabled the rise of yet another scary, Apple-like behemoth.

We all know what happened next. Within months (October 2006), Google read the tea leaves and plunked down a nice little pile of cash to buy the renegade startup – $1.65 billion (actually in the form of stock.) Google's move certainly wasn't about YouTube's financials. The company hemorrhaged money hosting and serving all of those "heavy" video files that it served to the world for free. And, it certainly wasn't about the content rights from all of the NBCs out there whose content YouTube increasingly featured all over its site (and the IP exposure that went with it). Google ultimately inherited YouTube's IP risk and Viacom's $1 billion lawsuit in 2007, but the dye had already been cast. YouTube was already too massive, and that lawsuit quietly settled in 2014.

Google's brilliant, audacious move – which was a head-scratcher to most in the media and entertainment business at the time – was simply driven by the realization that conditions were finally "right" for Internet video at scale. Online video represented Google's next great frontier. And YouTube was the biggest kid on the block. In YouTube, Google found the answer to what most others didn't see (and didn't see for several more years in many cases) – a new platform for the next massive wave of consumer engagement and the advertising to support it. Video-driven advertising. Advertising more deeply engaging and, therefore, more lucrative.

YouTube's #1 competitor, Veoh, wasn't so lucky. Whereas 800 pound gorilla and sugar daddy Google stood behind YouTube – and could soak up all of its child's shenanigans (operating losses and IP risk) – Veoh was swallowed up by them. It sucks to be second to market. And it sucks to go it alone. Sure Veoh had its own massive audience, but no dance partner approached it to protect it from its similar risks. Yahoo! could have, and should have. Same could be said for AOL and several others. But, they didn't. They froze.

Sensing vulnerability, the major media companies seized that moment, attacked Veoh's privately-held company Achilles heel, and went in for the kill to stop YouTube's second coming (a highly questionable strategic move, since content suppliers should seek to promote competition amongst as many distributors as possible to drive up value). They sued, rather than supported *(or better yet, bought)*, Veoh. Sued it into oblivion. Veoh's series of court victories years later against these forces essentially didn't matter. Litigation won. But, Veoh*(ver)*, and a possible mega-opportunity lost for media companies in the new UGC video world.

Sometimes, that's just how it goes. Doesn't mean that Veoh wasn't worthy. Doesn't mean that YouTube was better than Veoh (or the other Veohs out there). Just means that the stars aligned for YouTube in ways that few could have predicted. Timing. Fortuity. And, a series of bold actions. Sequoia Capital. *Lazy Sunday*. Google. And on the flipside, a series of missed opportunities. No real, well-resourced Hulu threat. No retaliatory lawsuit *(at least not immediately)*. No similar sugar-daddy for Veoh (could have been the studios, but wasn't). Fearless ... and fearful.

And, here we are today, living in a YouTube world. A "YouTube economy," as we insiders call it ... or, should say, *called* it.

Things began to change significantly a few years ago, yet again. Because they always do in Media 2.0 land. YouTube itself now faces major new challenges and challengers in a YouTube-only economy no more.

More on that in Part III.

6

NETFLIX SEIZED THE DAY

(THE RISE OF PREMIUM OTT VIDEO)

PIPES got fatter. Mobile networks bigger, better. Content delivery and consumption possibilities multiplied. This fast-evolving, tech-driven reality transformed the video world once again, as the streaming of movies and television became both commercially feasible and consumer friendly.

Whereas YouTube already owned the predominantly short-form UGC video market, Netflix jumped onto the high quality, long-form premium video end of the streaming spectrum – and never looked back.

But, why Netflix and not someone else?

Because someone had to do it. And no one else did – even though the company's name screams Internet for god's sake – *NETflix, anyone? Not enough of a clue for you?* Netflix became the first well-funded company of scale that *believed.* Truly believed. And boldly pursued that belief while others waited for the world to evolve, which it inevitably would. CEO Reed Hastings didn't freeze like others held back by accountants who were too afraid to sacrifice legacy revenue streams and couldn't make traditional financial models pencil out in a newly digital world.

Netflix launched in 1997 with DVD rentals of course. But, Hastings always saw what others (like cautionary tale Blockbuster) didn't – that the Internet would get faster and faster over time. It was inevitable. Kind of obvious when you really thought about it. So, Netflix got in early, staked its claim, and waited patiently until the backbone infrastructure was just right. Subscription revenues overtook its DVD rental revenues in 2010. *(Soon after in 2011, in a bungled move reminiscent of the "New Coke/Coca-Cola Classic" fiasco years earlier, Netflix tried to officially separate its now-secondary DVD rental business into "Qwikster" – a moniker that met the same "New Coke" fate only three months later. See, even mighty Netflix isn't infallible!)*

Netflix embraced technological advancement and possibilities, even though evolving technology threatened its then highly lucrative core DVD rental business. Netflix went all-in despite challenging new economics that fundamentally differed from the more comfortable established media and entertainment economics of the time. It chose to define the rules of the new game, rather than be defined by them, because its executives knew technology ultimately would demand it. It reinvented its core strategy and laid down price points that still impact virtually all other premium OTT video services today. Netflix defined the rules of the new game. Fearlessly! Meanwhile, Blockbuster, which was positioned well to capture it all (or at least, a significant portion of the new premium streaming video opportunity), stuck its head in the sand.

All of us jumped onto the Netflix bandwagon, despite its strange content brew at the time. It featured a relative jambalaya of movies, television and anything else it could muster, because Netflix was beholden to media and entertainment companies that controlled its content. These content owners treaded softly into that deep night and refused to give Netflix everything it wanted. You see Netflix, like Apple and Google before it, scared them. And, as Netflix grew and became even scarier to media execs, those execs began to do two things. First, they demanded significantly more money for their valuable content – dollars that Netflix couldn't justify, given its new world economics. And second, media execs began to take back – even hold back – content from Netflix, further limiting Netflix's ability to succeed on its own terms.

So, what did Netflix do? Throw in the towel? No, ever the rebel, it changed the rules of the game once again. Since Netflix couldn't control the flow of premium video content available on its service, it took action and brilliantly decided to develop and control the content itself. Borrowing from HBO's "originals" playbook (which ultimately made HBO a juggernaut), Netflix shocked us all in 2013 when it developed and launched its first original series – *House of Cards* – and made it available exclusively to Netflix subscribers. And, the company paid up big time to do it right. There was no skimping here. Netflix used top marquee talent – now-disgraced Kevin Spacey, Robin Wright, director and producer David Fincher – to make a statement and fundamentally change our perception of what it was.

But, Netflix didn't stop there. The company did another thing that was equally radical. Downright unthinkable to many traditionalists. It broke ranks with the entire rest of the entertainment world and shattered one of the fundamental rules of the episodic television series game. It released the full season of *House of Cards* to its customers *all at once*. And, *abracadabra*, the phenomenon of binge watching was born!

Most in the media and entertainment world stood in silent disbelief *(okay, many screamed and stomped because it is the media business after all)*. A kind of collective shock and awe. Netflix, developing its own content? And, releasing all of it at once, sacrificing valuable next-day water cooler talk and word of mouth (which was thought to be critical for commercial success under traditional media's traditional weekly release cycle)? What the hell was Netflix doing? Who did these technocrats think they were? *Netflix was bound to fail!*

Or maybe not. Those audacious moves changed everything for Netflix, and the company retains its pole position because of them. Before its grand *House of Cards* experiment, Netflix counted 33 million paid subscribers worldwide. Today, that number stands at 137 million. Netflix is Media 2.0's HBO, and now consistently ranks as one of the top winners of prized industry awards each year. This year its Emmy haul equaled HBO's, in fact. And now its exclusive content is *the* primary reason all of us have made Netflix a part of our lives without even thinking about it. *"$9.99 per month? Who cares!"* As a result, Netflix holds significantly more power today than it did when it acted purely as a distributor for the content of others. It increasingly controls its own destiny.

And, check this out, because this is incredibly important. Netflix collects a critical ingredient that the traditional guys don't. Data. Unlike traditional media and entertainment companies, Netflix knows precisely who watches what – and precisely how much of that "what." Netflix owns a massive treasure trove of data about its subscribers, and it develops its programming strategy (and programs some of its individual creative choices, such as directors, actors) because of it.

Traditional media, on the other hand, still essentially green-lights development based on subjective tastes and historical performance, rather than using more precise data that doesn't lie. And, in the immortal words of Tony Montana – twisted a bit to fit this context – *"Once you got the data, you got the power. And once you got the power, you get the viewers!"* Now, Netflix not only leads the "television" game in the U.S., it is the leading force by far globally, available in 190 countries.

So, it's essentially a given that Netflix owns the world of premium video streaming of movies and television, while YouTube owns the UGC side of the video spectrum. Right?

Of course not! *(You knew I was going to say that).* Much like YouTube and Apple, Netflix faces its own challenges. No one is immune or invincible in the world of Media 2.0.

Stay tuned for more in Chapters 10 and 11.

7

APPLE STRIKES AGAIN!

(THE IPHONE'S MOBILE-DRIVEN, SHORT-FORM VIDEO REVOLUTION)

As we saw in Chapter 4, Apple single-handedly transformed the music industry in 2003 when it launched iTunes. Apple changed the game once again in 2007 when it followed up its iPod/iTunes main event and released its first iPhone amidst a significant sea of doubters. Most questioned why Apple was getting into the communications space at all. It simply made no sense.

But, ever-wily Apple thought "different," and its iPhone was never about communications. That's why Apple happily handed that part over to AT&T in a highly lucrative deal that ultimately benefitted both parties, much to Verizon's chagrin. Apple, instead, smartly recognized that mobile computers – so-called "smart phones" – represented its next great frontier amidst a world then dominated by humdrum dumb ones. We already clutched our simple phones wherever we went (*hell, many of us in the business world still clutched our now-extinct Blackberry devices – ahh yes, Blackberry, yet another Media 2.0 cautionary tale*). So, why not give consumers a single device that could do it all, including enabling rich media and entertainment experiences. How could we say "no" to that?

We couldn't. And we haven't ever since.

To be clear, the iPhone certainly wasn't the first "smart" phone. Apple rarely is the first in anything. Remember the music world before it? Clunky consumer electronics company Creative *(now, there's any oxymoron!)* launched an unattractive, brick-looking iPod-like device years before Apple, but no one really cared until Apple perfected the form factor and customer experience. Same thing happened in the world of mobile phones. Apple's all-in-one iPhone was *the* game-changer. It was powerful, truly smart, fun, and sexy too. Could any previous mobile device really say that? And so, Apple created the mass consumer smart phone market. Boldly. Audaciously. Fearlessly.

Apple's timing was impeccable. Just like Netflix always anticipated the rise of fatter Internet pipes that would enable high quality movie and television streaming, Apple saw the dawn of a brave new powerful 4G wireless age that would finally enable high quality video streaming on mobile devices. That came in 2008, only one year after iPhone 1's launch. Remember, prior to the iPhone, few of us used our mobile phones to do anything but talk. In the U.S., we rarely even used them for texting due to limited button functionality *(yes, actual physical buttons millennials, can you imagine that?)*. We certainly didn't watch high quality premium video on our phones, because the experience … what's the word … oh yeah, *"sucked!"*

Virtually no one in the ranks of traditional media and entertainment believed that a mass audience would ever watch movies and television on mobile's small screens. They were downright adamant about that. I remember those conversations vividly. More like debates, really. But the kids changed all that. They didn't care what we older folks thought *(do they ever?)*. They flocked to Apple stores like never before amidst an iPhone frenzy that made the iPod's launch years earlier look quaint in comparison. This was the era of overnight camping vigils outside Apple stores, remember?

The iPhone single-handedly changed mobile possibilities at mass scale. Young consumers began to obsess over Apple's new truly smart phones and demanded higher quality mobile-first video content to satisfy that obsession. Real professionally produced, premium video content. Conditions were ripe, therefore, for an entirely new class of mobile-focused video content creators (and the companies supporting them) to serve this new mobile-first audience. The media and entertainment industry had its next big win!

But, for the most part, traditional media didn't see it. So, new digital-first, mobile-focused media companies led by young Turks took action and rose up to seize the day. And, voila, an entirely new category of media company called multi-channel networks (or "MCNs") was born. Built on top of YouTube.

MCNs essentially took the chaos of YouTube and aggregated related individual channels and YouTube celebrities, most typically under a new brand with a specific content focus. The goal of MCNs was two-fold. First, to help fund higher end video production and make the overall YouTube consumer experience better. And second, to give more revenue-generating power to individual YouTube channels and creators via scale. These pioneers produced mostly short-form, "bite-sized," snackable video that spoke a completely different language to a completely different mobile-first video audience. And, MCN executive DNA was fundamentally different than that of traditional media and entertainment creative executives because of it.

All of these MCNs focused on mobile and millennials first, and marketers certainly were eager to reach that target demo. The working theory at the time was that these advertisers would pay higher ad rates due to the MCNs' more targeted, precise focus and coveted youth demographic. That, in turn, meant that MCNs would drive more overall revenues from that content for all involved.

The modern MCN era began around 2009 when gamer-focused Machinima essentially relaunched to become the digital-first media company we know today. Then, in rapid succession, broad-based Maker Studios, Fullscreen and Collective Digital Studio (now Studio71); kids animation-focused AwesomenessTV; young girl fashion and beauty-focused Style-Haul; dance-focused DanceOn (now izo); sports-focused Whistle Sports; food and travel-focused Tastemade; Latino-focused Mitu; urban-focused All Def Digital. The list goes on and on.

Leading MCNs scaled massively and achieved viewership that dwarfed that of traditional media, and traditional media didn't know what hit them. By the time some of them did, it was too late to build these youth-focused Internet-driven media companies themselves. They most likely would have failed anyhow because the mobile-first content development process – and overall economics that go with it – were entirely different than traditional motion picture and television economics. So, what did the traditionalists do? They began to gobble them up *(more on that in Chapter 13)*.

But, it soon became apparent that the original MCN aggregation strategy and ad-driven business model didn't work. The times had changed significantly once more.

And, alas, even Apple's almighty iPhone – the device that first popularized it all – was not immune to changing times as it headed into 2019. In what Wedbush analyst Daniel Ives called a year-end *"jaw dropper,"* Apple surprised industry pundits this past November 2018 when it announced 0% iPhone sales growth and broke the news that it would no longer report individual iPhone, iPad and Mac numbers each quarter. Apparently, detailed sales reports and overall transparency no longer served the company's purpose. Always-invincible Apple, apparently wasn't.

Changing times indeed ....

8

FACEBOOK
– THE ORIGINAL SOCIAL ANIMAL

(& THE RISE OF SOCIAL MEDIA)

APPLE, Google/YouTube and Netflix revolutionized the business of music and video – at the risk of using an overused word, "disrupting" the music, motion picture and television industries .... digitally.

But perhaps the biggest revolution of all, apart from the Internet itself that enabled all of it, is the Media 2.0 "tissue" that connects all of it and all of us, globally. That, of course, is social media. And, that, of course, means Facebook.

Facebook didn't launch focused on the worlds of media and entertainment in any meaningful way. That came later. Facebook instead was (and continues to be) the place we shared our hopes and dreams, showcasing our fabulous and carefree lives, complete with sunny vacations and envy-producing parties. Because, you see, on Facebook and in our virtual social media lives, all is always good with the world. "Sharing," of course, is the key concept here.

From a media and entertainment standpoint, Facebook's unique (and downright revolutionary) potential was for us, its users, to do the distributor's work. Facebook held the promise of expanding the industry's reach across our collective individual networks.

Others beat Facebook to the punch in social-driven media and entertainment (just like others beat Apple to the punch over and over again). Consumers, of course, already shared videos all the time via YouTube, so YouTube certainly was social. But, YouTube's social utility is far more limited. Think about it. YouTube collects very little actual data about you. On the other hand, we use Facebook almost reflexively as an integral part of our lives, and Facebook happily collects more and more data about all of us all along the way *(not always a good thing, as discussed earlier in Chapter 1)*. Facebook knows everything about us. Our hopes and dreams. That means that its potential to engage with us as individuals, intelligently, is significantly greater than YouTube's.

But, Facebook moved too slowly to capture the Media 2.0 opportunity and was late to the mobile-first video party (just like Apple was late to the music streaming soiree). Twitter first entered the scene and became a media and entertainment favorite second-screen companion. A hash-tag here, a hash-tag there, a hash-tag everywhere. And that was nothing compared to some of the other "new guys" on the block that focused first on mobile-first consumers, especially tweens and teens. New mobile-first social media behemoths – most notably, Snapchat and Instagram – smartly focused on images and video first, rather than on Facebook-ian text, due to the rise of smart phones and their embedded cameras. (As an aside, smart phones predictably killed off both stand-alone digital cameras and Flip-like mobile video cameras ... *remember Flips and that great $590 million price Cisco paid to buy the company in 2009? Yet another Media 2.0 cautionary tale).*

These new, young, brash social giants seized on the fact that constantly-portable cameras gave rise to a new selfie *"ME"* generation obsessed with capturing and sharing virtually every moment of every day. That reality accelerated the rise of mobile video as well. And, video's deeper inherent ability to engage young audiences accelerated the need and desire for advertisers and brands to reach them.

Facebook's strategy to combat these forces of destruction? Take action! Evolve. First, it fully embraced mobile. And, when it did, its user base skyrocketed. Next, to maximize its mobile-first opportunity, Facebook looked to expand beyond its older and largely U.S.-centric user base. The company used M&A to accelerate that path. Facebook bought Instagram for $1 billion in 2012, thereby immediately transforming itself and broadening its user base. As a result, images and video became leading players in its overall strategy. Facebook now conquered text, still images and video. But it wasn't done yet. Facebook looked even further into the future, becoming an early believer in the ultimate power of immersive media. Facebook bought virtual reality (VR) pioneer Oculus-Rift for $2 billion in 2014 *(more on VR in Chapter 22)*.

So, after initially faltering in the aftermath of its 2012 IPO, Facebook found its mojo and became the Media 2.0 juggernaut we know today.

But, just like other innovative juggernauts before it, Facebook now shares the social media space with other giants. And, as we have already seen, Facebook faced its own demons in 2018 and now must find ways to exorcise them.

More on that in Chapter 14.

PART III

AND SO, HERE WE ARE
– THE STATE OF MEDIA 2.0 IN 2019

(CROSS-PLATFORM, CROWDED & CONFUSING)

PART I laid out 2018's Media 2.0 headline stories. Part II took us on a journey that laid out how we got from there (the past) to here (the present). Now, in Part III, we get to the heart of the matter – the state of Media 2.0 in 2019.

In this section, I do a deep dive and analysis of our tech-transformed multi-platform world of media and entertainment. I begin with a detailed overview of the video industry, including its leading, boldest and most innovative players (and their strengths, strategies and vulnerabilities). I then move on to the now streaming dominated music industry. Next, I immerse you in the tantalizing brave new world of extended reality (virtual reality, augmented reality and mixed reality). I follow that up with an introduction to the somewhat surprisingly robust new world of eSports.

And finally, I conclude with a deep discussion of the world of live events and experiences. After all, we cannot live by online interaction alone. Real, human contact and non-virtual real world experiences matter.

Kind of obvious, right? Well, it should be.

PART III, SECTION 1
SETTING THE STAGE

LET's first set the stage for our deep dive multi-platform discussion that follows. Let's start with the content itself. After all, it's the artists and creators – their songs, stories, and experiences – that drive the Media 2.0 opportunity in the first place. And, never have great creators and storytellers and their content been in such high demand, in whatever platform they choose to reach and engage with us.

Content is king. Always has been. Always will be.

9

WELCOME TO HOLLYWOOD'S NEW "GOLDEN AGE"

(IT'S THE CONTENT, STUPID!)

A MIDST the maelstrom of technology shattering decades-old media-centric business models – a reality that continues to frighten many in its wake – often lost is the fact that we are now in the midst of a new "Golden Age" of content. Yes, it's true. There has been too much doom and gloom, and not enough of the content creators' boom. We will look back at this era decades from now as being a period of creative boom, not bust. And you already know why – the Internet, mobile, social media trifecta is already ubiquitous in much of the world. Creators have new power to reach just about anyone, anywhere around the globe, at any time with their stories. And we, the audience, help them expand that audience.

But, it's not just about new distribution models and engagement that are enabled by these new technologies. New forms of content – new artistic freedom – are now possible. Gone are the days of creativity being locked into serial 22-minute segments dictated by traditional broadcast time slots and ad spends. Digital media has shattered those constraints, unleashing a torrent of unprecedented creativity. Content creators have more ways than ever before to express themselves. Those ways are truly unlimited, because mass storytelling has been democratized. All of us can have a public voice – and most of us now do. We can tell the stories we want to tell. Some may be "traditional" in form, but others most certainly are not.

And, here's the deal. An audience exists for *all* of it – both the traditional and the new. These forms don't necessarily compete with one another. The mere fact that our mobile phones are with us and connected 24/7 means that each of us has more (not less) of an opportunity to consume. And, consume we do – voraciously. All of us like to experience a good story, and we enthusiastically embrace new ways of telling them. Traditional notions of scripted series *(hell, traditional notions, period!)* have been disrupted, upended.

And that's a good thing!

Yes, we are in a new "Golden Age" of content. Great for creators – more demand for their services, more opportunities to tell new stories, and more ways to tell them. And, great for consumers – who now have more content choices than ever before and can (and will) judge for themselves whether specific content is worthy of their time. Have you seen so-called "TV" lately? In 2017, the scripted series count reached 500, essentially doubling the total count just six years earlier. Netflix developed about 10% of those at that point. But, ever-audacious Netflix pressed Tesla's "insane mode" button in 2018, alone bringing us 700 original television shows and 80 feature films in 2018. That's a lot of content experimentation. As a result of that kind of OTT video bravado, Media 2.0 storytelling is significantly *less* formulaic and *higher* quality than it was in the past. How could it not be?

Gone (or, at least certainly fleeting) are traditional cookie-cutter sitcoms and dramas of the past. Now we live in an entertainment world where the most celebrated scripted series, *Game of Thrones*, kills off lead characters with reckless abandon and where *Fargo* (one of this Minnesota boy's favorites) serves us with a brand new hot-dish storyline and cast each season *(I am thrilled that a new season starring Chris Rock is coming)*.

We sample this, binge that. Binge viewing – and other new Media 2.0 phenomena – work precisely because some consumers want it that way. Not all, but some. Netflix offered a new type of content package, a new mode of consumption. But, it's not binge viewing versus traditional scheduled viewing. It's not a zero sum game of either/or. It's simply a new game with different experiences.

Yes, after wearing the crown for most Emmy wins for 16 consecutive years, traditional media's HBO managed to only squeak out a tie in 2018 with new media's Netflix, which shared *The Crown* (each captured 23 Emmy wins, although Netflix actually beat back HBO with more Emmy nominations and broke HBO's 18 year streak on that front). So, although it's not just a volume game – where those that produce the most, win – sheer numbers certainly don't hurt. And, to put it mildly, Netflix flooded the market with content in 2018 to the tune of $13 billion.

There certainly is more video clutter and "noise" out there this year as a result of this content arms race. But, there's also more quality than ever before, and we consumers can and will decide what *we* like. What speaks to us. What is worthy of our time. We can be discerning. Not surprisingly, Netflix agrees. At *Vanity Fair*'s 2017 New Establishment Summit, never afraid to be controversial (in other words, fearless) chief content officer Ted Sarandos proclaimed that *"the notion of Peak TV is a completely backwards idea, which is that somehow you can have too much of things. That's like having too many choices at the buffet. You're only going to eat the things you like."*

Bottom line – high quality content creation and ownership have never been in so much demand. And, it's not just a video phenomenon of course. On the music side, new Media 2.0 dynamics fueled Sony's $2.3 billion deal to up its ownership in EMI Music Publishing to 90%, thereby adding EMI's 2.1 million song catalog to Sony's 2.3 million. Why? Because at long last, industry insiders understand that music publishing rights are big business – an ongoing revenue stream, annuity and overall gift that keeps giving in a burgeoning high volume streaming world. Sony's new CEO Kenichiro Yoshida underscored this point when he announced the deal. *"We are a technology firm, but the technology [today] means not only electronics but also entertainment and content creation."*

And, if we do like something (music, movies, television, immersive experiences), we will share it with our friends. Frequently with real conviction and passion. And, in never before possible, digitally-fueled ways via our social networks, blogs, and Twitter *(just ask larger than life TV star of The Apprentice … I mean, The White House)*. That's how Media 2.0 works. That's the beauty of it all. Media democracy in action.

So, perhaps overall audience size for each program will be smaller amidst the increasing volume and choice of stories. But, perhaps these audiences will be more global. More engaged. More meaningful. And, accordingly, more monetizable. Listen people, these possibilities are real!

But, creators, don't expect your audience to do all the content discovery heavy lifting. It's your responsibility too. Challenge yourselves to lead the charge, get your voices heard, your stories seen. Media 2.0 gives you innovative new marketing tools that you should *(scratch that, must)* try. Learn by doing. Social media's impact goes without saying, with new innovations popping up all the time. Unearth them. Study them. Use them. Data can be a friend here, and should not be simply dismissed as being anathema to the creative process. Data holds the power to better target audiences with content that speaks to them in a voice they want to hear.

Take that quest for data and multiply it with the promise of artificial intelligence (AI) and machine learning, because ready or not, they are here to stay. AI holds potential tantalizing power to deliver the ultimate audience feedback loop. Stories and marketing messages can be precision-tuned in real-time, making them more relevant and meaningful to distributors, advertisers and we, the people, who need to deal with far less clutter and noise as a result.

And don't even get me started on the promise of blockchain technology for creators and owners of content. Think of blockchain as a tamper-proof, transparent digital ledger. Blockchain technology holds the potential to fundamentally transform the content industry through the use of cryptographic "hashes" of original media files. According to Deloitte, *"a blockchain would ensure that copyright theft and illegal file-sharing become all but impossible."* In other words, the end of piracy. Creators, just think about that. More money in your pockets to fuel more creation!

Despite what you may think amidst all of the Bitcoin and initial coin offering (ICO) hype, blockchain technology serves as the foundation for much more than financial transactions (although crypto-currency will ultimately open up new media and entertainment monetization possibilities). Suffice it to say that blockchain holds the disruptive power to create a direct creator-to-consumer path, thereby squeezing out middlemen distribution services. Think about that YouTube and Netflix *(or maybe you don't want to)*. That means more money for you, creators. Potentially much more.

So, embrace this new Golden Age!

Yes, many traditional voices may fade away amidst challenging new Media 2.0 economics *(a harsh reality, I know)*. Production budgets for high end, premium dramas on HBO and Netflix now regularly range between $15-$20 million per episode *(yes, episode)*. Which players can sustain those new Media 2.0 economic realities? FX CEO John Landgraf strikes a sobering tone. In response to questions from *Variety* about Netflix, Amazon and the new Media 2.0 world order's impact on traditional cable networks, he laments, *"Platforms will damage or destroy a lot of brands."*

But, the not necessarily satisfying Media 2.0 response to Landgraf's point is that several more innovative, quality, fearless voices will rise up to be heard. Voices, big and small, that may be more personalized to each of us and, hence, more impactful. Even traditional notions of "celebrity" have been up-ended in this new Media 2.0 world. Yes, millennials still obsess over Kanye and Kim, but many of the celebrities that matter most are digital-first creators. Why? Because these new celebs are relatable. Approachable. They are just regular kids who somehow amassed frenzied grassroots followings using new Media 2.0 platforms like YouTube, Facebook, Snapchat, and Instagram. These new Media 2.0 celebs rose to the top by starting at the bottom. They weren't anointed from the top down. And, that makes them and their voices authentic to their fans.

This is all part of Media 2.0's great promise and potential.

It is also Media 2.0's simple reality. Don't fear it. Embrace it. It's your choice.

PART III, SECTION 2
TODAY'S MULTI-PLATFORM VIDEO WORLD

APART from when we actually spend time together in the real physical world, video is now our primary mode of engagement. How frequently do you see your kids with their heads down posting to Instagram, live streaming with friends on Snapchat, or simply watching a video, even when their best friend sits right there next to them on the same couch?

Part III, Section 2 gives an overview of our wonderful new Media 2.0 world of video.

10

NETFLIX AND OTHER PREMIUM OTT PLAYERS (OR WANNABES)

("THE NEW FACES OF THE CONTENT INDUSTRY")

INTERNET-DELIVERED premium video services are no longer just the "new normal." They are now, without question, the media and entertainment industry's dominant transformational force. 2018 underscored that with the M&A bullet discussed in Chapter 1. These are the disruptors – the so-called broadband-driven "over-the-top" (OTT) services.

OTT streaming video services are not alone of course. Traditional live broadcast TV, pay TV, and transactional on-demand download and rental services continue to be major players. But, given their increasing takeover of our viewing lives, leading OTT-first video players Netflix, Amazon, and Google/YouTube now audaciously anoint themselves as being the kingmakers. In their own words – as expressed in a notorious summer 2017 letter to the White House – *we are the new faces of the American content industry.* Provocative, to be sure. And also very true. A not-too-subtle knock on the legacy media and entertainment industry.

I. AN INTRODUCTION TO THE LINGO & VARIOUS FLAVORS OF OTT VIDEO

OTT players come in three primary "flavors" that continue to grow market share. Significantly. These include "all-you-can-eat" paid subscription video on demand streaming services ("SVOD"), advertising-driven video on demand streaming services ("AVOD"), and *virtual* multi-channel video programming distributors ("MVPD") that generally offer stripped down live pay TV-like packages called "skinny bundles" for streaming over the Internet. In contrast, actual, non-virtual traditional cable and satellite MVPDs deliver content across their own network infrastructure.

Not so long ago (just a few years, really), most media and entertainment execs scoffed at the notion of "cord-cutting" – consumers ditching pricy and bloated pay TV packages for skinny bundles that give them more of the targeted programming they want for a lot less money. Well, even the most ardent doubters don't doubt that anymore. How could they when leading industry trade publication *Variety* screamed *"Cord-Cutting Keeps Churning"* in a July 2018 story that reported that 33 million U.S. adults would leave the traditional pay TV fold by year's end – a number up 33% from the 25 million who ditched their cable and satellite packages one year earlier.

We are, in fact, now well beyond cord-cutting. Now even media traditionalists fully understand and acknowledge that we have raised an entire generation of "cord-nevers" – those refusing to enter the traditional pay TV world in the first place. Most are millennials, so-called "digital natives," who can't even comprehend a world with no broadband Internet and smart phone-driven premium video. Analyst Digital TV Research projects the global SVOD market to more than double by 2023, and analyst eMarketer projects that the number of traditional pay TV subscribers in the U.S. will plummet from 205.4 million to 169.7 million during that same general time period. And, *Variety* reports that the number of cord-nevers will equal cord-cutters by 2021, for a combined traditional pay TV-snubbing audience of 81 million U.S. adults. Those cord-nevers, according to analyst firm Kagan, will in turn essentially triple today's $2.82 billion cordless MVPD market to $7.77 billion by 2022.

Once again, the premium OTT wars escalated in 2018, as some very big names finally prepared to enter the premium OTT video ring. Disney made the year's biggest splash when it beat back a late run by Comcast to acquire a controlling stake in Hulu, as part of its master plan to launch its own Disney+ branded "Netflix-Killer" in 2019. But, Apple also finally prepared to enter the fight this year too. So, even mighty Netflix feels the heat from increasingly intense competition (although neither Reed Hastings, nor Ted Sarandos would ever admit that).

And then there are a growing number of other kinds of premium OTT video players that focus on specific content segments for underserved markets. Examples include WarnerMedia's DC Universe for superhero content, Fox's Fox Nation for those who just can't get enough Hannity, Nickelodeon's Noggin for preschoolers, AMC Network's Shudder for horror-focused programming, Acorn TV for British comedies and drama (acquired by AMC Networks in 2018), Turner's FilmStruck for classic and Indie films (killed off by AT&T at year's end as part of its post-M&A pruning), and U.K.-based Channel 4's Walter Presents for the best independent television programming from around the world.

Still others focus on specific geographic territories rather than trying to blanket the world. Examples here include emerging market-focused iflix (backed by Sky and Liberty Global) and HOOQ (the Southeast Asia-focused SVOD joint venture of international telco Singtel, Sony Pictures Entertainment and Warner Bros.).

In these hyper-competitive premium OTT times, one thing is for certain – we consumers aren't lacking for choice to satisfy our video appetites. Perhaps Reed Hastings, CEO of Netflix (the video behemoth amongst all behemoths) says it best: *"We're competing with sleep … sleep is my greatest enemy."* And, I know from my own frequently too-bleary eyes that Hastings is frequently winning.

This is the backdrop to the frenetically paced, increasingly crowded and competitive premium OTT video world. And, here are some of its leading players, together with their relevant strengths, weaknesses, strategies … and hopes and dreams.

II. Pure-Play Premium SVODs – And Then There Was One …

As 2018 began, two premium pure-play SVODs led the charge in the U.S. – Netflix and Hulu. But, the media and entertainment world changed dramatically this year when Disney acquired a 60% controlling stake in Hulu as part of its overall 21st Century Fox entertainment assets megadeal. So, now Netflix stands alone in this "Pure-Play" section.

Netflix – The (Seemingly) Invincible One

Netflix, of course, dominates the premium SVOD market in the U.S. and overseas in more than 190 territories. We all subscribe to Netflix – about 57 million of us in the U.S. and 137 million worldwide as of Q4 2018. International streaming subscribers surpassed U.S. subs for the first time one year earlier in Q2 2017 and outpaced U.S. subscriber growth about 6:1 in Q3 2018. And now, Netflix is reported to be the place U.S. consumers go most often to watch TV, and eats up 15% of all Internet bandwidth globally in the process. Pretty astounding, when you think about it.

Research firm eMarketer estimates that, as of July 2018, nearly 148 million viewers in the U.S. watched Netflix at least once per month, followed by Amazon Prime Video with 88.7 million, Hulu a distant third with 17.1 million, and Dish's Sling TV in fourth with 6.8 million.

We almost instinctively pay Netflix a low monthly subscription fee ranging between $8-$14 to get unlimited ad-free on demand viewing that covers all programming bases – essentially all genres, something for everyone – and with a mind-boggling (and frequently jarring) array of high-quality, expensively-produced, exclusively-available original programming (*I call this content category "Originals" as a short-hand throughout this book*). And, unlimited streaming we do. Collectively, worldwide, we watched more than 140 million hours of movies and television daily on Netflix as 2018 began (350 million hours on one day alone). Originals have become Netflix's calling card, continuously winning many of the industry's most prestigious awards. The SVOD giant captured 23 Emmy Awards in 2018, matching HBO's count and dethroning HBO as the sole champ for the first time in 16 years.

Due to its sheer size, Netflix earmarks massive dollars to fund development of its Originals. In 2017, that number climbed to $6-7 billion and created industry shock and awe. But, that was nothing. For 2018, *Variety* reports that Netflix's investment in content ballooned to $13 billion to bring all of us an astounding 80+ original features and 700 exclusive TV shows (*The Crown* alone cost Netflix $140 million for one season). The company released 676 hours of Originals in Q3 2018 for god's sake, more than doubling its number from one year earlier and up 50% from Q2 2018.

Chief content officer Ted Sarandos has revealed that Netflix spends 85% of its massive content budget to fund its Originals, even though those Originals account only for 20% of Netflix's total viewing time. That's the critical strategic importance and marketing power of its Originals and the increasing number of awards they win. No other company on the planet comes close to spending that kind of money on content. Few even have the means to do so.

But, why stop there? As of Q4 2018, Netflix has an astounding $18.6 billion in off balance sheet content commitments already locked and loaded, not to mention over $10 billion in long-term debt. Netflix's ultimate goal is to feature a massive video library that is equally split between its own Originals (the costs and commercialization of which it can control) and the licensed content of others (which it can't).

Sarandos concedes that Netflix has no choice. The major studios, on which Netflix had historically depended for the majority of its movies and television, increasingly lock Netflix in their sights. As a result, they either significantly raised their licensing rates, or withhold valuable programming altogether *(that would be you, Disney)*. In Sarandos's words, *"The more successful we get, the more anxious I get about the willingness of networks to license their stuff to us. That's why original content is critical."* Originals. Plain and simple. *That* is Netflix's fundamental strategy.

Netflix owns a treasure trove of data about what we watch and how we watch it – and uses that data to inform its content decisions. How much? No one except for Netflix really knows, although Nielsen announced in October 2017 that it can now measure and report Netflix and other SVOD viewing in what it called an industry game changer. Netflix, in turn, dismissed Nielsen's initial reporting as being *"not even close"* to reality and has no plans to release its own data, because why would it? Those traditional metrics hold little relevance to Netflix and its subscription model.

Only subscriber numbers, customer acquisition, churn (customer retention), revenues and profits matter. Even Netflix's A-list talent isn't clamoring for that data, because they are more than content developing their passion projects and getting paid handsomely to do it. It's kind of *"Don't ask, don't tell"* – Netflix style.

Interestingly, despite the fact that mobile video now represents approximately 60% of all online video consumption, only about 20% of total Netflix viewing worldwide streams on mobile devices. No surprise then that up to now, Netflix has focused only minimally on mobile-first, mobile-friendly programming that is typically more "bite sized" in length. But, this year, Netflix openly acknowledged for the first time that mobile presents a significant opportunity, especially as it expands internationally into emerging markets where mobile is essentially the only screen. And, lo and behold, by year's end, Netflix confirmed that it was testing low cost mobile-only subscriptions ($4 per month) in select emerging markets like Malaysia.

But, here's a major risk to Netflix. Unlike many newly aggressive competitors like Hulu, YouTube TV and DirecTV Now *(all discussed below)*, Netflix has no plans – at least no publicly revealed plans yet – to offer a virtual MVPD experience that offers live television programming. That's significant. Very. After all, despite Netflix's seeming invincibility, Hub Entertainment Research reports that half of Americans still see live TV as being critical. Yes, it's true that comScore reports that only 5% of U.S. households subscribed to new virtual MVPD services like DirecTV Now as of April 2018. But, that number represents 58% growth in just one year. In other words, it's still very early.

Netflix's fundamental Achilles heel, however, remains its one-dimensional business model. Netflix monetizes only its content. That's a world away from mega-competitors Amazon, YouTube TV, Apple, AT&T/DirecTV Now and others discussed below, all of which can use content purely as marketing due to their fundamentally different multi-faceted business models. So, Netflix's long-term viability as an independent is dependent on both extracting more from its existing customers via ongoing price hikes, and expanding (and retaining) its customer base amidst an increasingly crowded playing field. And, that's a field where others hold more pricing freedom and where consumer-switching costs (i.e., the costs of terminating an existing service and moving on to another one) are essentially zero.

Netflix's continuing pressure to attract more customers (and retain them) means "feeding the beast" – our continuous expectation for more and more new expensive, A-list-driven Originals upon which we can feast. And, as we have already seen, that beast is expensive to feed. That's why Netflix's losses (negative free cash flow) continue to mount and are expected to reach between $3-$4 billion in 2018 after reaching $2.5 billion in 2017. But, apparently that's nothing. CEO Reed Hastings unapologetically conceded to Wall Street that Netflix expects *"to be free cash flow negative for many years,"* as the company announced another $2 billion debt offering in October 2018 (adding to its existing $8.34 billion junk bond rated debt load as of Q4 2018). Ouch!

And, the costs for Originals most assuredly will only rise over time. They already have amidst hyper-competition in the overall premium video space, in which Netflix and HBO regularly invest $15-$20 million per episode for *The Crown* and *Game of Thrones*.

Netflix, of course, has a nice little accounting trick up its sleeve to help Wall Street deal with its sobering reality. Netflix amortizes the cost of its Originals over time *(it's not alone in doing this by the way)*, essentially pushing off that adverse impact and offsetting some of its tax bill in the process. Analyst firm Midia Research points out that these machinations cause Netflix's margins to actually increase as it spends more and more on its Originals. In Midia's words, this *"creates the intriguing dynamic of the U.S. Treasury subsidizing Netflix's business model. Welcome to the next generation of state funded broadcaster!"*

But, wait. There's more. Netflix doesn't own the rights to many of its most popular Originals. It licenses them. That goes for *Orange Is the New Black, House of Cards, Iron Fist,* and *The Crown.* That means that Netflix can't really control those costs. Even more, the ever-expanding playing field of premium OTT video competitors aggressively fights for access to a limited supply of A-list marquee talent that they hope will attract new customers to their competing services (and keep them there). That means Netflix can't control those costs either, which already have skyrocketed.

Meanwhile, that A-list talent will smile all the way to the bank as they get pulled in multiple directions. In the words of Jeff Wachtel, chief content officer for NBCUniversal Cable Entertainment, *"Actors and writers and directors who used to compete for jobs are now having studios compete over them."* Good time to be an artist or creator, indeed *(remember what I said in Chapter 9).*

So, here's the thing. Netflix climbed to new heights in 2018 and continues to try to prove me wrong. But, know one thing. In order to keep climbing and maintaining Wall Street's bullishness, it's gotta keep doing lots of things right and threading the needle. If user growth begins to slow down in the U.S. due to already-deep market penetration. If international growth begins to slow down or foreign obstacles grow due to increasingly powerful international SVOD competition (as an example, Netflix is second to Amazon Prime Video in Germany). If customer retention begins to slow down and reverse itself due to increasingly hyper-competition amongst giants. If consumers begin to switch over to "the other guys" due to a perception of more compelling content "over there," and non-existent switching costs. And if, amidst these forces, Netflix continues to borrow more and spend more than it makes due to its one-dimensional business model. If any one of these things happens, and those trends continue, investor confidence will shake.

Can Netflix prove long-term that it is more than a *House of Cards*? Lots of bears out there. And, if even Amazon CEO Jeff Bezos believes that his multi-faceted business model can fail (something he famously told his troops in 2018, when he predicted that ultimately *"Amazon will go bankrupt"*), that should give Netflix investors pause. But, from the look of it, still definitely more bulls. One media analyst who isn't worried is Bank of America's Nat Schindler, who expects Netflix's global subscriber count to nearly triple by 2030 and reach 360 million (280 million of whom he expects to be international).

One thing is certain until then. Netflix's biz affairs execs will collect lots of frequent flyer miles to prove Nat right.

III. THE NETFLIX "KILLERS"

Netflix is now the sole major U.S.-based pure-play that monetizes one thing only – the content itself. Each of these mega-players below, on the other hand, use premium OTT video as marketing vehicles to drive their very different underlying multi-pronged business models. In that way, they are fundamentally different animals. This year, we welcome Disney-controlled Hulu to this list. Donning its new mouse ears, Hulu really isn't a pure-play service anymore. It's now a critical new weapon in the multi-faceted Disney arsenal.

Let's first start with Netflix's PRIME competitor – Amazon. Tantalizing Amazon. Why tantalizing? Well, check this out.

AMAZON PRIME VIDEO

Behemoth shopping mall-in-the-sky Amazon launched Amazon Prime Video a few years back and has become a shocking premium OTT video contender, second only to Netflix. Amazon Prime Video lacks the deep motion picture and television catalog of Netflix and Hulu, but it too funds development of its own exclusive Originals that draw customers in and have been surprisingly successful (2018 Emmy Award-sweeping *The Marvelous Mrs. Maisel* and Academy Award-winning *Manchester By the Sea* being just two examples).

Amazon really stepped up its all-out assault on Netflix in 2018 by investing $5 billion on its own Originals and exclusive programming, more than doubling its expenditures just two years earlier. In one *prime* example *(okay, I'll stop now)*, Amazon reportedly committed $500+ million for two seasons of its upcoming *The Lord of the Rings* series. And, Amazon Prime Video undoubtedly will continue to up its content ante in 2019 like Netflix and all others.

Just like everyone subscribes to Netflix, everyone shops at Amazon. And, if you're an Amazon Prime subscriber *(because why wouldn't you be … free shipping!)*, then you're already an Amazon Prime Video subscriber, although you may not even know it. That's right. The good folks from Seattle toss in this perk for "free" to Primers – and they do it in over 200 countries *(take that, Netflix which advertises a mere 190)*. But, make no mistake. Amazon doesn't toss us this bone altruistically. Oh, no, no, no. There is most definitely a method to its madness. It uses Amazon Prime Video to draw us in – and keep us there. That's it. End of story.

Amazon Prime Video is a fundamentally different SVOD animal than Netflix in two critical respects. First, you don't pay more for it. For this reason, it's difficult to pinpoint actual video subscriber numbers (although in early 2018, Amazon reported that the number of U.S. subscribers for Prime itself had crossed the 100 million mark, and *Reuters* estimated that 26 million of those watched Prime Video). Second, unlike Netflix, Amazon doesn't need to make money directly from Amazon Prime Video itself. You heard me right. Just like Apple used iTunes music as a hook to lure us into Apple stores for years to buy iPhones, iPads, and Macbooks, Amazon primarily uses Amazon Prime Video to lure us into becoming Prime customers who dutifully pay our annual fees and "shop 'til we drop." CEO Jeff Bezos makes no bones about this. *"When we win a Golden Globe, it helps us sell more shoes,"* he proudly proclaimed at a 2016 industry conference.

And that fundamental difference gives Amazon a massive advantage over – and significantly more business freedom than – pure-play SVOD Netflix. That freedom includes significant freedom to undercut pricing, as Amazon already is doing in the streaming music world with its Amazon Music Unlimited service *(discussed later in Chapter 19)*.

Meanwhile Netflix's Ted Sarandos dismisses the Amazon threat almost entirely. *"I frankly don't understand their strategy,"* said Sarandos in a 2017 interview with *Variety*, citing what he deemed – at least at the time – Amazon's unfathomable strategy of releasing some of its Originals in theaters first, which, in his view, *"perpetuat[es] a model that feels more and more disconnected with the population."* I violently disagreed with those sentiments at the time because, to the contrary, Amazon's actions reflect a brilliant, fully fleshed out multi-platform strategy *(I discuss this at length in Chapter 26)*. Apparently, one year later, Sarandos v.2018 does too, because Netflix changed its tune this past November. Now, Netflix also plans to give some of its feature films the full exclusive theatrical run treatment. Ahh, yes. Imitation *is* the sincerest form of flattery!

In any event, Amazon also holds tantalizing data about each of us, including our individual shopping habits. It knows what we browse, buy and watch and, therefore, can determine what content is most profitable in fueling coveted Prime memberships. Amazon is also arguably in a better position to give us better customized content recommendations. Further, because we are already programmed to have our credit cards ready and waiting when we enter Amazon's stores (now both online and off), we also may be more open to paying for additional content and related commerce in all of its non-SVOD forms. *Digiday* reported in August 2018 that Amazon surpassed both iTunes and Google Play in transaction-based content revenues (digital downloads and rentals).

On the broader video-driven e-commerce front, no one is in a better position than Amazon. You can bet this mega-player will make it drop dead easy to buy NFL merchandise as we watch our favorite teams battle on Thursday nights (Amazon now controls those streaming rights). How can we resist? Alexa's helpful, soothing voice will make it so easy that we won't need to take our hands off the remote. "She" likely will even offer flash incentives to get us to buy more – all from the comfort of our couches. How helpful is she?

Amazon Prime Video is intriguing. Very. Amazon is simply, well, just everywhere – including everywhere Netflix can't be (at least, not yet). Don't forget that Amazon finds itself on all four major connected TV platforms – Roku, Chromecast, Apple TV and, of course, its own Fire TV – while mighty Apple always goes it alone. iTunes lives on Apple TV only. That gives Amazon much broader distribution in our living rooms. So, no one – not even mighty Netflix or behemoth Apple – is a lock. Amazon is knocking. And it has a mighty powerful fist.

The "industry" is beginning to notice. Tim Goodman of *The Hollywood Reporter*, in a feature piece from August 2018, screamed this headline: "*A Redefined Amazon Studios Is Primed to Disrupt Its Rivals' Plans*." True that.

Stop. Watch. Listen to Amazon in 2019. It is an incredibly powerful Media 2.0 force that is still not fully appreciated. Even if its CEO, Jeff Bezos, predicts that it ultimately *"will fail"* and *"go bankrupt"* (something he (in)famously told his troops in a 2018 company meeting).

HULU

Hulu – the #3 player in the U.S. premium OTT video world – officially launched in 2008, backed by NBCUniversal and News Corp. (now 21st Century Fox). Disney joined the party in 2009 and, as we now know, beat back Comcast to wrestle 60% control in 2018 via its $71 billion mega-purchase of Fox's entertainment assets. As a result, Hulu is not the stand-alone pure-play premium video service that it used to be. Hulu now plays a central strategic role in Disney's overall global multi-platform media machine. Disney's acquisition justifies itself if Hulu helps Disney's overall cause. Long-term stand-alone profitability, in other words, no longer represents an existential crisis.

This new Disney/Hulu reality, of course, inevitably makes for strange, very strange, internal company dynamics. Just think about those Hulu board meetings? Yes, Disney now controls Hulu strategy and execution with its 60% stake. But, the Mouse House still must cooperate with vanquished Comcast NBCUniversal's continuing 30% stake. And, to top things off and make things even more complex, Time Warner joined the Hulu party in 2016 when it bought a 10% stake in a deal that then valued the company at $5.83 billion. Remember, AT&T now owns Time Warner (rechristened WarnerMedia), which means that AT&T essentially competes with itself via Hulu and its own Direct TV Now premium OTT service. Do Comcast and AT&T really want Disney-controlled Hulu to "win," even though they continue to be part owners who help fund its operations?

Confused yet? Well, welcome to our wacky, wonderful world of Media 2.0!

In any event, let's get back to basics. Hulu offers multiple subscription tiers. Some are VOD only to compete with Netflix pricing. But one tier (Hulu With Live TV) gives 50+ channels of live and on-demand television programming, plus the full Hulu VOD treatment for $40 monthly – a fraction of the cost of a traditional cable or satellite bundle. The full Monty of live and on demand streaming is Hulu's major differentiator from Netflix as it tries to move up from its distant third place position amongst U.S. subscription streaming video services. Hulu crossed the 20 million paid subscriber count in May 2018, and later in September announced that it had signed 1 million subscribers to its new Hulu With Live TV service.

And now, with Mickey at the helm – and all of his priceless friends in tow (including the *Star Wars*, Marvel and Pixar universes, not to mention the Disney Princesses and new friends *X-Men* and *Avatar* from Fox) – Hulu is ready for its close-up. Let's face it, membership has its privileges. And, Disney's Magic Kingdom is some kind of private club. Just think of its massive resources. Hulu is Disney's long-anticipated adult-oriented, R-rated direct-to-consumer (DTC) premium OTT video service that augments its younger, mousier new Disney+ SVOD that will launch late 2019.

Even before Disney's big move this past year, Hulu stepped it up big time when it shelled out massive dollars to license the rights to exclusively stream iconic television shows like *Seinfeld* and *South Park* – $180 million and $192 million, respectively. At that time, Hulu also accelerated the pace of its own Originals to keep up with the Jones's *(I mean, Netflix of course)*. To that end, Hulu is reported to have spent $5 billion in 2018 for its own Originals, essentially doubling its number from the year before. That's a lot of *Handmaid Tales*. Not quite global Netflix-ian numbers, of course, but massive still in their own right. *The Handmaid's Tale (one of my personal favorites)* became Hulu's 2018 calling card – akin to Netflix's *House of Cards.*

But, the Originals game is a costly one, of course, and Hulu's losses doubled to $357 million in Q2 2018 alone – and were projected to reach $1.5 billion for the full year. That made Disney's new, larger controlling stake a costly affair, to be sure. 2019 represents a pivotal year that will demonstrate whether Disney can catch up to Netflix and control those losses.

Up to this point, one of Hulu's major weaknesses vis-à-vis Netflix (and Amazon Prime Video) has been that it is available only in the U.S. (Hulu Japan is a separate licensed entity operated by Nippon TV). Disney hopes to change that, and international expansion represents Hulu's most significant growth opportunity. Disney's massive international brand and cash hoard certainly won't hurt in that cause. Disney can also do what Netflix can't – i.e., bundle multiple OTT video services (Hulu, Disney+, and ESPN+) for one low monthly price. In the words of CEO Iger, *"If a consumer wants all three, ultimately, we see an opportunity to package them from a pricing perspective."*

Compelling.

DISNEY

Ahh, yes. And then there's Disney itself, apart from its new Hulu child. As discussed above, Disney boldly threw its mouse ears into the OTT subscription video ring with not one, but two major "Netflix-Killers" (in addition to its new ESPN+ service). Disney, as they say in Vegas, doubled down on its DTC premium OTT video ambitions, with Disney Chairman and CEO Bob Iger calling his twin OTT services the *"biggest priority of the company during calendar 2019."* That's some kind of call to arms.

But, let's be clear. Disney isn't exactly starting from scratch here in its DTC ambitions. It's a long-time massive, proven player in the world of DTC with its Blu-ray and DVD business (not to mention videocassettes before that). Disney at long last is simply now digitizing its DTC ambitions.

Disney will launch its Disney+ SVOD late 2019 at a monthly subscription price reportedly lower than Netflix's monthly price tag. We already know that Disney plans to hold back some of its most valuable programming from Netflix and keep it for itself, no matter how much Netflix is willing to pay for it (which is a lot). Disney is reportedly kissing about $300 million in annual revenue goodbye from Netflix alone.

Disney brings some massive guns to this epic premium SVOD battle royale. The company already has the single most powerful entertainment brand on the planet. Trusted. Beloved. All around the globe. Disney, of course, also owns many of the most powerful content franchises on the planet *(I identify them above in my Hulu discussion)*. That's a pretty damn powerful sales pitch. Maybe that won't make us ditch Netflix entirely. But, it certainly may motivate us to sign up and pay Disney too. We may have no choice. After all, our entitled kids can be quite demanding.

Still, even behemoth Disney, with its uniquely powerful pedigree and IP assets, can't bank on immediate widespread adoption in a sea of Netflix, Amazon and other giants. No one gets a free pass anymore. So, whether Disney's twin premium OTT video services become Bob Iger and his merry shareholders' "happiest places on earth" remains to be seen.

Disney versus Netflix. A battle so big that it deserves its own chapter. You will find it next in Chapter 11.

APPLE

What about Apple? After all, as of 2018, Apple is the first $1 trillion company in the U.S. *(Amazon followed suit just weeks later)*, so you know it has quite a lot going on. But, as 2018 ended, Apple shockingly still had not launched its own much-anticipated "Netflix-Killer" – something I have anticipated for years. By year-end 2018, however, it was widely reported that Apple's long-awaited subscription OTT video service would launch in the first half of 2019.

Apple absolutely wants to control our overall television experiences with its own DTC video service that will undoubtedly offer both on demand streaming and live skinny bundles when it does launch. Steve Jobs' DNA permeates the Cupertino crew, and he was nothing if not both hyper-competitive and a control freak. It's not in Apple's core fabric to see others win in a game in which it wants to play. And, get this. Even before it launches, Morgan Stanley predicts that Apple will ultimately rival Netflix. According to Mr. Stanley, Apple's Netflix challenger will generate $500 million in 2019 alone, $4.4 billion by 2025, and count 50 million paid subscribers by that time. I, for one, believe those numbers are extremely conservative. After all, Apple already reaches us across 1.3 billion active devices today.

In any event, we have already seen how this has played out on the music side. Apple first resisted music streaming services (*remember when Steve Jobs completely rejected them?*) – then waited too long when reality set in – and then failed when it finally launched its own Apple branded music streaming service. So, what did it do? It bought its way into the music streaming game in 2014 for $3 billion with Beats, and is now a top music player again.

Will Apple buy its way into the video game too? You may think not, given that its Apple TV OTT video service isn't far off at this point. But, an M&A strategy still has plenty of time to play out here too – and it need not happen before the launch of its own branded Netflix-ian service. After all, Apple bought Beats only after it had launched its own branded music subscription service and failed to impress the world in the process. So, if Apple can't succeed in getting entirely what it wants on its own as it increasingly battles the other behemoths, why not buy its way in to become an immediate player that already has everything it needs?

Hmmmm, who could that be? No Dana Carvey, not Satan.

How about Netflix? That would certainly be an audacious Media 2.0 move, and Apple certainly has the cash. But, with its ballooning market cap, Netflix no longer seems like a real possibility. Other more humble Beats-like players exist, however, that already operate proven technology platforms and feature a depth of valuable premium content. fuboTV *(yes, lowercase "f", a company I discuss further below)* is one such company that could fit the bill.

In any event, Apple's subscription-based DTC video service is coming, and Apple began to prep for that inevitable event by investing big time in its own Originals in 2017 to the (i)Tune of $1 billion. As of October 2018, Apple had 24 Originals in production and development. And, lest we forget, Apple's unchallengeable competitive edge over all other major SVODs is its unique, undeniable power to inject its upcoming "Netflix-Killer" into our daily lives. Expect Apple to be relentless when it enters the ring, bundling its new OTT video service in all of our Apple TVs, iPhones, iPads, and Macs (a strategy that was confirmed late 2018). Unlike competing services, no separate install or sign-in will be needed. That's some massive automatic and instantaneous distribution. Some would say, its very special (Apple) sauce. Who can compete with that?

Yes, that's right. Crickets. No one can. That's precisely why Apple Music is fast catching up to Spotify in terms of paid subscribers worldwide, even though Spotify previously seemed untouchable. In fact, Apple Music's paid subscriber count in the U.S. now eclipses Spotify's.

But wait, there's more. Apple likely will steal a *prime* page from Amazon's playbook *(there I go again)* and offer a single subscription price that combines its Originals, music and magazine offerings. Sure, Apple won't be able to offer free next-day shipping. But, Apple does offer immediate digital access to content, and Cupertino cool!

Formidable. Apple will be an immediate video force when it launches. If it builds it, we will come. To a certain extent, we have no choice.

GOOGLE/YOUTUBE TV

YouTube – still the giant amongst giants in the world of Media 2.0 video – took a Hulu-like path in 2017 in a bid to become your premium paid video service provider of choice and take a bite out of Netflix. YouTube launched its own virtual MVPD service at that time, not so creatively named simply YouTube TV. This OTT video service features both premium on-demand and live TV programming. Unlike Hulu and other virtual MVPDs discussed in this chapter, YouTube TV keeps it simple, offering only one paid tier of service at $40 per month. No "good, better, best" options here. YouTube TV reportedly hit the 800,000 paid subscriber count by October 2018.

YouTube also operates its $11.99 monthly YouTube Premium subscription service (previously called YouTube Red), which gives ad-free YouTube video, YouTube Music and access to YouTube Originals. YouTube Premium-driven Originals typically star YouTube's top digital-first celebs, not traditional marquee Hollywood talent – so it's not really an "apples to Apple" comparison (so to speak).

YouTube now hopes to extract our subscription dollars, not only the endless ad dollars we generate. But, that's harder than it sounds. After all, it's always tough to get consumers to pay for something that they've always used for free, even if that "something" is now a very different thing. *(You will see in Chapter 19 that Pandora faced similar challenges when it first launched its Spotify-like service)*.

Still, YouTube's definition of "success" with its premium OTT video ambitions can be very different than Netflix's. Does it really matter whether YouTube's virtual MVPD is stand-alone profitable? Remember, Google/YouTube is a lot like Apple and Amazon when it comes to content. Sure it's nice to have users pay for it. But that's all gravy. The main course is to keep us search, search, searching for more to fuel its very different core business model. For Google, it's all about keeping us "in the family" in order to barrage us with ads. Keep us coming, and they'll do just fine.

YouTube is still the dominant overall OTT video player as you look across the entire spectrum of Media 2.0 video companies. But, it certainly no longer plays alone and faces serious challenges of its own.

SONY CRACKLE AND PLAYSTATION VUE

Sony also plays in the premium OTT video game with two very different services. Crackle is Sony's AVOD-driven Netflix-like VOD service, whereas PlayStation Vue is its virtual MVPD that offers live television skinny bundles. Up to this point, Sony has kept those two OTT services separate.

But, big changes are afoot in Sony land. Faced with the reality that Crackle barely "crackles" and rises above the collective Netflix, Amazon, and Hulu din, Sony announced in 2018 that it is looking to sell a major equity stake to the right partner. Maybe it's the right time for one of the major media companies so far largely frozen out of the premium OTT video world (like Comcast) to buy into Crackle's AVOD opportunity, an opportunity that gets significantly less attention than today's SVOD battle royale. After all, for consumers potentially reaching a breaking point once they pay for 2-3 SVODs and virtual MVPDs (Netflix, Hulu, HBO Now, YouTube TV, CBS All Access, etc., etc.), their next best option is an AVOD service that costs them nothing out of the gates.

Unlike Crackle, PlayStation Vue is very much in the vein of Hulu, offering both VOD and live programming packages. But, PlayStation Vue is also a distant player with only 500,000 paid subscribers as of October 2018. Some of that stalled growth may be caused by the service's confusing name itself. Despite its moniker, you can find PlayStation Vue on Roku and Amazon – i.e., no Sony PlayStation needed.

At least you can find PlayStation Vue for now. *The Motley Fool* painted a pretty bleak picture as 2018 ended, concluding that *"PlayStation Vue is probably destined for failure"* and the *"eventual shuttering of the service is arguably already baked into Sony's stock price."*

Yikes.

WALMART VUDU

Remember Vudu, Walmart's long-time attempt to stay relevant online in the world of media and entertainment? Neither do I, but Walmart reports that Vudu surprisingly counts 25 million registered users as of late 2018. This past year, Walmart vowed to expand its focus on Vudu's Movies On Us AVOD service in an attempt to hold onto its offline customers and keep them out of the still mostly virtual hands of Amazon. To fuel those ambitions, Vudu struck a deal with MGM to develop Originals based on beloved franchises like James Bond. Vudu also planned to add a new shoppable video ad format that enables viewers to make instant purchases on Walmart.com.

But, don't expect Walmart to do a full Amazon Prime Video on us. Scott Blanksteen, Vudu's VP of product, underscored this point. *"We are not going to be a studio. We are not going to have 300 or 400 originals."* You will, however, inevitably be able to happily stream NBC's *Superstore* on your phones as you cruise through Walmart's big box aisles.

Stay tuned for that!

IV. BEHEMOTHS WITH VERY DIFFERENT DNA - THE ACTUAL MVPDS

But wait, there's more. With traditional pay TV packages under siege, it was only a matter of time before the *actual*, non-virtual, big cable and satellite MVPDs entered the premium OTT video game. After all, each of them holds the secret weapon of built-in distribution via massive customer bases. They are "locks" to be successful, right?

Well, not so fast. First, before we introduce these Netflix "wannabes," time for another Media 2.0 cautionary tale – this time, starring once seemingly invincible Samsung.

Samsung – an undeniable behemoth with a massive customer footprint – launched its own premium OTT services a few years back and came out swinging. It first launched its streaming music service, strangely called Milk Music *(even befuddled Samsung execs conceded to me that they didn't know quite what that name meant or why they chose it)*. It later doubled down with that enigmatic brand and launched its premium OTT video twin – Milk Video – to great fanfare and investment, including top executive talent. But, alas, nothing happened. Both services fizzled. Samsung first dropped Milk Video in 2015, and then pulled the plug on Milk Music one year later in 2016.

Lesson here? Massive distribution alone does not guarantee massive results, or even meaningful results. After all, consumers can already get the services they really want – like Netflix and Spotify – on virtually any platform. So, why would they sign up for yet another new service, especially if it comes from a name like Samsung that doesn't exactly scream content and storytelling? There must be more to make a dent, and that's where the focus needs to be. A library of exclusive premium Originals is the most obvious answer, and Samsung didn't have it. One more key lesson from Samsung's experiment gone awry – far too much bureaucracy and too many layers of management. Samsung hired experienced content execs to lead the charge, but failed to empower them. That leads to low morale, and low morale leads to diminished results. Every time.

But, don't feel too bad for the giant traditional MVPDs below if they fail in their bids for OTT video dominance. Yes, their pay TV subscriber numbers and content-generated revenues may continue to shrink (*in fact, they will shrink – there is nothing "may" about it*). But, many of these companies are now more profitable than ever. Yes, it's true. All of that great high quality premium movie and television video content that streams from other OTTs demands fatter, more expensive broadband pipes. We content-hungry consumers absolutely will pay big-ly for that without even thinking about it. And, no end is in sight for these purveyors of pipe amidst our never-sated thirst for faster and faster broadband that delivers the bountiful premium video content to which we feel entitled (and delivers significantly higher margins to these plumbers than offering royalty-laden content services).

With this backdrop, let's see which of the major actual MVPDs moved aggressively into the Internet-driven virtual MVPD world in 2018.

AT&T/DirecTV Now (& Even More, Later, With WarnerMedia)

AT&T, that's who. Not exactly trying. More like massively doing. AT&T made 2016's boldest and brashest Media 2.0 bet when it inked its deal to buy venerable Time Warner and its treasure trove of Warner Bros., HBO and Turner content for $85 billion. AT&T later launched its all-out premium OTT video assault on Netflix in November 2016 under its DirecTV Now banner, after acquiring DirecTV for $50 billion in one of 2015's boldest moves. 2015's bold, followed by 2016's bold. Bold squared! And, that bravado finally paid off in 2018. Yes, it took about 18 months to get there, but AT&T's acquisition of Time Warner finally closed. A federal judge finally ripped it out of the The Donald's tiny hands in June.

As a result, AT&T now owns the premium video trifecta of Warner Bros., HBO and Turner under its new WarnerMedia banner. That's some powerful content ammunition that it can deploy in new and exclusive ways – and also withhold from those with whom it does battle a la Disney with Netflix.

DirecTV Now counts a relatively modest 1.86 million subscribers as of Q3 2018, about double from one year earlier. How much of that growth comes from cannibalizing its much higher-priced traditional DirecTV service? Unclear. But what is (clear), is sobering. In Q3 2018, AT&T shed 346,000 DirecTV satellite and AT&T Uverse video customers, and only signed 49,000 new DirecTV Now customers. Just pause for a second and let that soak in.

In any event, DirecTV Now – like Hulu and PlayStation Vue – features both VOD and several live TV skinny bundle options. In fact, its top tier bundles aren't too skinny at all. They are, in fact, some of the fattest in the virtual MVPD industry. Meanwhile, its base price caused shock and awe when AT&T first announced it in 2016 ($35 monthly), and placed tremendous pricing pressure on all others when it entered the ring. Not surprisingly, Hulu and others had little choice but to price their new live skinny bundles at roughly the same price point.

These relatively reasonable "a lot for a little" monthly fees likely mean that AT&T operates its DirecTV Now virtual MVPD service as a loss leader to build overall market share and play an Amazon-like long game in a hyper-competitive market. And, in a competitive edge, AT&T mobile wireless subscribers can stream DirecTV Now on their mobile phones without dinging their wireless plans. Net neutrality be damned! AT&T also announced its new mobile-first WatchTV service, available free for its best wireless customers and $15 monthly for all others. WatchTV significantly features WarnerMedia content, of course, because AT&T now owns it. No licensing costs there.

For those of you skeptical of AT&T's ambitions and likelihood of premium OTT video success, I'd offer a word of caution. AT&T already is everywhere in many of your lives, and DirecTV itself is a long-time content-focused mega-player largely due to the NFL package. And, don't forget AT&T's continuing 10% ownership stake in Hulu. That means AT&T already rides two major horses in the premium OTT race. Remember further that AT&T acquired full control of digital-first Otter Media in 2018, buying out The Chernin Group's 50% stake for a deal valued at $1 billion. Because Otter Media itself operates a number of millennial-focused fan-centric SVODs, including anime-focused Crunchyroll *(which I discuss later in Chapter 13)*, AT&T's tentacles already run very deep indeed.

But, why stop there? As year-end 2018 approached, WarnerMedia CEO John Stankey unveiled new plans for its own upcoming "Netflix-Killer" that it plans to launch late 2019. Stankey will use HBO as the SVOD's lead actor, and boldly announced that his content spend would be *"competitive"* to Netflix's. So, AT&T has placed multiple premium OTT video bets and is a real multi-brand, multi-platform video player. An extremely formidable one.

One of the big questions for AT&T is whether its new "whole" will be greater and more valuable than the sum of all of its massive individual parts. It will be fascinating to watch, especially since AT&T also hopes to change the rules of the game when it comes to the licensing of premium content to run on OTT platforms. As an example, AT&T now experiments with so-called "engagement pricing" based on actual viewership, rather than subscriber count. According to AT&T Communications CEO John Donovan, *"The content industry has declining viewership but increasing pricing ... A person who watches 10 hours a day paid the same as one who watched one hour a day ... Is that a good value proposition for customers? So you have to change the model."*

There certainly is no denying that this formerly stodgy telco has fundamentally transformed itself in just the past few years and is now a fearless Media 2.0 leader.

VERIZON

AT&T's arch-nemesis Verizon entered the premium OTT ring big time itself in late 2015, when it launched its mobile-first go90 OTT streaming video service focused on younger millennials. But, those millennials never "got" the name, nor did they ever really "get" the service (literally or figuratively). And, Verizon faced the music in 2018 when it shut it down after spending hundreds of millions of dollars.

Word on the street from the creative community in go90's "go go" days was that Verizon seriously overpaid for exclusive rights to content, spending up to $4 million per bite-sized show in an effort to differentiate its service from the others and fuel adoption (much like Netflix did when it first launched its Originals strategy). So, yes, Verizon certainly built it. But, subscribers certainly didn't come (at least at sufficient scale). Much like Samsung before it, Verizon learned the hard way that mega-reach and a mega-dollar-fueled content strategy do not a successful service make.

What remains for Verizon in these contentious Media 2.0 video days? Don't forget Yahoo! and its content portfolio. Verizon acquired the sleeping *(nay, essentially comatose)* giant back in 2016 at a comparatively bargain basement price of $4.8 billion – a price that was discounted further to $4.48 billion by the time the deal finally closed in 2017 due to its highly-publicized hacking woes. And this was after Verizon had acquired AOL just one year earlier for $4.4 billion in another heavily-discounted, content-driven Media 2.0 mega-move.

With all these big bets, it's certainly no surprise that Verizon also threw its hat into the AT&T/DirecTV Now-ian ring by year-end 2017, announcing that it too plans to compete more directly with premium content on all platforms and to a mass audience via its own "Netflix-Killer" *(or at least maim-er)* – not just to young mobile-first millennials via go90. As 2018 ended, however, no such premium SVOD had yet materialized.

Verizon does play in the OTT video space in smaller ways. Together with Hearst, it operates mobile-first Complex. It also previously owned a major stake in AwesomenessTV, but sold that off to Viacom for a song in 2018 *(more on that in Chapter 13)*.

Many industry insiders remain skeptical of Verizon's ambitions as a result of go90's failure and the ghosts of Verizon's content initiatives past. To counter the naysayers, Verizon is banking on its new Media 2.0 AOL and Yahoo! executive DNA which sits under one roof in Verizon's media unit, Oath *(a name which, as one industry insider joked, might not be the worst name ever, simply because Tribune Media's truncated – and now properly-discarded – Tronc still is)*. Both AOL and much-maligned Yahoo! still possess serious content chops. They just didn't make the most of them on their own. Maybe Verizon can help those ambitions materialize, even as its overall strategy remains opaque.

Verizon throws a lot of spaghetti against the wall to see what sticks – a strategy that I don't condemn at all. Better to experiment and act, rather than simply stand frozen in time. And, this behemoth certainly has the resources to experiment.

All I can say is, keep trying.

Comcast NBCUniversal

Like Verizon, massive media and cable conglomerate Comcast NBCUniversal is all over the map in this brave new digitally-fueled and increasingly cord-nevered video world. And, like Verizon, this corporate behemoth has little real success to show for it so far. Well, 2018 certainly didn't help its Media 2.0 cause.

First, Comcast lost out very publicly to Disney in its bid to buy Fox's entertainment assets. That meant that Comcast failed to gain control of Hulu, which would have made it an immediate play-ah (#3) in the U.S. premium DTC streaming video wars. Comcast, of course, still owns a 30% minority stake, but the question is how that benefits Comcast when Disney now charts Hulu's course. Will Comcast NBCUniversal be motivated – authentically – to support Hulu's continued growth and success by offering up its valuable movies and television? Or, will Comcast instead interfere with Disney at every turn? Perhaps it simply decides that enough is enough and sells its minority stake to Disney, and uses those proceeds to buy some other premium DTC subscription service (fuboTV, perhaps).

In a fascinating reversal of fortunes later in the year, Comcast managed to exact a little revenge against Disney when it beat back Rupert Murdoch to buy a 61% controlling interest in prized British pay TV giant Sky for $39 billion. Because Fox still owns Sky's remaining 39% – and Disney will inherit Fox's stake as part of its acquisition – that means that this time Disney is the "odd man out." So, ultimately, the question here is whether Disney will act as a productive partner with Comcast. The most logical answer is that Disney and Comcast will ultimately agree to *Trading Places*, swapping their respective minority stakes in Hulu and Sky, and calling it a day.

In any event, Comcast's OTT video experimentation to date has been largely unsuccessful. The giant has learned the hard way that monetizing digital-first video is hard. Very hard. After shutting down both its SeeSo comedy SVOD and its Flixster video streaming and download service in 2017 due to lack of traction, NBCU added its mobile-first AVOD Watchable to that dead pool when it gave it the axe too. Apparently, few consumers did (watch). Kind of a 1-2-3 strikeout.

So, now what? Well, Comcast still plans to enter the premium SVOD game to compete against Netflix and other giants, even as it already prominently bundles Netflix on its X1 set-top boxes. Alas, Hulu could have been that player. Instead, for now, Comcast has launched Xfinity Instant TV at a monthly $34.99 to $49.99 price, but that is available only for those willing to buy its broadband as well. It also has teased a new low-priced $15 monthly mobile-first, millennial-focused subscription video service. But, CEO Dave Watson explains that Comcast has no plans to go wide with it. In his words *"this is going to be very targeted, primarily digital in nature."* Hmmm. Sounds a lot like Verizon's failed go90 strategy.

Beyond these moves, late 2017, NBCUniversal announced a new 50/50 joint venture with Snap to produce mobile-first scripted content. Comcast also laid out plans a couple years back to become your wireless carrier of choice, using its valuable NBCUniversal content as its "special sauce."

We didn't hear much more about these audacious wireless plans in 2018. But, if the company does move forward, then you can bet that Comcast will efficiently bill you for that privilege in your overall wireless data plan. And, don't underestimate the power of convenience.

Comcast NBCUniversal's "everything but the kitchen sink" strategy has not generated hoped-for results to date. Nonetheless, I continue to applaud this giant for trying, experimenting, and hopefully learning. That's the key part – i.e., learning. After all, we are still relatively early in these tech-transformed Media 2.0 times. Early failures can lead to long-term successes.

DISH NETWORK/SLING TV

I discussed DirecTV already in the context of AT&T. So, how about DirecTV wannabe DISH? That's an interesting question, because DISH hedged its Media 2.0 bets earlier than most. In 2015, and in a bold move to appeal directly to the accelerating number of cord-cutters and cord-nevers, DISH brashly launched its skinny bundle-laden virtual MVPD service. Notably, Sling TV was the first to offer ESPN a la carte, in a snub to all pay TV services out there that counted ESPN as the glue to hold those supersized bundles together. Sling, like most others, offers various tiers of skinny bundles, the lowest being $25 monthly.

Sling TV is reported to have reached the 2.5 million subscriber count as of Q3 2018, which sounds pretty good. But, early returns lead many to believe that DISH essentially cannibalizes itself with Sling TV. Kind of what AT&T seems to be doing with DirecTV and DirecTV Now.

But, then again, would you rather cannibalize yourself, or passively let the OTT competition cannibalize you? I'll take door #1 please!

The Roku Channel

Let's not forget about Roku, a company that has surprised from its very beginning. 2018 looked like it would be one for the books (in a good way) for Roku. First, its stock more than doubled throughout the year after its successful IPO one year earlier. And second, this "David" continued to grow its connected TV dominance over all of the Goliaths out there hell bent on crushing it. Roku's connected TV market share grew to 40% mid-year and surpassed Amazon Fire TV, Google Chromecast, and Apple TV (which surprisingly languished a distant 4th with only 15% share).

But, Roku's stock tanked year-end, wiping out virtually all of its 2018 gains. And, although the company launched its own AVOD (The Roku Channel), it has not yet revealed how many viewers watch it.

Hard to say whether Jekyll or Hyde will appear for Roku in 2019.

V. Mobile-First Netflix Challengers – One Stands Apart

Jeffrey Katzenberg launched enigmatic, massively-funded Media 2.0 venture firm WndrCo in 2017. He upped his own ante in 2018, when he raised an additional $1 billion *(yes, billion!)* to incubate NewTV, an entirely different kind of mobile-first premium video company – one that took ambition and audacity to an entirely new level. Later in the year, he changed the service's name to Quibi (short for "*Quick Bites*").

Quibi

Quibi is an entirely different kind of mobile-first premium video service that plans to launch (vertically) late 2019. Yes, you are right. Both Verizon's mobile-first SVOD go90 and Comcast's Watchable AVOD preceded it, as did others like VC-backed darling Vessel. All crashed and burned. But, those were very different short stories.

Quibi is entirely different. It looks and acts a lot like good old-fashioned TV – high-end primetime TV-like storytelling from A-list top-line and bottom-line talent *(in other words, expensive)*. But, unlike Netflix and the other major SVODs, Quibi's high-end programming will come only in small increments, no longer than 10 minutes each, to suit an audience of 18-34 year old mobile natives. These snackable episodes will cost as much as $125,000 per minute to produce and feel like *Game of Thrones* in terms of Hollywood production quality. While Netflix offers binge-worthy premium content for a rainy day or weekend, binging Quibi will be possible while you wait in line at the DMV *(a place that features its own very interesting cast of characters)*. Its bold mission is to become the first mobile-first Netflix-like SVOD. When it launches, Quibi plans to use a two-tier Hulu-like subscription model ($5 monthly with ads, or $8 monthly without).

Katzenberg's particular small screen vision for premium, Hollywood quality content requires massive amounts of investment, significantly more than anything before it. And, as mentioned above, he didn't disappoint. Katzenberg's jaw-dropping $1 billion flowed from Chinese giant Alibaba and all of the "big six" studios (Disney, 21st Century Fox, NBCUniversal, Sony Pictures Entertainment, Viacom and WarnerMedia) in a financing round that only Katzenberg could call "seed" with a straight face. And, he ain't done yet. He hopes to reach $2 billion, and I wouldn't bet against him. Katzenberg also enlisted former HP and eBay CEO Meg Whitman to add overall technical chops to his story. In Whitman's words, the Katzenberg/Whitman combo *"bring[s] together the best of Hollywood and Silicon Valley."*

Quibi's major media investors likely see the upcoming mobile-first service as being somewhat of a hedge, representing a "throw-back-ian" view of the media world. They also undoubtedly love the fact that they will supply all of its expensive premium content. Surprisingly (at least to me), Quibi won't produce or own any of its own programming. The company will license all of it. Academy Award-winning director Guillermo del Toro, for one, is developing a modern zombie tale exclusively for the service.

Quibi certainly represents a contrarian blueprint to the Media 2.0 world, and execs across both old and new media scratched their heads when it was first announced. But few place bets like Katzenberg, or can raise capital like Katzenberg. And, no one else has gone "all-in" in pursuing a premium mobile-first Netflix-ian SVOD vision as audacious as this.

So, are times now "right" for Quibi's bold new vision, or will its more traditional Media 1.0-ish economics and overall ethos strike it down? Well, remember, Netflix, Amazon, Hulu and the other major SVODs still largely ignore mobile. So, Quibi has a moment in time, right now, to at least try.

Place your bets.

VI. THE SVOD "DAVIDS" AMONGST A FIELD OF GOLIATHS

FUBOTV

And then there's fuboTV – far away from Hollywood, but hiding in plain sight in New York City. Talk about ambitious. fuboTV launched in early 2015 as a sports-centric OTT video service primarily focused on kicking global soccer matches across territorial goal lines to a U.S. audience. But, over time, fuboTV somehow amassed $150 million to finance its operations (including a massive $75 million infusion in 2018) and significantly expand its entertainment faire to compete more directly on the virtual MVPD pitch.

Does fuboTV stand a chance amidst industry Goliaths? Well, the company certainly experienced significant growth in the past year, reaching 250,000 paid subs in October 2018 (up 150,000 from one year earlier). Significant, but still a drop in the bucket compared to the giants. fuboTV also hit new personal heights on the financial metrics side, with its annual run rate exceeding $100 million at that time and average revenues per user (ARPU) climbing 80% year-over-year to $49. And, CEO David Gandler certainly has enlisted giants of his own to beat back his mammoth competitors. He counts 21st Century Fox, Scripps Networks Interactive, and U.K.'s Sky as strategic investors. Insiders tell me that even DirecTV Now, now takes fuboTV seriously.

The fundamental question remains how this upstart can become a significant premium video force in a field of massively-deeper pocketed players. That's a tough "ask" for any independent. Gandler lays out his strategy to me this way. *"We plan to solidify ourselves as a total cable replacement for the home. In 2018, we focused on building our entertainment and news offerings that, combined with our sports-centric programming, is a real alternative to cable or satellite. We continue to differentiate by consistently being first to innovate in our industry across a number of areas, including product and technology."* Gandler points to the following data points to back up that claim. *"We launched 4K HDR Beta in July ahead of anyone else, we launched dynamic ad insertion in January, and we offer better customer service, billing and content."* Tough to verify Gandler's points, but no reason to doubt him.

In any event, ultimately, I expect fuboTV to be bought. Earlier, I mentioned Apple as one possible buyer. And, how about Comcast? After losing out to Disney for control of Hulu, Comcast needs some kind of major premium OTT video shot in the arm. Although fuboTV pales in comparison to the other "usual suspects" out there in terms of reach or impact, it does own a proven tech platform that delivers the premium content goods. It also owns an established, differentiated sports-centric brand that attracts a meaningful and impressively growing audience.

For Comcast, that may be better than starting from scratch.

PLUTO TV

AVOD upstart Pluto TV is another Indie worth knowing. Here's why. First, Pluto TV does things differently than virtually all others. Rather than offer typical VOD access to programming, the service recreates the classic old-world TV channel guide and gives users more than 100 channels of programming in a familiar linear manner (just like your typical broadcast channels on cable). These channels include a mix of major studio programming and premium content from new Media 2.0 brands like finance-focused Cheddar, as well as Pluto TV's own branded channels generally defined by themes curated from a library of tens of thousands of titles from over 130 major media partners.

Second, Pluto TV continues to surprise. This AVOD now quietly counts more than 10 million monthly active users. The company fuels its growth via strategic partnerships with television manufacturers like Vizio and Samsung, in which a bundled TV channel guide-like interface makes perfect sense – both for couch potato consumers that crave passive laid-back experiences, and for Pluto TV's television partners that split resulting ad revenues. By powering instant, free plug-and-play programming, these consumer electronics partners drive revenue beyond point of sale, at least theoretically.

While the majority of Pluto TV's channel lineup is now driven by premium long form programming, select short-form publishers also increasingly use Pluto TV to expand their footprints. *"What Pluto provides for us is access to a lean-back viewing experience on connected TVs,"* according to

Steven Oh, chief business officer of The Young Turks Network. Cheddar CEO Jon Steinberg is even more bullish. *"We love it. They are a much better partner for news video in terms of discovery, revenue and a high-quality environment than Facebook."*

That's right. More Facebook bashing (a recurring theme this past year).

FULLSCREEN

Prior to 2018 and AT&T's acquisition of full control of Otter Media, Fullscreen was an ambitious young SVOD that sprung out of the world of multi-channel networks *(I discuss those later in Chapter 13)*. Fullscreen looked to stake its claim in the crowded SVOD market with its own slate of premium Originals that targeted a young mobile-first millennial audience. Many of those Originals came from Rooster Teeth, a leading digital studio Fullscreen acquired earlier in 2014. But despite Fullscreen's not so secret weapon AT&T and its massive mobile customer base, Fullscreen, as an SVOD service, went dark early 2018. Game over. Only Fullscreen, as a content producer and provider of tools for other creators, lives on.

It's tough being a newbie in this SVOD game of thrones.

VII. INTERNATIONAL PREMIUM OTT VIDEO PLAYERS

Those are just the major U.S. players in the global premium OTT video game. But, even in today's disarmingly nationalistic political climate, let's not focus on domestic players alone. After all, it's a big, borderless world out there *(don't worry Donald, am talking about the Internet here – no need to send the troops)*. So, yes, while Netflix operates in over 190 countries, and Amazon ups the ante to 200, here's at least a taste of major international players, many of which have their own designs to win beyond their own borders.

CHINA

Let's first take China – the biggest international prize of them all – where multiple mega-companies vie to be the "Netflix of China." By May 2018, paid streaming video subscriptions ballooned here to 140 million, essentially doubling in less than two years and exceeding Netflix's global count.

Netflix itself first tried to conquer China. On its own. But, then reality set it in, and Netflix held up the white flag of surrender late 2016. Rather than fight the inevitable, it smartly chose to switch strategies and partner – finally cracking the code (at least to a limited extent) in the process. Netflix chose China's popular video platform iQIYI (a subsidiary of Chinese search giant Baidu) as its dance partner in 2017, which made Netflix programming – but, importantly, not the Netflix service itself – available to this new mass market.

So, Netflix chose to hit a single rather than keep swinging for the fences alone. iQIYI, on the other hand, now holds a particularly strong claim of being the coveted "Netflix of China." After all, it now features the Netflix content to prove it. And, you guessed it, iQIYI plans to build on that claim via an aggressive Originals strategy of its own. But wait, there's even more. iQIYI successfully went public in the U.S. in a Q2 2018 IPO.

Other China behemoths are investing massively to beat back iQIYI and take the pole position. They include the usual suspects – uber-brands Tencent and Alibaba (the latter, through its Youku Tudou division), both of which now absolutely consider entertainment to be core to their overall business. In the words of Tencent VP Sun Zhonghuai, *"Platforms with strength in both quantity and quality content will be the most popular."* And, Tencent put its money where its mouth is, shelling out $2 billion itself for content in 2017, while Alibaba's Youku Tudou reportedly spent $1.1 billion. Both are eyeing aggressive international expansion as well, focusing first on emerging markets India, Latin America, Russia and Eastern Europe.

Wanda Cinema Line, the world's largest cinema exhibitor, also entered the SVOD theater in 2017 via Mtime (China's answer to Fandango and IMDb), in which it made a $350 million investment. And, in an interesting twist, Hong Kong-based Bison Group acquired a majority stake in U.S.-based OTT platform Cinedigm to not only conquer China, but also bring Chinese content to a U.S. audience. You know, the old "what's good for the goose is good for the gander" play *(what's a "gander?" I ask, with my best George Costanza impression).*

In yet another Media 2.0 cautionary tale *(this time, international edition),* LeECO – another major Chinese player at the time – arrogantly proclaimed itself to be the "Netflix of China" in 2016. And, from the outside, life looked good for LeECO, as it boldly announced that it would introduce its new SVOD service both in China and in the U.S. to compete on Netflix's home turf. The company had even acquired a 50-acre site from Yahoo! in Silicon Valley for $250 million to do it. How audacious is that?

But, in a stunning fall from grace, LeECO crashed and burned less than twelve months later. It first scuttled its highly publicized $2 billion acquisition of television-maker Vizio. Then, the floor completely dropped when the company essentially cancelled all of its plans for U.S. OTT market domination and laid off hundreds of U.S. workers.

Two lessons here kids. Lesson #1 – effectively launching and monetizing digital-first video services beyond domestic borders is increasingly hard amidst the growing field of international behemoths. Case in point, LeECO. And, Lesson #2 – internationalizing your customer base is even harder. Netflix's failed attempt to go it alone in China is proof positive of that. So, if you want to be a formidable player outside your home turf, the answer is to not go it alone. In the poetic words of 2018 Pulitzer Prize winning artist Kendrick Lamar, *"Sit down, be humble"* and partner.

EUROPE

Netflix and Amazon already play to win in Europe, with Amazon reportedly catching up to Netflix and now becoming a real threat. But those U.S.-based giants certainly aren't alone either. U.K.'s Sky – now fully-owned by Comcast – is a major Euro-focused pay TV player, of course. Sky counts 23 million subscribers across the U.K., Ireland, Italy, Germany, Austria and Spain. It too plans to launch a stand-alone box-less SVOD service. And, when it does, its strategy naturally will be to beat back Netflix and Amazon with its own slate of localized Originals.

Other players – both obvious, and some not so much – either joined or plan to join the Euro dance party. Deutsche Telekom unveiled its own SVOD called MagentaTV to compete in the land of lederhosen. German media giant ProSiebenSat.1 announced a 50/50 joint venture with Discovery Communications to launch a new premium OTT video service in 2019. Meanwhile, in France, three major television groups – public broadcaster France Televisions and private broadcasters M6 and TF1 – announced their own Netflix (and Amazon) "killer" SALTO. Finally, in a nod to my Magyar D.N.A. *("Magyar" is what we Hungarians call ourselves),* and underscoring the need to be hyper-local in order to succeed amidst global giants, services like Hungarian-based MoziKlub sprinkle in their own local content flavor *(in its case, paprika). (By the way, here's my Hungarian lesson for you – "Mozi" means movie, and "Klub" means, well, think you can figure that one out).*

EMERGING MARKETS

HOOQ is the joint venture of major telco Singtel and competing media giants Sony Pictures Entertainment and WarnerMedia. HOOQ launched in 2015 as a mobile-first SVOD service focused primarily on Southeast

Asia. HOOQ crossed the 1,000,000 paid subscriber mark in 2017, and recently announced a major new partnership with India's Hotstar to expand significantly into India.

And then there's iflix *(no, that's no typo – the company uses no caps)*, a premium OTT service that operates in Asia, Southeast Asia, the Middle East, and North Africa. iflix reported 15 million subscribers as of July 2018, experiencing 250% growth in the first half of the year alone. Backed by international media giants Liberty Global, Sky and Hearst (as well as CAA-affiliated Evolution Media Capital), the service hopes to beat back Netflix with its hyper-focus on hyper-local emerging market content, as well as lower pricing that is more in line with economic realities in those challenging consumer markets. That means $2-$3 per month, a far cry from Netflix's customary $10-ish monthly pricing (something that Netflix now plans to address in Malaysia, at least, when it tests a $4 monthly mobile-only plan).

In 2017, iflix's outspoken CEO Mark Britt, in true audacious, contrarian and fearless fashion, confidently proclaimed that he and his team *"don't believe the thesis that Netflix is going to achieve a global monopoly."* He pointed out that iflix launched well ahead of Netflix in *"places nobody else cares about"* and identified Vietnam, Myanmar, Sri Lanka, Pakistan and Saudi Arabia as specific examples. He also claimed to take a country-focused approach to content, rather than viewing broad territories monolithically (which means more localized and culturally-specific content). Smart. Very smart.

Ever-sly Disney is helping iflix in its counter-Netflix-ian cause. Specifically, while Disney plans to hold back flagship content from Netflix, it did a George Costanza-like opposite *(yes, there he is again)* and actively helped iflix launch a Disney branded channel that features its biggest franchises, including Marvel and Pixar.

Other hyper-local competitors in Southeast Asia include Tribe (an SVOD owned by Malaysian pay TV group Astro) and Catchplay (which launched in Taiwan but now also operates in Indonesia and Singapore at a low sub-$10 monthly fee). Meanwhile, in an interesting twist, three of Korea's largest broadcasters partnered to launch a new OTT service called Kocowa that is laser-focused on a U.S. audience hungry for Korean dramas and K-pop (you know, the same audience WarnerMedia reached with DramaFever, an SVOD it surprisingly shut down late 2018).

Not surprisingly, the Japanese market is also crowded. Japanese e-commerce giant Rakuten operates Viki, a two-tiered AVOD and SVOD service that is available in nearly 200 countries and boasts well over 1 billion viewers. And, in 2017, six of Japan's biggest media companies, together with TBS (an interesting Media 2.0 mélange, to be sure), announced plans to launch their own premium video service called Premium Platinum Japan. But, their combined $72 million investment is downright microscopic compared to investments made by other. And, you gotta go big to have a real chance to win big (or even make a dent).

How about India? Netflix and Amazon already play hard there, of course. But, others to consider include Spuul (which features premium video content from Bollywood), BIGFlix, BoxTV, YuppTV and Star TV's Hotstar (which launched less than four years ago and already claims over 350 million downloads and 150 million monthly active users). Meanwhile, in Russia, that tundra-laden country's Google is Yandex, which is now very much focused on video in an effort to confine Netflix to Siberia. China behemoths Tencent and Alibaba discussed above also eyeball both India and Russia for themselves.

From the sidelines, at least one international SVOD insider – iflix's CEO Mark Britt – is not afraid to stir the pot with his predictions for ultimate international OTT streaming video victory. *"My corporate view is that the Chinese services will end up dominating the global media landscape."*

Now *that's* a bold statement. Downright fearless of the repercussions it will generate!

VIII. WHAT DOES THIS ALL MEAN?

The list of Netflix wannabes is long, and we have just scratched the surface. Several other premium OTT video players try to rise above the premium OTT video din, including Fandor (an Indie and international film-focused SVOD) and Tubi (a broad-based AVOD), just to name two. All of these contenders hope to use Originals to lure us in and keep us there, adding different localized approaches to personalization along the way.

One thing is absolutely certain. This proliferation of premium OTT video services – literally hundreds of them now exist – shows no signs of abating. Others will rise up, several most certainly will fail, and bigger fish will eat many of those caught in the middle. 2019 promises to be yet another major, and frequently painful, shake out year in these global premium OTT video wars.

So many choices, so little time to watch and pay for them all. Perhaps Showtime president & CEO David Nevins summed it up best to an October 2018 industry gathering, at which he predicted more than $100 billion to be spent on content within two years. *"There's no question – it's an arms race."*

That it is, David. That, it is.

11

DISNEY V. NETFLIX – WHAT IT MEANS

(AND IS THE THREAT REAL?)

As discussed in Chapter 10, Disney rocked the premium DTC subscription streaming video world in 2018 when it acquired its 60% controlling stake in Hulu and marched toward the launch of its separate Disney+ SVOD in order to compete head-to-head against Netflix. This followed Disney's separate edict in 2017 that it would no longer license much of its prized content and franchises to Netflix. With these mega-moves, Disney looked straight into Netflix's eyes and pronounced, *"Game On!"*

So, how concerned should Netflix and its investors be about the Disney threat and what it represents? In a word, *"Very."*

Here are three reasons why.

(1) DISNEY IS SUPREMELY MOTIVATED TO WIN.

Disney had likely wanted to buy – not fight – Netflix to become an instant global SVOD juggernaut. But Netflix apparently held too high of an opinion of itself (in the eyes of Disney, at least). And, Disney doesn't like to lose. So, now the gloves are off.

But, more fundamentally, Disney had no choice but to prioritize DTC OTT video platforms by either buying or competing with Netflix, given the cut-the-cord bleeding of traditional cable and satellite television packages that historically have served as Disney's cash cow. ESPN's downward slide in traditional pay TV packages has been well publicized, and the Disney Channel has been right there with it. Subscription streaming video is Disney's plan to make up for that lost ground, and you can bet that CEO Bob Iger will ignite all of his multiple businesses, platforms and channels to promote Disney's new *cause celebre* to consumers.

He certainly made no bones about that in 2018, calling Disney's DTC video ambitions the company's highest priority for 2019. And, let's not forget, Disney is a long-time champion in the world of DTC, with its powerful global brand that still drives significant Blu-ray and DVD sales. Disney's one-of-a-kind brand undoubtedly will draw us into its digital Magic Kingdom. Scary indeed.

A bit daunting for Disney too, by the way, precisely because ESPN is widely seen as being the glue that holds traditional pay TV packages together. ESPN is the home for sports, of course, and sports remain one of the last bastions of premium content that consumers feel they need to experience live, rather than on demand. That's why the major pay TV players pay Disney handsomely for that privilege. Extremely handsomely. To a certain meaningful extent, those lofty traditional ESPN economics prop up an entire professional sports ecosystem, including the skyrocketing professional athlete salaries that go with it. And some pundits believe that Media 2.0's unbundling forces will cause those overall industry economics to come tumbling down. So, Disney's OTT moves, at least to a certain extent, bite the hands that feed by competing directly against its traditional pay TV sugar daddies.

(2) DISNEY KNOWS THAT "CONTENT IS KING" LIKE NEVER BEFORE AMIDST THIS EXTREMELY HEATED DTC PREMIUM VIDEO COMPETITION, AND NOW PLANS TO USE ITS CONTENT MIGHT AS A WEAPON TO WIN.

Amidst the massive global SVOD land grab and overall shift to DTC OTT video viewing, exclusive content is the great differentiator. That's why each massive player hopes to capture our hearts and minds (and most importantly, our eyes and wallets) with high-priced, premium quality Originals. Well, guess what, Disney already owns the rights to the most valuable entertainment brand, franchises, content and characters in the world. Due to massively astute strategic moves over the past decade plus, ESPN and the Disney princesses now share the stage with the Marvel, *Star Wars* and Pixar holy trinity – not to mention massive Fox-born franchises *X-Men* and *Avatar*. So, why give industry-leading Netflix the keys to its content castle when Disney can deliver those crown jewels directly to consumers itself via Hulu and its upcoming Disney+ SVOD?

Exactly! And Disney won't. Not anymore. And, make no mistake, that will hurt Netflix. Disney-esque kids-focused programming is increasingly strategic to Netflix, since about half of Netflix's subscribers regularly watch it with their obsessive kids over and over and over again. That programming is frequently animated and "evergreen," which means kid-friendly content cost-effectively travels and never gets old.

That's precisely why Netflix immediately countered Disney's gut punch in 2017 by buying Millarworld, the comic book creators of characters and stories that include *Kick-Ass*, *Kingsman* and *Old Man Logan*. Although not exactly A-listers, those franchises are now critically important to Netflix now that Disney is gone and its primary focus is international expansion.

Out of either spite or necessity (most likely a little of both), Netflix also shelled out $150 million to television creator Shonda Rhimes of *Grey's Anatomy* and *Empire* fame to steal her away from Disney/ABC. Netflix managed this feat with promises of creative freedom that ABC's traditional media system simply couldn't match. In rapid fire, Netflix also pilfered Robert Kirkman, creator of *The Walking Dead*, from pay TV player AMC and Ryan Murphy, creator of *Glee*, from Fox Television (in a deal reportedly worth as much as $300 million).

And, in 2018, in perhaps its biggest coup yet, Netflix grabbed Barack and Michelle Obama to exclusively produce television series and movies. In the words of the former President, *"We hope to cultivate and curate the talented, inspiring, creative voices who are able to promote greater empathy and understanding between peoples, and help them share their stories with the entire world."*

Do I actually smell idealism in these highly cynical and divided times? I think so. And, I like it!

In any event, Netflix's fearless *(shameless?)* moves represented major retaliatory shots across Disney's bow. Some industry insiders called them blows to traditional broadcast and cable TV in general.

They absolutely were.

(3) DISNEY IS JUST THE LATEST IN A LONG AND GROWING LIST OF INDUSTRY BEHEMOTHS HELL BENT ON TAKING NETFLIX DOWN.

That list now includes Amazon, YouTube TV, AT&T's DirecTV Now, and soon Apple – all of which have resources that dwarf Netflix's. None of these giants will likely be "Netflix-Killers" alone, of course. Certainly not anytime soon. But, together, this colossal cabal may result in "death by 1,000 cuts" to Netflix (or at least heavy bleeding). Netflix is too big to fail, of course. But, that doesn't mean it is a lock to survive long-term on its own, even though Netflix's market cap is comparable to Disney's as year-end 2018 approached.

After all, as we see saw in Chapter 10, Disney and the other "Netflix-Killers" bask in the glow of holistic, multi-faceted business models. In Disney's case, it can monetize multiple divisions with multiple product lines and revenue streams (movies, television, theme parks, merchandising, licensing), all on a global scale. Netflix can't. Remember, its business model is one-dimensional. Netflix's very existence is justified by content subscriptions alone.

So, Disney's forthcoming DTC subscription video services just need to play their parts in Disney's overall smooth-running, multi-platform machine. That gives Disney and other mega-competitors like it tremendous freedom that Netflix doesn't have, especially as budgets for Originals continue to skyrocket amidst this hyper-competition. Let's not forget that Netflix spent a whopping $13 billion in 2018 alone on its programming. It soon will have more than $10 billion in junk bonds on top of its existing $10 billion debt to keep the hits coming. And, let's not forget that it holds long-term content commitments of nearly $19 billion. How long can it keep all of that up?

Disney's call to arms certainly doesn't help Netflix's cause, especially when Disney can, and says it will, undercut Netflix's subscription pricing when it launches Disney+. It also plans to offer each of its services (Hulu, ESPN+, Disney+) individually, or together at some discounted "package" price. Well played.

Naysayers no doubt will challenge the notion that Netflix, with its global brand and massive head start, faces any real existential crisis from Mickey and his fellow cast of giant OTT characters. After all, all of us reading this undoubtedly count ourselves as being part of the Netflix faithful (that's why Netflix experienced heady market gains this past year). Would any of us ever really leave Netflix?

Well, chew on this. Each of these three meta-forces discussed above represents a significant new threat, the likes of which Netflix has never seen before. First, the onslaught by Disney and the burgeoning list of other major players – all of which can afford to play the long game – now offer real choice to consumers for the first time. Take Amazon for example. Amazon Prime Video outperforms Netflix in Germany, India and Japan. So perhaps, in increasingly critical international markets where the Netflix brand is not so deeply entrenched, neither is viewer uptick or loyalty in the face of compelling alternatives.

Even in the U.S., consumers face no real switching costs in an OTT world. If they lose interest in Netflix Originals or simply prefer those of Amazon or others, all they need to do is cancel their monthly subscriptions. Yes, many will pay for more than one. But, Netflix's U.S. market penetration already exceeds 50%, and its long-term bet on continuous international expansion faces major headwinds related to significantly higher overseas customer acquisition costs and significantly lower ARPU. Not much room for error here in a market that gets ever closer to saturation.

That leads to the second disruptive factor of ever-escalating Herculean budgets for Originals in order to both acquire and retain customers. Amazon, with its more ironclad and resilient checkbook *(more like bottomless pit)*, spent $5 billion itself on programming in 2018. Ultimately, Netflix foes like Amazon can afford to out-spend the reigning champ – or undercut its pricing – if they choose to do so. Will Netflix be able to keep it up long-term?

Finally, Disney's internationally beloved franchises, characters, and over-all brand are marketing goldmines that can be used to attract new users – but are now apparently out of Netflix's reach forever. It's not too much of a stretch to assume that WarnerMedia will follow suit and hold back its franchise movies and television shows as well, now that it is part of the AT&T family. Other major media companies have already significantly upped their licensing fees to Netflix or pulled back their content significantly as well.

Together, these daunting forces amount to a perfect storm that may stunt Netflix's growth and depress its shares. Maybe not overnight, or even in 2019. But, ultimately, Netflix may not be able to go it alone, whereas Disney can (go it alone) due to its myriad lines of business and revenue streams. And to think, had Disney successfully bought Netflix a few years back, Reed Hastings likely would be Iger's successor – something the Street most certainly would have loved.

At this point, however, I gotta think that a Disney/Netflix combination is off the table (*although, is anything really off the table in our frenetic Media 2.0 world?*). The new reality is Disney versus Netflix. Scratch that. Disney, Disney-fied Hulu, Amazon, DirecTV Now, Sling TV, Crackle and soon Apple – essentially the world of premium OTT video players – versus Netflix.

That should give all investors pause.

12

HBO Now, ESPN+ & The Unbundled Stand-Alone OTT Video Players

(Less Taste, More (Ful)Filling?)

MEDIA 2.0's great unbundling! That's what I called the new world of once pay TV bundle-only channels that emancipated themselves a few years back to either go it alone, or be part of stripped down skinny bundles. Whereas Netflix, Amazon Prime Video, Hulu and the others discussed in Chapter 10 offer an endless stream of content across multiple "channels," stand-alone pay DTC OTT services *are* the channel – frequently focused on a specific genre. You can now access them without being forced to pay for other channels or content you don't want.

Sounds so simple. But it took so long to get to this point. Now that it has, the number of these newly emancipated OTT services continues to multiply. Here are just some of the key market leaders amongst the many, each with very different DNA.

HBO Now

Pay TV darling HBO, renowned for premium high-quality storytelling, really started this "great unbundling" in a big way a seeming eternity ago

– back in 2015. That's when it boldly stripped itself out of pay TV bundles to offer itself as a stand-alone HBO Now SVOD at a price-tag of $15 per month. At that time, HBO's move represented a major digital-first shot across the traditional media bow – the first domino to fall in a lengthy line of other individual premium pay TV channels that followed. Just months before, many media and entertainment executives predicted that such a move by a major pay TV player wouldn't happen for years. After all, the major cable and satellite providers pay HBO handsomely for carriage. So, why would HBO bite the hand that feeds?

Because HBO saw Media 2.0's writing on the wall, that's why. As already discussed, the accelerating number of cord-cutters and cord-nevers hit home as the industry began to realize what many consumers already had – why pay for the full content cow when you can buy the milk for free *(well, not free, but certainly for a fraction of the cost)*? HBO risked losing an entire generation of digital natives who simply wouldn't consider buying what many perceived to be overly filling, bloated pay TV packages. HBO wanted to reach them, and has reached about 8 million HBO Now paid subscribers as of September 2018 (a number that still just scratches the surface of its roughly 150 million global subscriber count). Hence, the big, bold bet that threatened HBO's relationships with its big cable and satellite partners who shelled out big bucks to carry it and make it the brand we all know today.

HBO held the cards in this poker game. As upsetting and unsettling as HBO's game-changing play was to the major traditional MVPDs, they knew that consumers would bolt to the OTT streaming world even faster if HBO were missing from their traditional pay TV packages. And, once HBO broke free from those pay TV ranks to go it alone, others followed in rapid succession. CBS, Showtime, Cinemax, Starz, TNT, Nickelodeon and a growing parade of others. Even slow-moving Viacom joined the stand-alone SVOD club in 2018 when it acquired AwesomenessTV and launched its Philo SVOD at a bargain basement $16 monthly price point. If Viacom is doing it, you know virtually everyone else is. Now the exception is *not* to unbundle.

The great unknown, of course, is how many stand-alone SVODs or stripped down skinny pay TV bundles the market can bear. After all, $10 here, $15 there, $40 over there (to add live TV programming) – pretty soon consumers end up being at the same place they tried to escape from in the first place when they caught the cord-cutting bug. A certain critical mass element can't be denied. Parks Associates reports that only 17% of U.S. broadband subscribers pay for three or more OTT services.

And now, HBO Now faces a major new threat in the form of the SVOD onslaught discussed in Chapter 10. HBO invented the Originals game "back in the day" to compete and win against traditional cable movie channels and broadcasters. But, now all the SVOD behemoths have stolen that Originals page from HBO's playbook *(more like the whole damn playbook!)*. The students have become the masters (or, at least peers), as high cost, high production value Originals are the weapons of choice to win in our new Media 2.0 OTT video wars.

So, with consumers awash in a sea of premium award-winning programming from the likes of Netflix, Amazon, Hulu and others, even prestigious HBO feels the heat. And, it boasted a relatively meager $2 billion budget to fund its programming for 2018 compared to Amazon's and Hulu's respective $5 billion budgets, and Netflix's gargantuan $13 billion budget. How will HBO's new owner AT&T react? In Q3 2018, CEO Randall Stephenson offered clues when he acknowledged that HBO needs *"a more fulsome lineup and schedule"* to effectively compete. He conceded that many subscribers abandon ship when the *Game of Thrones* season ends (a universal industry peril in a Media 2.0 "cut the cord" world with $0 switching costs). But, he added, *"We're not talking about Netflix-like investments."*

Suffice it to say that the pressure is on at HBO. WarnerMedia CEO John Stankey, who directly oversees HBO, amped up his team and their overall stress levels in a June 2018 internal town hall meeting. In true *Lorax*-ian fashion – with demands to get "bigger-er" with more, more, more HBO viewer engagement – Stankey issued the following edict. *"We need hours a day. It's not hours a week, and it's not hours a month. We need hours a day."*

Don't we all.

ESPN+

ESPN+ is another major stand-alone player in these ruthless DTC subscription video wars – and a major Disney bet at only $4.99 per month. I already discussed ESPN+ at length in Chapter 10, so I'll keep it short here. This critical new DTC video addition to the Disney family launched in April 2018. And, by September, Disney reported that it had reached the 1 million paid subscriber count. CEO Bob Iger eagerly trumpeted this growth to the Street, pointing out that initial conversion rates from free trials to paid subscriptions exceeded expectations. He did, however, also place an important caveat on his statements, conceding that those were *"relatively modest expectations."*

The critical question, of course, is whether ESPN+ SVOD revenues will make up for traditional ESPN's significant lost ground in legacy cable and satellite packages. Kevin Mayer, who now oversees Disney's entire digital strategy and portfolio, has much work cut out for him in 2019. But, Mayer and his seven Disney senior execs certainly aren't Dopey (*yeah, I said that*). They are smart, seasoned, and flush with coveted live sports programming that can't be found anywhere else.

At least, for now.

STARZ

Lionsgate's Starz SVOD generated significant and somewhat surprising growth in 2018. CEO Jon Feltheimer reported more than 3 million paying subs in the U.S. alone as of September 2018 (at $9 per month) – up from 1 million one year earlier. He reported an additional 1 million subs overseas.

What is Starz's "special sauce" to attract new subs? Unlike most others, Starz focuses on content that resonates deeply with certain underserved market segments. According to Feltheimer, *"At Starz, we spent the year continuing to invest in content for African-American, Latinx, female and LGBTQ audiences."*

CBS ALL ACCESS

CBS charges surprisingly hard in the stand-alone DTC subscription video theater with its All Access service, which boasts 2.5 million paid subscribers as of September 2018 – reportedly doubling its count year-over-year. This traditional broadcaster hopes to serve 8 million paying subs with Originals of its own when all is said and done, including Jordan Peele's upcoming reimagined *The Twilight Zone* series and more *Star Trek* for you Trekkies out there.

Kudos to CBS. Its digital efforts and multi-platform strategy seem to be working. CBS's digital revenues, which include All Access, rose a healthy 32% in Q3 2018 and drove overall CBS revenues skyward. Marc DeBevoise, president and COO of CBS Interactive, is bullish about his company's long-term prospects against Netflix and others. *"We're feeling very competitive. This isn't a winner-take-all market."*

While I wholeheartedly agree, consumers *do* have their limits.

VICE

Vice, a darling amongst darlings in the Media 2.0 world over the past few years, seemingly could do no wrong prior to 2018. But, much like with Facebook, 2018 was not particularly kind. #MeToo moments and flat-lining revenues (reportedly $600-$650 million), together with continuing losses (expected to reach $50 million-ish), rocked this former wunderkind. By year's end, newly-installed CEO Nancy Dubuc announced major austerity measures and overall business realignment.

Vice launched "angry" originally as an underground print publication, featuring counter-culture, frequently shocking news stories that turned the traditional news world on its head. It later fundamentally changed its stripes to focus significantly on video. Think of it this way. If ESPN is video's jock, and HBO its artiste, Vice is the video industry's rebel – the dangerous bad boy.

And it largely worked. Until this year. The company's unprecedented middle finger-ian approach appealed to an entire generation of young millennials, many of whom felt nothing but apathy or even contempt for traditional news outlets. And, since Vice was where the coveted young audience was, Vice was where both Madison Avenue and Hollywood felt they needed to be. Even family-friendly Disney couldn't resist, investing $400 million (which couldn't have been easy, given that Vice's form of storytelling isn't exactly told from *"the happiest place on earth"*). Vice also attracted a whopping $450 million cash infusion in 2017 from mega private equity firm TPG at an even more whopping $5.7 billion valuation, in order to accelerate Vice's own video-first and Originals strategy.

But, Vice's particular brand of danger caught up with it in 2018. And, reality frequently bites. So, whereas industry insiders were generally bullish at year-end 2017, 2018 ended with Disney writing off $157 million of its original investment (about 40%). Many now paint a very different picture of Vice. Some even tell me privately that they expect the sky to fall further on its unicorn valuation and long-time growth story, a story that previously went largely unchallenged.

What that means, no one knows for sure. But, it certainly may mean that a big fish pays a previously unthinkably low price largely for the brand's very different kind of cache. Vice's swagger isn't completely vanquished yet, of course. But, its star certainly has significantly diminished.

VEVO

Music-focused Vevo is premium OTT video's privileged high school musician who gets accepted to Juilliard because of mommy and daddy's connections. You see, Vevo shares similar pedigreed big traditional media roots as its cousin, Hulu. Two of the three major record labels own Vevo – Universal Music Group and Sony Music. The third, Warner Music, is not yet an actual owner, but finally did join the party in 2016 when it agreed to license its music to Vevo for the first time. Like Hulu discussed earlier, Vevo used its parents' deep pockets to begin to spend aggressively in 2016 in order to be taken seriously as a premium OTT video contender.

But despite boasting a massive user base that watches more than 25 billion videos every month, Vevo also faced tough times in 2018. Here's why.

Vevo has always been a free AVOD service like YouTube. And, in a little known fact (except to industry insiders), over 90% of Vevo's traffic comes directly from YouTube. That reality means that YouTube first collects Vevo's advertising dollars and gives back only a fraction (although a better fraction than YouTube's typical 55% revenue split with video creators). And, that's only the half (or nearly) of it. Vevo must then give the lion's share of its fraction to the music labels and publishers. All this sharing doesn't leave much left for Vevo, which is why Vevo claimed revenues of only $650 million in 2017, a relatively small sum for a service so big and with such reach. Bottom line – Vevo's economics are deeply challenged, a recurring theme for pure-play video services as we have seen.

Prior to 2018, Vevo loudly signaled to the world that it wanted to change all that. In 2016, then-CEO Erik Huggers very publicly announced that Vevo would launch its own paid SVOD service later that year in order to accelerate its monetization path. But, that SVOD never materialized. Even more surprising *(and downright shocking to many, myself included)*, Vevo dropped its own DTC channel in 2018. In other words, Vevo did the exact opposite of what it had told the world it would do. It reverted to its original failed strategy of exclusively distributing through YouTube and other social channels.

So, Vevo – which had previously committed to weaning itself off its YouTube heroin addiction *(its mass traffic high)* in order to take back control of its own destiny in its bid to be profitable *(directly monetize its content so that it doesn't need to share with its pusher)* – succumbed to its addiction this past year. Vevo is now fully hooked. An addict. With no rehab in sight (at least for now).

What does this new reality mean for Vevo as it goes forward? Does this mean that its major label owners – who now operate in an industry on the upswing – have resigned themselves to Vevo serving purely as a marketing platform for their artists (rather than a real stand-alone business)? Or, will Vevo's owners now consider an outright sale, something they had previously entertained, but later abandoned, a few years ago?

Watch (and listen closely to) Vevo's machinations as the major labels press "play" for 2019.

SPOTIFY

Since we're talking music, we gotta talk Spotify, the world's biggest stand-alone music streaming service. Spotify finally went public in 2018 at expected lofty valuations, meaning that it now has money to burn to fund major new strategic initiatives in its endless quest for profitability. *"But, Spotify isn't an OTT video streaming service,"* you insightfully say. Well, that was true up to 2016. But then, Spotify announced that it too was moving full throttle into the world of Originals. And it wasn't just talking good old-fashioned music videos at the time. Rather, Spotify announced a video strategy focused on producing expensive premium scripted series. Sure, Spotify had featured clips from ESPN and others for quite some time, but its newly-announced Originals strategy represented a whole new world.

Since then, however, Spotify's video actions have been nothing if not schizophrenic. Late 2017, Spotify significantly narrowed its focus on Originals, and its global head of content, Tom Calderone, exited stage left. In his place, former head of Maker Studios, Courtney Holt, entered the scene to refocus Spotify's video dreams on smaller, simpler influencer-driven videos. That transformed, less audacious video strategy made sense to many industry insiders. But, just when these pundits thought they knew where Spotify was heading in 2018, in comes traditional media exec Dawn Ostroff as its new chief content officer, who – you guessed it – was charged with once again developing high-priced long-form premium Originals. Talk about déjà vu, all over again.

Maybe Spotify's bipolar behavior can simply be explained away by its very different pre-IPO and post-IPO realities. Pre-IPO, Spotify was forced to reign in its lavish spending (at least to a certain extent). But, once its IPO successfully hit and the company was flush with cash, perhaps it was time to go back to the good old days of dreaming big. Spending big. Premium video big.

In any event, no matter how massive it is – and Spotify certainly is massive – big questions remain whether the music giant can break through the collective premium OTT video wall of sound. After all, we subscribe to Spotify to listen. Will enough of us choose Spotify to satisfy our more video-centric urges? Is it even possible for Spotify to dramatically change its audio stripes in our eyes *(er, more accurately ears)*? That's a real existential question analogous to Google's fundamental challenge with YouTube to get us to rethink its long-time brand and pay up for looking down at previously "free" ad-supported content.

WWE Network

Since we're talking about bold and brash video strategies, why not mix in some body-slamming? Professional "wrestling" *(if you can call it that)* operates its surprisingly successful WWE Network SVOD service and (body)counts 1.8 million paying subscribers globally as of mid-2018. WWE Network's content travels well internationally, and these entertainers *(er, wrestlers)* now find themselves in over 180 countries. After all, a body-slam is a body-slam in any language.

WWE is a surprising technology innovator. Always has been. It helped create the still-massive pay-per-view television market in the first place. Its successful SVOD service proves that targeted specialized programming can be both lucrative and global in its appeal.

The Bottom Line

Stakes are extremely high. But, at least the players discussed in this chapter have built established brands and amassed real audiences at scale. By taking action. Taking risks. Boldly. Frequently fearlessly.

Place your bets on which stand-alone services have a real chance of winning. Odds are long, and the list of winners will be short.

13

DIGITAL-FIRST, MILLENNIAL-FOCUSED VIDEO COMPANIES

(THE ARTISTS FORMERLY KNOWN AS "MCNS")

THE earlier chapters laid out some of the leading big ticket video players in the premium motion picture and television-focused DTC OTT video game, all of them backed by massive dollars or traditional media companies – and most *not* with a mobile-first millennial audience top of mind.

Now, let's move to the other side of the spectrum – the digital-first new media companies that primarily feature mobile-friendly video content (most frequently focused on a defined content theme or lifestyle) and specifically targeted for a millennial audience (in other words, content for a generation growing up, looking down). These services most typically started in the world of ad-supported YouTube-ian UGC.

Just a few years back, most of these new media companies were known as multichannel networks (MCNs). These were those quaint aggregators of YouTube channels that generally focused on a specific vertical audience or market segment. Their roots are fundamentally different from those of the major OTT video players discussed earlier. But, MCNs are now a thing of the past. They are now simply new media companies focused on producing and distributing compelling digital-first content that can be monetized in multiple Media 2.0 ways and across multiple platforms.

And, 2018 was a very tough year for many of them. Whereas several new media pioneers achieved massive early exits during the MCN "best of times" a few years back – most notably, Maker Studios which Disney acquired in 2014 for a price ultimately pegged at $675 million – valuations fell to Earth fast in 2018. Daunting downward forces included an ever-increasing stream of deep-pocketed competitors, ever-changing ad algorithms, and plummeting advertising revenues. In one notable example, once promising creator Little Things experienced a 75% drop in its organic traffic as a result of Facebook "tweaking" its ad formulas that now favor content shared and created by friends over that offered by publishers.

Even previous new media darlings felt the hurt. AwesomenessTV – once the poster child for a next-gen media company doing it right – experienced its own "come to Jesus." Viacom scooped it up at a fraction of its earlier lofty valuations (reportedly $50 million) during the unkind summer of 2018. Viacom Digital Studios' president Kelly Day called its buy *"the bargain of a lifetime."* Just a couple years earlier, the company had been valued at $650 million.

But, there was more. As year-end approached, AT&T pulled the plug on not just one, but two of WarnerMedia's high profile digital-first companies as part of its post-merger pruning. First, the axe dropped on Korean drama-focused DramaFever, just two years after Warner Bros. had acquired it from Japan's SoftBank (which, in turn, had bought DramaFever just two years before that for a reported $100+ million). Then, in rapid succession, AT&T killed off WarnerMedia's digital studio division Super Deluxe.

Tough times indeed. New media's mood swung to depression.

I. The Rise and Fall of MCNs – A History Lesson & Cautionary Tale

MCNs – that specific moniker and that specific aggregation "play" – were all the rage 4-5 years ago (*I wrote about them constantly myself*). But, then, something curious happened. All of these digital-first video companies shied away from that acronym. Some, violently, contending they were never MCNs in the first place. And, they – at least the leading digital-first video companies that I discuss below – were right. The world in which they played (and how they played in it) had changed dramatically since those earlier heady days.

First, the MCN business model ultimately didn't work. Initially, MCNs focused almost entirely on audience scale. Once that scale was achieved, virtually all category leaders turned to the question of revenue and chose an advertising-driven model to monetize their frequently hundreds of millions of subscribers (and for some, billion-plus). But, while that ad-driven strategy sounded so logical at the time, it never effectively monetized, especially since these new media companies also shared 45% of their ad revenues with YouTube. High view counts simply didn't translate into high revenue.

And, because these MCNs had to monetize for themselves of course, they took their additional cut (typically 20-30%) from the remaining 55% and returned only the remaining fraction to their video creators. That made nobody happy – neither the MCN and its investors, nor the creators they represented who had significantly higher revenue expectations. And so, pure aggregation plays became suspect. On top of that, many creators who were not amongst the MCN's top performers felt marginalized – that they were not getting the attention they deserved. That certainly didn't help. That's when, out of necessity, these companies pivoted. Some MCNs sooner than others.

Case in point, tween and teen-focused AwesomenessTV. At the time, as noted above, industry insiders revered this Media 2.0 video pioneer for building a digital-first media company right. Early on in its life, AwesomenessTV stole a page from the HBO playbook *(sound familiar?)* and began to develop and distribute its own premium Originals, and it had the proven creative DNA chops and credibility to do it right. Then-CEO Brian Robbins came from the traditional media world and launched AwesomenessTV after he saw his kids obsessively watching animated videos on YouTube *(a perfect example of using your kids as your own personal Petri dish)*. AwesomenessTV poured significant resources into developing – rather than just aggregating – its own exclusive characters, content and special brand of storytelling.

AwesomenessTV also understood the value of building its own brand first. Many other "artists formerly known as MCNs" *(an homage to Prince from a fellow Minnesotan)* didn't recognize this strategic imperative until much later. Several initially marketed their top individual creators and shows first, and their own brands second. This led to audience confusion. What kind of content did the company's brand stand for exactly? Audiences didn't really care. They simply wanted to watch the individual shows they liked. And, that mattered to advertisers, potential distribution partners, and ultimately to investors.

AwesomenessTV's strategy worked (at least initially). The brand developed a compelling library of exclusive content, properties and characters that it exploited and monetized for big bucks in myriad ways, including licensing for movies and television. Add brand-funded and brand-integrated videos – so-called "branded content" or "content marketing" – and you had a powerful 1-2 punch that knocked down the former advertising-only model. Seeing AwesomenessTV's success amidst the existential economic challenges they faced, virtually all MCNs smartly followed suit.

They, in essence, simply evolved into being digital-first studios that aspired to be their Awesome(nessTV) idol.

Finally, the term "MCN" simply no longer fit our ever-evolving Media 2.0 landscape. "Multi-channel networks" literally meant companies that aggregated multiple YouTube – and essentially only YouTube – channels together under a new media brand. Well, it certainly ain't a YouTube-only world anymore. Now we have Facebook, Instagram, Snapchat, Twitter and myriad other social platforms that have become Media 2.0 powerhouses themselves and are increasingly strategic to video creators and the former MCNs supporting them.

And, there's the rub for these new more niche, smaller digital-first media companies. While all of these former MCNs smartly pivoted in the past 2-3 years to more closely follow the AwesomenessTV model, now – in 2019 – they face an uncertain reality of competing for premium OTT video ad dollars in a field of giants who out-premium them by a massive order of magnitude with their gargantuan content budgets. They also now face newly gun-shy advertisers wary of videos linked to "fake news" and unsafe content in their more open, less controlled, video environments. And, to add insult to injury, platforms like Facebook continuously changed the rules of their game (their advertising algorithms). So, while real "here and now" monetization is paramount, it is increasingly elusive for many of these companies.

The best bet to win for these new media companies is to position themselves narrowly and be lifestyle-focused, monetizing all elements of an underserved market via content, community and commerce … lots of commerce. In other words, to establish brands steeped in "fandom." Rabid fandom. Lifestyle brand Goop *(yes, Gwyneth's Goop)* is a new poster child here. Goop focuses on six areas of content – wellness, travel, food, beauty, style, and work – for a largely female audience. And, it monetizes all of it.

II. DIGITAL-FIRST, MILLENNIAL-FOCUSED VIDEO LEADERS

YouTube, of course, is the mother of all of these digital-first media companies, having birthed our entire UGC video world and getting paid handsomely for it with its 55/45 revenue split. As we have already seen, YouTube is almost everywhere millennial viewers want to be (music, sports, fashion, beauty, comedy, cats – *lots of cats* – you name it). But, its tremendous breadth is also its principal weakness. It is frequently challenging to navigate its ever-deepening ocean of content and ever-proliferating number of brands (YouTube "classic," YouTube Premium, YouTube TV, not to mention all of the relevant Google offshoots like Google Play).

Here are some of the biggest and boldest new digital-first and millennial-focused media companies that aim to solve YouTube's challenges. All have achieved significant scale, most are still primarily ad-supported, and most now have big name traditional media investors behind them – established players that frequently invest to learn more about a brave new world they don't yet understand and "try before they buy." You see, strategic investors frequently become buyers as they get more comfortable in an unfamiliar space.

Many of these strategic investors are significantly more skittish in 2019 than they were just one year ago. Ironically, that may actually accelerate M&A activity if new media company pain continues and valuations continue to be pushed downward amidst current challenging video ad dynamics.

A. AWESOMENESSTV – THE O.G.

You already knew this one would be first on my list, given its pioneering Media 2.0 role. AwesomenessTV launched in 2012 and soon became one of the first highly successful and highly targeted digital-first media companies, hoping to build a better mousetrap in an increasingly mobile-first world. And when it did, Gen Z tweens and teens came to the party, happily led by their exhausted parents who got some much-needed peace because of it.

DreamWorks Animation took notice and ultimately bought the company in 2013. Kudos to Jeffrey Katzenberg for being amongst the first traditional media execs to understand that the world had changed and he needed to get on board. And, because Comcast NBCUniversal later swallowed up Dreamworks Animation for $3.8 billion in 2016, the Peacock owned its part ownership of AwesomenessTV, together with joint-owners Verizon and Hearst (both of which had made investments of their own in AwesomenessTV just before the sale). So, Katzenberg's early action paid off big time. What cost him about $115 million back in 2013, cost NBCUniversal about 4X that number as part of its overall DreamWorks Animation deal only three years later. Not a bad Media 2.0 return on investment for him.

Fast forward to 2018. Not such good news for Comcast NBCUniversal, which – together with co-owners Verizon and Hearst – sold off AwesomenessTV to Viacom for a bargain basement price reported to be about $50 million. In other words, for about 1/13th of its $650 million valuation just two years earlier. Certainly some of that deflation flowed directly from AwesomenessTV's complex joint ownership structure. Suffice it to say that joint venture partners frequently don't share the same vision or optimize strategy and decision-making. But, industry dynamics played the biggest part.

Ahh, how sentiments and resulting fortunes change from year to year in our Media 2.0 world. By externalities frequently impossible to control. There it is again. Timing.

Let's see what Viacom can do with its shiny new Awesome(ness) toy that boasts an audience of 158 million unique users and 300 million monthly views as of August 2018. It already owns MTV and Nickelodean, brands that resonate with a similar demographic. It just might be a natural "fit."

B. THE BROAD-BASED DIGITAL-FIRST PLAYERS

The digital-first video companies below cover extensive ground, not specifically focusing on any particular content, lifestyle or demographic market segment. Sometimes that works, but many times it doesn't due to an overly-ambitious agenda that frequently pits them against giants with much deeper pockets.

MAKER STUDIOS

Maker Studios helped pioneer the original MCN space. Up until 2017, it was one of the few digital-first media companies that covered multiple bases – not just one specific content category or market segment. Maker launched early 2009 and immediately became a juggernaut at least in terms of reach, if not in terms of compelling stand-alone economics. Video creators themselves made Maker (hence, the name), inspired by the story of traditional media's United Artists a long, long time ago and in a media galaxy far, far away. OTT video-inspired Disney bought Maker Studios in 2014 for what ultimately proved to be around $675 million (the deal had the potential to cost Disney up to $950 million with certain performance milestones). So, Maker has now been part of Disney's burgeoning Media 2.0 Magic Kingdom for several years.

Many scratched their heads when Disney opened its coffers wide to buy Maker. In fact, most scoffed. And many *(most?)* still do. Those naysayers felt vindicated in 2017 as virtually all of Maker's senior executives exited stage left, and Disney officially placed Maker into its Disney Digital division. Its new mission is to exclusively focus on acting as a marketing and distribution engine for Disney-related franchises, movies, television and characters – which certainly wasn't a fundamental part of the original plan. *Or, was it?*

Buying Maker was never about stand-alone economics. Traditional media M&A metrics of revenue and EBITDA multiples were thrown out the window (just as they generally have been in all other major digital-first media acquisitions to date, since this nascent industry still has few real "comps"). Rather, Maker's massive digital, millennial footprint gave Disney an ability to reach a heads down, mobile-focused generation of digital natives that it otherwise likely would not reach with its treasure trove of classic franchises, titles, characters and stories. And, that mega-marketing benefit alone may be enough to justify Maker's price tag, even if the going has been rough in these first few post-acquisition years.

Disney CEO Bob Iger said as much when he announced the deal in the first place, underscoring that Disney primarily viewed Maker as being a distribution platform for the marketing of its storytelling. It's a basic point that is frequently lost on the deal's naysayers. A highly successful Maker-driven, mobile-centric, millennial-focused marketing campaign for one Disney mega-movie property alone (like *Star Wars*) holds the potential to generate hundreds of millions of incremental dollars at the box office – not to mention hundreds of millions more in all of Disney's ancillary channels. Do that a few times and the $675 million price tag doesn't sound too bad, does it?

So, yes, these new digital-first, millennial-focused media companies face challenging stand-alone economics. And, yes, unanticipated M&A integration challenges muted Disney's and Maker's initial success. But, those significant challenges confront any party in M&A, and those realities do nothing to diminish the strategic value of the right digital-first new media company in the hands of the right, more traditional, strategic buyer that looks at the world with a much broader and longer-term ROI lens. After all, established digital-first media company brands and audiences matter.

Evaluated in that light, Disney's acquisition of Maker still may prove to be a smart, savvy move. First, with one stroke of its pen, Disney entered the mobile-first, millennial-focused video world at mass scale and with the right DNA that Disney sorely needed to jump-start its Media 2.0 ambitions. To its credit, Disney humbly conceded to the world that it needed that DNA. Yes, most of those Maker execs have now left the building, but they undoubtedly made their (Maker's) mark *(a drink they still may be toasting to celebrate their M&A good fortunes … and timing)*. The Maker buy also sent a message both to Wall Street and Disney employees that its top brass took this brave new Media 2.0 world seriously. And, those signals matter. They set the tone. Impact culture.

I still like the deal and what it represents.

STUDIO 71 (FORMERLY COLLECTIVE DIGITAL STUDIO)

Collective Digital Studio (CDS) "suffered" a fate similar to Maker in 2015, selling to German-based media conglomerate ProSiebenSat.1, which then merged it into its leading German-based digital-first media company Studio71 in an overall deal valued at $240 million. CDS always had a relatively broad focus compared to most other digital-first media companies, and is best known for its *Fred, Annoying Orange* and *Video Game High School* series that it successfully monetized across multiple platforms, including television. CDS proved it could monetize. But, CDS never really built a consumer brand while doing it. ProSieben hopes to change that and use Studio71 as one of its secret weapons to penetrate the U.S. market.

Other European media giants joined ProSieben for this ride "across the pond" in 2017. France's leading commercial network TF1 and Italian broadcaster Mediaset together invested $56 million at a valuation that essentially doubled ProSieben's investment valuation less than two years earlier. *"Not bad for a nine-figure business,"* CEO Reza Izad tells me. He further points out that Studio71's growth rate since acquisition has been 65+% each year. According to Reza, *"1 in 3 Americans watch our content every month for 1.5 hours plus according to ComScore and we only have 900 U.S.-based channels. That is way less than Vevo and everyone else playing the scale game. This means Studio71 represents the largest number of hit channels on YouTube, Facebook, Instagram etc. out of all of our competitive set. Since we are in the culture business, that is really important and a significant distinction between us and the competition."*

Studio71 sounds like it's playing its part in ProSieben's overall media machine. Could it do it alone? Doesn't really matter anymore. Doesn't need to.

COMPLEX NETWORKS

This one is a 50-50 joint venture from our friends at Verizon and Hearst that promotes a broad-based "youth culture" *(whatever that means)*. Not surprisingly, given its Verizon DNA, Complex develops high quality (code for expensive) mobile-first programming. It also produces and distributes content under its own brand across YouTube and other channels, boasting nearly 300 million monthly video views. One of its channels, *Rated Red,* is aimed at millennials in U.S. red states, something sure to please a certain someone presently in the White House.

VRV

Otter Media-born VRV, an SVOD launched in 2016, is now officially part of AT&T's video universe as a result of its acquisition. VRV focuses on a broad range of channels with deep fandom at a monthly $9.99 price point. Nickelodeon's animation fan-focused Nicksplat was one such channel that joined in 2018, featuring hits like *The Wild Thornberry's* and *CatDog*. NickSplat joins VRV standouts Crunchyroll (*discussed below*), Nerdist and Mubi. In the words of VRV general manager Arlen Marmel, *"We're building a basecamp for unique fandom experiences within the VRV universe. By rallying and connecting fan communities, we make it easy to be a fan."* Sounds logical to me. And monetizable.

C. TARGETED, SO-CALLED "NICHE" CONTENT PLAYERS

And then there are the more focused digital-first new media companies that cater to a specific underserved market segment that craves a specific category of content. Many of these audiences become superfans, for whom the content becomes deeply personal and resonates at a visceral level. If done right, these so-called "niche" video services can generate massive numbers on a global scale in our borderless OTT world.

Here are some focused, so-called "niche" new media companies worth knowing.

MACHINIMA

Nearly one decade ago, Allen DeBevoise, short-form video's godfather of soul, essentially created the gamer-focused Machinima we know today and birthed the entire modern MCN movement. Machinima quickly became one of the new MCN world's shining stars in terms of audience, both in its size and in its coveted young male demographic. Warner Bros., keeper of the young male-focused DC Comics flame, invested more than $40 million over time. Finally, Warner Bros. pulled the trigger and, in true superhero style, lifted Machinima to safety from its subsequent monetization challenges, buying the company and giving it a logical new home in its DC Comics universe. A collective sigh of relief could be heard from the Machinima faithful as final papers were signed and the deal was sealed just in time for the 2016 holidays *(Thanksgiving indeed!)*.

Perhaps not the best financial result, but a good result nonetheless. Machinima found itself a nice warm home, which sure beats the alternative.

CRUNCHYROLL

Crunchyroll is all anime and manga, all the time – 25,000-plus episodes of the best-licensed programming Asian media producers can offer. And, this Sensei serves a massive audience of 40 million who eat it up. Voraciously. Most view for free, but 1 million pay for more wasabi (deeper content, additional features).

Berkeley college grads rolled Crunchyroll much earlier than most in 2006, and always focused on Asian-produced content for an audience primarily outside Asia. The Chernin Group bought a controlling interest in 2013 and then later contributed that stake to its Otter Media joint venture with AT&T. As a result of AT&T's acquisition of Otter Media in 2018, Crunchyroll now finds itself in the AT&T family as an individual branded service under Otter's Ellation umbrella brand.

Former Otter Media president Sarah Harden (now CEO of Reese Witherspoon's female-focused new media company Hello Sunshine) told me last year that Crunchyroll did not, like most other mobile-first new media services, suffer from the Media 2.0 *"Adpocalpyse."* Here's how. Harden explained that Crunchyroll's parental unit, Ellation, is *"all about building identity brands with multiple revenue streams and built around emotional connection."* In other words, passionate communities, fandoms, characterized by what she calls *"brand love."*

Harden's test for whether any service has succeeded in building that kind of loving feeling with its fans is whether they become brand loyalists who show up at brand-sponsored live events, wearing brand t-shirts. If they do, then brand love translates not only into advertising and subscription dollars, but also into live event and merchandising dollars. And, Harden tells me that those somewhat under-the-radar revenue streams are substantial for Crunchyroll, as well as for other Ellation brands like Rooster Teeth.

We'll see how those multi-platform revenue streams scale for AT&T in 2019.

TASTEMADE

The innovators behind early short-form video pioneer Demand Media launched this foodie and travel-focused digital-first media company in 2012. Consider it a millennial and mobile-focused version of The Food Channel, with a healthy dose of Travel Channel sprinkled in. In fact, The Food Channel's majority owner, Scripps Networks (now owned by Discovery Communications), is a significant Tastemade investor, which ultimately makes it a very possible buyer. Amazon joined the investor party in 2018, participating in the company's $35 million Series E financing, bringing total investment to $115 million. That makes Amazon a potential buyer as well.

Like AwesomenessTV, at least up until the end of 2017, Tastemade carried one of the strongest Media 2.0 names and reputations amongst traditional media executives. Here's why. First, much like AwesomenessTV,

Tastemade focused first on developing its own Originals and building a library of evergreen content that it could license and monetize over and over again. It was never just an aggregation play. Second, like AwesomenessTV, Tastemade always built its brand first and the brands of its creators second. That meant that its audience and potential distribution partners knew what Tastemade content represented. Third, because of those two strategic pillars, Tastemade successfully achieved significant distribution across multiple key platforms like Apple TV much earlier than most – and, broad-based distribution is the name of the game in our multi-platform world, remember?

But, we saw how fortunes changed for AwesomenessTV in 2018. So, Tastemade's value in the eyes of external beholders likely followed suit and is very different today than it was one year ago. And, like all other independent digital-first media companies on this list, Tastemade's existential challenge is to effectively monetize at scale and, therefore, justify its $115 million in financing and long-term stand-alone story. Fandom and a Goop style makeover may hold the key here too. No surprise, then, that Tastemade hired Goop's former president in 2018 to be its new COO.

One of Tastemade's most tantalizing possibilities is video-driven e-commerce, which logically should generously flow from this particular food and travel category. Just think about it. You watch your favorite chefs. You see what they use to make your favorite recipes. And, *bam!* Up comes an instant, seamless buying opportunity with a stress-inducing time limit. Of course you'll buy! Tastemade moves ever-closer toward that holy grail with its online e-commerce marketplace. And, the fact that Amazon is now a strategic investor certainly doesn't hurt that cause. Makes perfect cents *(yes, intentional)*.

At a minimum, Tastemade is focusing more on wrapping itself in a multi-pronged business model story that at least theoretically generates multiple compelling and growing revenue streams. According to CEO Larry

Fitzgibbon, the company's primary goal in 2019 will be *"to continue to develop a strong connection with our core audience through their passions for food, home and design, travel, and bring new consumers into our worldwide community."*

Once again, our good friend fandom. Just the ticket to prepare for an ultimate sale. Still hasn't happened, but it is inevitable. And, Amazon may be the most logical buyer.

WHISTLE SPORTS

Whistle Sports launched in 2014 to bring a new and very different kind of sports-related entertainment to an audience of digital natives (26-34 year olds who watch across platforms) and even younger social natives (13-25 year olds who don't just watch, they lean in and actively engage). Rather than traditional sports, Whistle focuses on new millennial sports like basketball dunking, slack-lining, bottle tossing, cow tipping *(virtually anything you can imagine)* – all of which are a world away from ESPN. And that's the point. In CEO John West's words, *"Today's generation is developing new formats – authentic commentary, behind-the-scenes, comedic sports, trick shots, etc. They are also combining sports with pop culture and music, taking down the adult-created walls between genres and creating their own amazing, entertaining and inspiring video content."*

So, while Whistle won't bring Chris Berman to your living room TV, it *"will, go, all, the, way!"* to bring trick-shot basketball stars Dude Perfect and 500 other curated video creators to your mobile screens. Whistle counts an audience of more than 480 million subscribers, followers and fans (as of September 2018) who watch a library of over 800,000 videos. West tells me that the company is on track to join the *"$100 million revenue club in the next 2-3 years."*

Whistle's biggest strengths are its impressive war chest and the strategic media investors who delivered it. The company raised yet another major round of financing in 2018 (a Series D of $28 million), bringing its total haul to about $100 million – a sum that includes major investments from global sports powerhouses Sky and Liberty Global, as well as a small strategic infusion from Jeffrey Katzenberg's WndrCo. If these international media giants fully embrace Whistle's vision, global coverage is in its reach. The company plans to use its new cash stash to expand into Asia, Europe and Latin America in 2019.

Whistle's challenges? The same as most others on this list. First, effectively monetizing its content across multiple social channels and navigating the newly-skittish advertisers that support them. Second, developing Originals for other OTT services at scale. And, third, in West's words, *"constantly reimagining our company to remain relevant to today's generation."* Sound familiar? Whistle hopes that its new fandom-fueled strategic focus on DTC monetization via multiple pathways (SVOD, AVOD, live events, merchandising) will deliver it to the promised land.

Whistle, like Tastemade, ultimately will be bought. Its brand is too big, and its reach is too extensive. It's merely a question of who, what valuation, and when.

The "who" most likely will be one of its current strategic investors.

StyleHaul

StyleHaul is a major digital-first media brand focused on young millennial females interested in fashion and beauty. It too launched relatively early (2011) and broke out fast, aggregating thousands of individual YouTube channels and creators (the company now counts over 23,000 of them). But, StyleHaul did what several others didn't – it told its own story well, thanks to charismatic founder Stephanie Horbaczewski. Horbaczewski enticed brands with the prospect of reaching a rabid audience smitten by YouTube stars who peddled fashion and beauty tips and the relevant products that go with them. StyleHaul reached 14.2 billion monthly views across all platforms during the first half of 2018.

StyleHaul achieved its own significant exit in 2014 when German media conglomerate Bertelsmann (via its RTL Group subsidiary) stepped up to take it out for $150 million after first being a major strategic investor *(see, try before you buy?)*. And, after three more years with the company, Horbaczewski finally exited to dream up her next big thing. Ex-MTV president Sean Atkins formally took over the reins as CEO in September 2018 and will also oversee RTL's new group that combines all of its digital network assets.

Atkins tells me this about his plans. *"The future for StyleHaul includes closer collaboration between our sister networks Divimove and United Screens, to support a digital video group that operates at global scale."* He remains optimistic amidst 2019's challenging digital video industry headwinds. *"The value of compelling content and talent is stronger than it's ever been and will only continue to grow."*

I agree with Atkins about the long-term market opportunity for all of these digital-first media companies – especially when they have the luxury of big media company backing that takes at least some of the pressure off.

IZO (FORMERLY DANCEON)

Originally called DanceOn and focused *solely* on dance *(get it?)* when it launched in 2010, this new media company changed its name to izo *(yes, lowercase "I")* in 2016 to signify that it had broadened its focus to include music. After all, this is the company credited with unleashing Silento's

Nae Nae craze loose to the world a couple years back *(is that a good thing?)*. That's its star-making potential.

izo's marquee investors include Nygel Lythgoe (of *Dancing with the Stars* and *American Idol* fame) and Madonna (yes, the "Material Girl" herself). izo's CEO Amanda Taylor tells me that her focus for 2019 will be to *"leverage its brand, audience and content capabilities to produce and distribute premium programming"* in all flavors. That means unscripted reality series, docu-series that profile major music artists, scripted series, and musical narratives.

Surprisingly, given its attention-seeking investor roots, izo flies under-the-radar, and its key challenge is to sing (not just dance) its own praises more loudly. But, I have always liked izo's music and dance category. Music alone is by far the single most popular content category online, driving 40+% of YouTube's video views. And, izo's infectious content combo of music and dance is truly global and universal, not bogged down by any language barrier.

izo also will find a much bigger dance hall in the not-too-distant future, perhaps most likely with strategic investor AMC Entertainment.

UPROXX MEDIA (FORMERLY WOVEN DIGITAL)

2018 was a big year for Uproxx (formerly Woven Digital). Warner Music Group (WMG) bought the company mid-2018 for an undisclosed sum. Uproxx primarily focuses on a young male audience and had positioned itself as being a "friendlier" version of Vice *(maybe not such a good idea anymore for the reasons I discussed earlier)*. The company raised $40 million prior to being swallowed up. It was great to have all that cash, of course, but that moolah also meant that Uproxx faced more pressure than ever before from its institutional investors to scale and monetize profitably. That likely drove its ultimate sale to WMG this past year. At what price? We don't know for sure. But, my guess is that it was likely for a song, and WMG certainly didn't overpay.

Now that WMG is its guide, where will Uproxx climb in 2019? Given WMG's new optimism in a fast-growing streaming-fueled music world, it likely hopes to use Uproxx for marketing. Yes, of course the music giant hopes to print money with its new service. At the same time, it recognizes the value in simply owning the Uproxx brand and the millennial audience it attracts.

CRYPT TV

Crypt TV is a relatively new digital-first media company that, as its name rather obviously suggests, focuses on the horror genre. Crypt TV appropriately comes from the minds of scare-meister Jason Blum (investor) and *Hostel* director Eli Roth. I love this genre for mobile-first millennial ADD appetites. First, compelling scary storylines can come in bite-sized, mobile-friendly packages that induce terror in minutes. Second, those short ghost stories frequently don't require much dialog and, therefore, travel well. Remember, "a scare is a scare in any language." Third, good frights – just like cute pets – are extremely viral. We share them incessantly.

Finally, and perhaps most intriguingly, short scares and new meme-worthy viral characters lend themselves to much longer treatment in movies and television, not to mention central roles in live events and merchandising – all of which means licensing cha-ching! Our small screens, in effect, become test grounds for much larger and more lucrative screens, where short stories and proven characters cost-effectively come to life in full big screen glory and with a built-in, thrill-seeking mass audience ready to spend.

CEO Jack Davis, also a founding father, laid out his strategy to me this way. *"Crypt is creating the next generation of iconic monsters, and in 2019 we are doing that in two ways. First, bringing long-form productions to the biggest streaming platforms in the world like Facebook, and second, growing our merchandising and live events business, bringing the experience of our monsters to our most engaged, paying fans. We are going to win because we are a consumer brand. Our moat is our fans' affinity for our original IP. We are the next generation producer."*

Jason Blum already cracked the code for making hit after hit in the theatrical horror movie world. 2018's incredibly successful resurrection of the *Halloween* franchise is proof positive of that. With his active involvement, I like Crypt TV's chances to scale. The potential here to develop a holistic multi-platform and highly monetizing media company fueled by fandom is downright scary … in the best possible way.

KIN

Female-focused Kin Community is now, as of 2019, simply Kin. I always thought of the old Kin, founded in 2011, as being a humbler and softer-spoken version of StyleHaul – a new video service for women, rather than tween and teen girls. New Kin 2.0, which debuted in the summer of 2018, doesn't seem all that different. Yes, Kin now refers to itself as being a *"neighborhood that brings together a group of brand-safe, like-minded diverse channels."* But, "Mr. Wayne's neighborhood" (Michael Wayne is CEO) is still female-first, catering to an audience that it refers to as "builders" – i.e., women in their 20's and 30's who are in the building stage of their lives (building their careers, families, homes).

Kin amassed over $40 million in financing over time. Its older female demographic is both a marketing blessing and a curse. Its core audience holds significantly more real "here and now" purchasing power. But, advertisers increasingly covet younger, always-on and mobile-focused millennial eyes. Based on Kin 2.0's new positioning, it sounds like the service is trying to expand the percentage of twenty-something's in its 'hood.

Like izo, Kin's major challenge is to build its profile and break out from its under-the-radar status in order to attract bigger brand bucks. Looks like the company took that kind of advice to heart this past year when it went on its all-out Kin 2.0 public relations and marketing blitz. How successful has that been? Hard to say so far. But, the company tells me that individual episodes of its anchor show – *Tia Mowry's Quick Fix* – reached as many as 8.8 million unique viewers. As Kin is quick to point out, those numbers beat top cable powerhouses like *Keeping Up with the Kardashians*.

Albeit under vastly different underlying economics, of course.

GROUP NINE

Group Nine actually consists of four digital brands: NowThis (news-focused), Seeker (technology, innovation and future), The Dodo (animal-centric), and Thrillest (for the curious and adventurous). The company focuses on producing brand-safe content for a mass audience, syndicating it as broadly as possible across all social platforms.

CEO Ben Lerer insists that, unlike most other ad-focused new media companies, Group Nine operates profitably. *"Even without selling premium advertising against it, we can create content profitably off of just what we call distributed revenue, which is just revenue generated off of [the major social] platforms."*

If true – and why doubt it? – that's quite a feat.

UPROAR

Uproar is a true startup that officially launched in 2018 with lofty, worthy ambitions – to be a new global video platform that enables individuals to make a difference in the world *(yes!)*. The company was founded by some of the leading voices and influencers in wildlife and conservation and produces authentic, inspirational and brand-safe social, short-form videos that grab attention, drive engagement, and connect at a deeply personal level. Its initial focus is the passionate and underserved wildlife and conservation community. So, at least initially, think of Uproar as being the new Media 2.0 version of *National Geographic*.

Uproar's primary goal is for its content to motivate us all to take action. In the words of co-founder Anthony Bay – no slouch in the world of video (he previously oversaw Amazon's entry into premium video content) – *"Uproar seeks to reach and inspire a global community numbering in the hundreds of millions and to engage that audience to directly benefit conservation."* To make that happen, each Uproar video gives viewers a clear path to learn more and positively impact the subject in question. Anthony further tells me, *"We founded Uproar based on what we feel is an opportunity to change the way conservation is funded. Harnessing modern audience acquisition and monetization techniques, Uproar can quickly grow to become a powerful new media company with a mission to revolutionize the way audiences engage with conservationists and conservation is funded."*

Uproar plans to build and organize the world's largest and most comprehensive catalogue of wildlife and nature conservation projects, professionals, entrepreneurs, scientists, and organizations. Their presence in the company's dedicated "conservation marketplace" enables viewers to directly connect, engage, and support them and their causes with donations, project funding, product purchases, and participation in one-of-a-kind real-world experiences. *"Our model is simple,"* Anthony tells me. *"In fact one of our lead conservation partners has called it a 'no brainer.'"*

Here's how he lays it out. *"Conservation partners give us video footage and stories, and we help them create a presence in the Uproar conservation marketplace to showcase their work. Uproar editors repurpose that footage into beautiful, powerful and compelling short videos – at no cost to the organization - which we distribute and promote (and partners can do as well). Viewers can click through to learn more in the marketplace and donate to the organization or individual or purchase products, arrange a visit, etc. We charge a small transaction fee to operate the marketplace like Patreon or Kickstarter and the balance goes to the conservation partner. In Amazon terms, it's a 'virtuous flywheel.'"*

I like it. A lot. This is the kind of new media company that can win.

D. TARGETED, IDENTITY-FOCUSED NEW MEDIA COMPANIES

MITU

Mitu launched in 2012 to serve a Latino and multicultural audience. In the words of founder and returning CEO Roy Burstin (this is his second deployment in that role), Mitu exists *"for "the 200%"* – content that has *"100% connection with American culture, and 100% with heritage culture."* Mitu was an early new media pioneer and darling but, as it was for many others, 2018 was not kind. Mitu shed 30% of its workforce before its board called Burstin back into action.

Some of Mitu's pain was due to its heavy reliance on Facebook (which had also faced its own unkind year in many respects). At first, this was a blessing. But, it soon became a curse, as that social giant first gaveth, but then tooketh away with its unpredictable algorithmic machinations. That's the danger of dependency. Over time, Mitu also got ahead of its skis in its plans to produce longer-form premium content. Burstin returned to the chalet late 2018 with $10 million in new cash (bringing Mitu's total haul to $52 million over time) and a more back-to-basics agenda. His focus for 2019 is to drive revenue from branded content, programmatic advertising, and merchandise that targets a young, U.S. Hispanic audience. *"I see the opportunity to evolve Mitu from a strictly content brand to a cultural brand,"* says Burstin. *"The unifying thread is, it will speak to you as a Latino."*

Like essentially all other remaining Indies, Mitu must find its "way" in an expanding sea of giants. But, Mitu's brand and audience are valuable.

It too will be swallowed up.

ALL DEF DIGITAL

Talk about a challenging year. Hip-hop-focused All Def Digital had one. Founding father Russell Simmons, who launched the new media company in 2013, became yet another big name swept up and away by the #MeToo movement.

Like Mitu, All Def is an identity brand. It focuses on what many still call an "urban" market that they believe is "niche." But, hip-hop is anything but, and continues to be at the center of the entertainment universe in its domination of the music charts and overall youth culture. Former CEO Sanjay Sharma underscored this point to me. *"Millennial and Gen-Z hip hop is a movement that transcends race ethnicity, socio-economic class, gender and geography."* And, he is absolutely right.

As of October 2018, All Def still reaches 4 million subscribers that drive nearly 300 million monthly views. The company has scored $18 million to date. Significantly, leading Silicon Valley blue-chip venture capital firm Andreessen Horowitz invested in its last round, demonstrating that the Northern California Silicon Valley-based tech world now finally takes the Southern California content-driven world seriously *(as it should)*. That's no small feat. Silicon Valley arrogance, after all *(I can say that, because I previously ran a Bay Area-based company and recognize the "vibe")*.

But, all that money flowed before All Def's 2018 #MeToo moment. So, the company's biggest risk is finding a way to move past its now-tainted legacy.

88RISING

88rising *(yes, one word)* is another identity-focused new media company. This one launched just a couple years back and focuses on Asian youth culture and creators across multiple Asian territories. Its mission is to showcase and share diversity from the East. Based in New York, 88rising closed its first significant round of financing in 2017, led by marketing giant WPP. My very own SAM CREATV Ventures fund also participated, so I am obviously a believer. And, for good reason.

While many others struggled in 2018, 88rising had no trouble raising capital and served as a beacon of new media optimism. The brand is hot, the critical ingredient of fandom exists, and investors like 88rising's multifaceted blueprint for success. The company represents some of Asia's top young social media influencers and musical artists who already have extensive global reach, and monetizes music, media, merchandise, and live events. It also boasts deep relationships with global brands (hence, the WPP connection) and is known for its high-end video production chops. That means both lucrative branded content and premium video, all of which can be licensed to others across multiple platforms.

88rising is definitely one to watch in 2019.

Mitu, All Def Digital and 88rising – three identity-focused new media brands that play to three different underserved demographic markets.

E. THE CONTRARIAN REBEL

And now for something completely different. This one is a fearless new media company that goes where virtually no one else dares to go – deep, deep, deep into the wonderful world of UGC video. And it does it with a very special and surprising ingredient – consistent profitability.

JUKIN MEDIA

UGC-focused Jukin Media is the quintessential bootstrapped start-up. Its founder and CEO, Jon Skogmo, started with an idea and an apartment. The company launched early on in this digital-first video game (2009) and initially focused almost-exclusively on highly viral so-called "fail" videos *(you know, those ones where a skateboarder slides down a rail, falls and lands on his crotch?).* Not particularly highbrow perhaps, but extremely effective and, importantly, global. As Skogmo likes to say, *"an ouch is an ouch in any language."* The company proudly celebrates its unique heritage. Its LA office features a sign that reads *"Failure is the Only Option!"* Love that.

Jukin started from that humble foundation and built up its expertise to efficiently spot and acquire UGC videos that showed signs of virality, adding its own "special sauce" to accelerate that growth. And it worked. Here's why. Unlike traditional MCNs, Jukin didn't just aggregate videos. Jukin bought and owned them from day 1. So now, years later, wily Jukin owns a massive library of frequently evergreen content that it lucratively licenses in myriad ways. Jukin feeds these clips to TV shows like *Ellen* and *Good Morning America*, while also licensing them to advertisers. According to Skogmo, *"Advertisers can see that UGC gives them authenticity and makes their brand relatable in a way that no other type of video content can."*

Jukin is a rare profitable stand-alone player in this new media space. Even so, it wasn't immune to 2018's new media challenges and scaled back its ambitions. But, as the year ended, Skogmo told me that the company returned to strong growth mode as a result of *"important growth initiatives like linear channels for our brands FailArmy and The Pet Collective."* And so, as of Q4 2018, Jukin reports 150 million subscribers and 4 billion monthly views across its individual consumer-facing brands.

Skogmo tells me that Jukin's greatest hurdles for 2019 are, *"Maintaining our focus and staying true to things that Jukin is better at than anyone else in the world – UGC-based storytelling, building brands, and growing audience."*

My prediction remains that Jukin will ultimately UGC itself into a much bigger home. Several potential buyers have tried and failed so far. But, contrary to Jukin's corporate mantra mentioned above, failure is not an option in this M&A context.

It's only a matter of time.

F. DIGITAL-FIRST STUDIOS

The new media companies I have profiled so far both develop and distribute their own content. In other words, they are essentially digital-first studios. Below, things are different. These companies do one thing, and one thing only – they develop premium digital-first content for others. They are essentially digital-first production companies.

NEW FORM DIGITAL

New Form Digital, from traditional media's dynamic duo of Ron Howard and Brian Grazier, is a different kind of digital-first media player (and not just because of its royal Hollywood pedigree). Founded in 2014, New Form pioneered premium quality, high-end digital-first production for publishers that were willing to pay top dollar for it. According to COO JC Cangilla, *"Unlike some other digital studios, we don't focus on advertisers. We know media companies and understand how to achieve their goals by telling great stories."*

New Form has produced 30+ multi-million dollar web series for multiple OTT video players. More traditional media players like NBC and MGM also increasingly look to New Form to produce and deliver high quality digital-first programming. Some examples in 2018 included *Final Space* for TBS, *I Ship It* for the CW, and *Dr. Havoc's Diary* for TruTV.

I asked Cangilla how 2018's highly-challenging new media headwinds impacted New Form. This is what he tells me. *"From conversations we've heard in the market, there is investor skepticism in digital media, especially as some of the bigger investments have yet to pay back returns. We hear a lot of 'business model pivoting' going on in the market. This, coupled with growing demand for investor profit, not growth. Fortunately, our investors [Discovery, ITV, and an investor group that includes Ron Howard, Brian Grazer, Ed Wilson, Craig Jacobson, and Jim Wiatt] have pushed us from day 1 to create 'a business that works.' We've seen steady growth since founding and are fortunate to have a war chest to weather market swings and turns."*

So, what's next for New Form? Top priority is to create great content, of course. But, other key priorities include producing its first feature film (financed by a major Hollywood studio), and developing more proprietary data and insights to share with its media clients. New Form also hopes to turn more of its incubated projects – like its *TXT Stories* series (which amassed over 2 billion views in 2018) – into popular shows on Facebook and other social platforms. *TXT Stories* tells its tales in the language of millennials – i.e., text *(bet you couldn't figure that one out)*. The series imagines real text conversations between very real people, as well as more fanciful conversations between characters that are not. New Form plans to develop longer-form programming for both digital and traditional platforms based on some of those *TXT Stories*.

Extending micro-text into long-form movies and television? Ahh yes, the surprising possibilities afforded by Media 2.0.

New Form established itself as an early leader in the digital-first production space. Now can it effectively monetize and scale?

NATCOM GLOBAL

Under-the-radar Natcom Global, tucked away in Miami, creates and distributes high quality premium mobile-first video content at scale and in multiple languages – Spanish, English, Portuguese and Mandarin. The company owns a library of 20,000+ largely evergreen titles, and produces more than 1,500 new premium short-form video segments each month. Natcom, highly profitable from day 1, works with leading consumer brands like Proctor & Gamble, Coke, Visa and McDonald's. It also works with major media companies like Warner Music and Conde Nast to maximize their reach, engagement and overall ROI.

Natcom made a major acquisition of its own in 2018 and is scaling rapidly under its multi-pronged business model. According to CEO Bob Rodriguez, *"We continue to see a lot of growth from consumer brands that want their messages associated with high quality brand-friendly video content. We are also witnessing more cross border synergies throughout the*

Americas, especially with larger media operations and intellectual property owners." As a result, Rodriguez is bullish for 2019.

He should be. His revenues more than doubled in 2018. And, those favorable trends should continue.

Natcom is a company that is positioned well and deserves to be noticed. I predict that it too will lose its Indie status in the next few years. Demand for its high quality, multi-lingual international content is too strong, and its content prowess and production efficiency are unique and uniquely compelling.

G. INTERNATIONAL DIGITAL-FIRST NEW MEDIA PLAYERS

A word about the global digital-first new media marketplace. It's already massive, with literally hundreds of players of varying shapes and sizes. But, for the sake of logistical necessity as I write this book – not to mention my own mental and physical health – I have essentially focused this chapter exclusively on U.S.-based players.

To give you at least a taste of what's hidden beyond U.S. borders, check out Vietnam-based Yeah1 Network. Of course you never heard of it, and I bet you are thinking right now to yourself that Vietnam is a market so small that you should just skip this section. How very American of you!

But hold on. Check those knee-jerk instincts. Yeah1 claims to be the fastest growing digital network in Southeast Asia, a market that is much bigger than you think.

Yeah1 is a broad-based mobile-first, youth-focused media company that plays mostly on YouTube and Facebook and, accordingly, calls itself a multi-platform network or "MPN" (a close relative to MCNs that have now largely been confined to Media 2.0's dustbin). Yeah1 aggregates thousands of channels on YouTube, counts 4 billion monthly video views and 162 million subscribers (90% from within Vietnam and Thailand), and boasts 60 million Facebook fans across all verticals. But, here's the best part. Yeah1 claims to be highly scaling, monetizing and profitable. The company's parent company successfully went public in July 2018 at a $300 million valuation.

How can that be? Well, former CEO and current advisor Brian Tiong tells me that Yeah1 caters to a mobile-first consumer base in the world's fastest growing region for YouTube and Facebook. Mobile Internet penetration in Southeast Asia is just over 50%, and Tiong underscores to me that this region is all about scale with its young population of 650 million. In Vietnam, for example, mobile video has completely leapfrogged over cable and satellite, where less than 5% of the population pay for pay TV subscriptions. These young people, instead, are hungry for small screen-focused ad-supported videos.

For 2019, Tiong tells me to expect Yeah1 to further expand throughout Southeast Asia via strategic M&A. *"Look at the ambition of Chinese companies like Tencent twenty years ago, and you get a good idea of the path forward for a company like Yeah1. The battle ground is now Southeast Asia."*

And, that's just Yeah1. So, yeah, the international opportunity is real.

So many territories. So few pages to cover them.

H. It's a Wrap

Other intriguing players in this digital-first, mobile-focused video space abound. These include startups like little known Heaven (from the leadership team of TrueCar, which does for cannabis retail what TrueCar did for car buying – i.e., bring product trust and pricing transparency), and new digital-first services from the big boys, like WarnerMedia's Stage 13 (which features content that spans horror, comedy and drama). Scores of others abound, including mini-giants like Reddit, the self-proclaimed front page of the Internet. Reddit launched native video uploads in August 2017 and streamed 13 million hours of video in October 2018 alone. Comcast NBCUniversal-backed BuzzFeed, which had high hopes for an IPO last year but saw those dreams dashed, also hopes video can resurrect greatness. The same can be said for Comcast-backed Vox Media.

Traditional media and entertainment executives should actively study and court the leading new media brands that remain independent. Many of them – like AwesomenessTV and Uproxx in 2018 – will not retain their Indie status for long amidst Media 2.0 video's increasing hyperactivity.

14

ALL MEDIA IS SOCIAL

(OR IS IT THE OTHER WAY AROUND?)

REMEMBER the mobile "second screen" talk of yore? Well, it ain't second screen time anymore. Mobile is now the first screen, especially for millennials who share everything they see. That means that all media is – or at least has the potential to be – social. And that reality presents a massive opportunity for content creators and the social platforms that support them. Those two notions of "social" and "media" are intertwined.

That's why Facebook and the other leading social media companies – no longer content to simply serve as our connective tissue in this Media 2.0 age – have transformed themselves into full-fledged new mega-media companies in literally just the past couple years. Now, as we have seen, these social animals have their sights set on developing and distributing their own premium Originals to differentiate themselves from the others, acquire and retain users, deepen their overall engagement and relationship with those users, and more effectively monetize them.

Does this content-driven strategy sound familiar? Sounds a lot like the major OTTs and digital-first media companies they increasingly target. The fundamental difference, of course, is that these guys already have the increasingly strategic community piece nailed. At least they did prior to 2018 and Facebook's somewhat stunning fall from grace, in a year in which we realized that lots of things were done wrong during social media's heady gold rush.

These are Media 2.0's major social players who now compete to win in the premium OTT video world.

FACEBOOK

Fortunes can change drastically overnight in Media 2.0 land. Literally. And, Facebook became the poster child for this reality in 2018. The bottom fell out for this behemoth at the end of July when it lost an astonishing $120 billion in market value in the course of less than 24 hours, which represented the single biggest drop in U.S. stock market history.

This once seemingly invincible giant lost its footing amidst the constant stream of fervent criticism about its privacy (or lack thereof), content policies, and "fake news." As a result, it faced increasingly skeptical and cynical advertisers justifiably concerned about brand safety. Facebook's response (and frequent non-response) to it all seemed downright arrogant to many, and served as a cautionary tale to all other Media 2.0 players. Nevertheless, despite a year it would like to forget in many respects, Facebook and Instagram still control 87% of U.S. social video ad spending.

2016 represented Facebook's "coming out" for its media ambitions, and 2017 brought it all home and made it 100% clear that this behemoth was all-in against all comers in the world of premium TV-esque video programming. In those friendlier times, Facebook launched its much anticipated premium OTT video service Watch with its own "special sauce" – its always-engaged and rabid daily billion plus audience who inevitably will find, view, follow and comment on those videos. CEO Mark Zuckerberg summed up his video strategy this way at the time. *"Watching a show doesn't have to be passive. You'll be able to chat and connect with people during an episode, and join groups with people who like the same shows afterwards to build community."*

Watch launched with hundreds of shows, including Originals that Facebook commissioned to seed its catalog. The company reportedly spent $1 billion for its initial premium content efforts and absorbed up to $3 million per episode for splash-worthy tent pole shows. Watch also featured premium programming from the likes of both traditional and new media companies such as Major League Baseball, A&E Networks, National Geographic, Tastemade and Whistle Sports. According to Facebook's VP of video, Fidji Simo, the common denominator here was a *"focus on building communities and connections around videos."* In other words, videos that spawn conversation and motivate its user base to watch socially, together, with their Facebook friends.

These videos were all relatively short (10 minutes or so), with many being episodic. Facebook announced that Watch would ultimately include thousands of channels from creators large and small *(undoubtedly including lots of cute and cuddly programming, because god knows we can never get enough of our favorite animal videos!)*. But, as 2018 ended, less than half of Facebook users even knew that Watch existed. And, of those who did, only about half had ever tried it. Apparently, all that content was drowned out by all the troubling noise of the year.

Facebook's sheer size and scope are its greatest strengths as it battles other video giants. It has the financial wherewithal to do just about anything it wants and expand its reach in ways unavailable to most. To a certain extent, the same can be said about archrival YouTube of course. But, we – the reported 2.23 billion-plus monthly active users as of mid-2018 – engage with Facebook far more actively than with YouTube. For many of us, it is woven into the fabric of our daily, if not hourly, lives. Check this out. 50% of Facebook's 1.47 billion daily active users worldwide go to Facebook even before brewing their first cup of coffee each morning.

Like Amazon, Facebook's other secret weapon is its reams of data about each of us who obsessively engage with it over and over again each day. Facebook certainly collects more information about us than just about any other service, a fact that became painfully obvious this year *(John Oliver, one of my favorites, famously railed against Facebook in one of his classic rants – extremely harsh, but dead on and worth googling)*.

Facebook's biggest challenge right now is credibility. Regaining our trust. The brand has been tarnished. No question about that. That's why we see very public efforts to crack down on fake news, and more transparency about its privacy policies.

2019 is a critical year for this once high-flying giant.

INSTAGRAM

Instagram is Facebook's child, of course, enabling our own children to connect and communicate via images and video. Facebook acquired Instagram in 2012 for $1 billion, and Instagram followed its parent's lead into video in a very big way in June 2018 when it launched Instagram TV (IGTV). According to head of product Ashley Yuki, IGTV re-imagines mobile video with longer-form videos served via channels in a vertical format. *"The way we think about IGTV is it's kind of the next generation's TV … It's not a set-top box, it's on their phones."* But, while Instagram's reach and rabid young user base certainly are attractive to creators, the path to monetization remains unclear (the same can be said for Facebook Watch well over one year after its launch).

Instagram competes directly with Snapchat, which led the way with social video at scale. But, here's Instagram's special power – it is shameless. Instagram makes no bones about the fact that it is willing to replicate *(let's just say "copy," because Instagram founder Kevin Systrom did)*. Instagram Stories anyone? And, get this. Instagram Stories passed 400 million daily active users by mid-2018 *(repeat, just for Stories)*, while Snapchat's total daily active user count *(repeat, total user count)* reached 188 million in that same time period (i.e., not even 50% of Instagram Stories).

Instagram's second not-so-secret weapon for success against Snapchat is its very special place in the Facebook family and the privileges that flow from that. Facebook brings its connected friends list to Instagram, making it much easier for users to find and retain new followers than with Snapchat.

Instagram is more than happy to be the fast-follower to Snapchat's first-mover status. After all, it's kind of nice and efficient to be able to use Snapchat as its product development team.

SNAPCHAT

Speaking of Snapchat, parent company Snap successfully went public in 2017 in an IPO valued at nearly $24 billion. But, times have been tough since then and, like the ghost that inspired it, Snap's market value dissipated steadily throughout 2018. As December approached, Snap alarmingly traded at only one-third of its IPO value. Now, *that* is scary!

To reverse that trend, Snap hopes to compete more effectively against arch-nemesis Instagram, expand its base and get "older," and monetize more effectively to get "richer" by attracting more TV-like ad dollars.

To that end, Snapchat announced its own slate of more than a dozen Originals late 2018, including its first scripted programming. This was all part of Snap's Shows initiative. Shows features serialized Originals that generally run 5 minutes in length and consist of 8-12 episodes, all shot in vertical format of course. According to Sean Mills, Snap's head of original content, *"We're building real relationships with viewers. To me, that looks a lot more like television than other tech platforms, which are tuned around 'here's a video that has an abnormal amount of views.'"* Take that Instagram. *"Oh, snap!"*

Shows functions as a companion to Snap's existing Discover feature that it had launched one year earlier. Discover, as you may recall, is Snapchat's gift to established old and new world content brands like *Cosmopolitan, People* and *Buzzfeed* – essentially a velvet rope portal where invite-only content partners hold the coveted privilege of creating new branded content for an entirely new audience that they otherwise would never reach. Snapchat launched Discover with a relative hodge-podge of initial content partners *(I scratched my head at the time about CNN's relevance to tweens and teens)*. But, that fact alone demonstrated how experimental Discover was. Several major (and perhaps more obviously logical) media brands just didn't "get" it and chose not to participate at launch. Well, guess what? They were kicking themselves after making those decisions. That's the price of taking a traditional "wait and see" attitude in this Media 2.0 age.

For its part, NBCUniversal is fully on board, investing $500 million in Snap's IPO, and increasingly investing in developing high-end, exclusive episodic shows. These not only include bite-sized versions of existing hit shows like *Saturday Night Live* and *The Voice*, but also entirely new Originals like twice-daily NBC News show *Stay Tuned*. NBCUniversal took things even further late 2017 when it announced a 50/50 joint venture with Snap to produce additional mobile-first scripted series. Not to be outdone, Time Warner handed Snapchat $100 million in cash to develop ten mobile-first Originals for its ADD audience. And, now most other media giants have followed suit – including ABC, BBC, Turner, Scripps, ESPN, Discovery and the NFL. Both for the "right" reasons (because it's smart). And, for some "wrong" ones (because everyone else is doing it).

Snapchat opens up tens of millions of young, obsessed daily users to those traditional shows and media brands. Many, for the first time. The great hope, of course, is for that massive promotional reach to pull Snapchat newbies into the more traditional television media fold and monetize them with more lucrative traditional media economics. Scripps' president of content distribution Henry Ahn lays it out plainly. *"Snapchat's distinctive mobile platform provides an ideal environment for us to touch millennials and centennials who may not yet be hooked on our premium offerings."* In other words, we don't have 'em, but we need 'em.

For those content creators like NBCUniversal and Time Warner that have embraced Media 2.0 and develop content specifically for Snapchat – rather than merely try to slice and dice existing content to make it fit – this grand experiment is paying off. And now, Snapchat counts Madison Avenue and the piles of branded money flowing from it as close friends. That's the great part. By October 2018, advertiser appetite for Discover had spiked more than 400%.

But, Snapchat continues to be challenged. Big time. Snap knows it. The market knows it. Even our kids know it. As we have seen, Snapchat's arch-nemesis is Facebook-backed Instagram. At first, Snapchat may have found Instagram's mimicking of its continuing string of powerful new differentiating features as being a little bit quaint. Downright flattering. But, no longer. Instragram's all-out assault on Snapchat and its most successful features has taken its toll. Hence, Snap's disturbing market declines throughout 2018.

For now, Snap investors must take solace in the fact that Facebook's stock dropped massively too post-IPO. That's when Facebook began to reinvent itself to become the multi-platform juggernaut it is today. Can Snap mimic Facebook this time?

So far, things don't look so good. 2018 was brutal. Let's hope that this social media pioneer has more up its sleeve than its flash in the pan Snap **Spectacles**. I bought one of those for my son a couple years back, and it is nowhere to be found.

TWITTER

Twitter is now absolutely a media company. And, after a brutal 2017, 2018 brought new hope (perhaps Snap's investors can use that as inspiration).

Twitter *(The Donald's bestie)* has been the media and entertainment world's second-screen companion for years. Entertainment companies aggressively use Twitter to promote their movies, television, and sports to an audience who demand to know what's happening *right now*! But, despite all the early morning Tweets that continue to bombard us from the White House *(who needs coffee to wake up anymore?)*, Twitter's growth stalled in 2017. That trend reversed this past year as a result of Twitter's massive bet on premium live video streaming – particularly, live sports events.

Twitter boldly announced a continuous string of content-fueled Media 2.0 mega licensing deals throughout 2018, paying up massive dollars to buy exclusive live streaming rights to premium sports programming from the likes of Major League Baseball and the PGA Tour. And, it worked. Twitter's overall video views more than doubled over the course of the year, and video now accounts for over half of Twitter's ad revenues. Underscoring Twitter's newfound video swagger, global VP of revenue and partnerships Matt Derella proudly proclaimed at the Digital NewFronts that *"Twitter is the only place where conversation is tied to video and the biggest live moments. That's our superpower."* And, he is right.

Twitter is betting its future on the power and growth of live video, the impact of which seems to be much greater than the sum of its original 140 individual parts.

SO MANY MORE SOCIAL CREATURES, SO LITTLE TIME

So many others to discuss. Let's not forget one of the hottest numbers from one year ago – Musical.ly, the wildly successful music video lip-syncing app that launched in 2014 and counted over 100 million users at one point. Musical.ly was on top of the world in 2017, so much so that Chinese telco Bytedance bought it for a cool $1 billion. Fast forward one year later. Bytedance pulled the plug on the Musical.ly brand this past August and merged the service into its own TikTok app. That was the day the Music(al .ly) died.

One final note of caution. Don't let this chapter's U.S.-centric discussion fool you. My focus here is on the major U.S.-based Media 2.0 social players simply because my task would be endless otherwise. Behemoth social media networks compete overseas and push boundaries everywhere, increasingly with video. And, remember we live in a borderless Media 2.0 world.

If nothing else, China's Bytedance tango with U.S.-based Musical.ly underscores that point.

15

Don't Forget About the Brands!

(Or, "And Now a Word ... I Mean, Video ... From Our Sponsors")

I N these mobile and millennial-focused Media 2.0 times, it's not just the traditional media companies that finally understand that the world of content has radically changed. So do major brands. Gone are the days of the brand hammer. We have used our DVRs to skip those ads for years even on our big screens. The trick is to engage and entertain with new storytelling that works within different Media 2.0 realities, new platforms, new audiences, and the new sensibilities that go with them.

For brands, Media 2.0 means structural new marketing challenges. Yes, even the kids still find time to watch TV on the big screens in their living rooms. But, even in that last hallowed bastion of traditional media, they increasingly look down at their mobile phones. So, brands too must transform their thinking of what engagement looks like in this Media 2.0 world.

"Branded content" (also known as "content marketing") gets most of the press. And, an effective branded content strategy is certainly a must in this day and age. Millennials almost expect branded messages now and accept them, so long as that content is entertaining, *authentically*. Digital-first media companies *(discussed earlier in Chapter 13)* offer the most obvious path to pursue those opportunities. Case in point, Whistle Sports' Dude Perfect boys use trickery to toss basketballs, instead of potato chips, into oversized Pringles cans *(that just made me hungry)*.

But, the boldest brands take things even further, transforming themselves into full-fledged media companies. No longer content simply making and marketing consumer packaged goods that touch consumers only sporadically, a few audacious brands look to establish an entirely different type of relationship and engage with their customers on an ongoing and deeply personal basis. They seek to associate themselves with a particular lifestyle category, and then become the voice and community for that category. These are what I call the new lifestyle media companies.

Red Bull is *the* prime example. The poster child. Red Bull is no longer just an energy drink, and hasn't been for a long time. It is now very much a media company focused on the lifestyles of aspiration and adrenaline *(which means a broad swath of us, because who doesn't want to be a fearless adventurer?)*. Red Bull promotes that lifestyle – and, therefore, ultimately itself and its products – via brilliantly-executed and expensive premium video content like space parachuting Felix Baumgartner, a video that has been viewed by virtually everyone on this planet. Cans of caffeine are only one manifestation of that lifestyle and the primary way Red Bull monetizes. If you have any doubt about Red Bull's media strategy, check out the company's main website. Not one can of Red Bull in sight! It's all about motorcycles, music festivals, and all kinds of cool places you'd rather be right now.

To underscore its versatility, Red Bull established Red Bull Media House in 2007, a completely separate media division that operates much more than just Red Bull's marketing arm. It actively courts outside clients and is measured by its own stand-alone financial success.

Other innovative major brands see Red Bull and this potentially game-changing Media 2.0 opportunity, and also hope to transform themselves into something much more than the products they sell. Marriott (*yes, that Marriott, the hotel chain*) boldly followed Red Bull's lead and launched its own major production studio in 2014, hoping to be the voice and home for millennial travel. Pepsi too has taken this route, building its own major studio in 2014 to produce digital-first content that speaks directly to a new generation of mobile-obsessed consumers who have grown tired of traditional marketing "speak."

In perhaps the most notorious Red Bull-inspired attempt, next-gen camera company GoPro positioned itself in 2014 to own the action-focused lifestyle vertical, a seemingly logical story given the fact that GoPro-captured videos fill YouTube. GoPro effectively preached its new media story to Wall Street, and drove a massively successful IPO in the process. At one point, investors valued the company at a mouth-watering $8.1 billion.

But, much like Red Bull's Felix Baumgartner, GoPro's ambitions dropped back down to Earth in 2016 as the company ejected its media strategy and jettisoned most of its media team. I still scratch my head about that one. GoPro's stock price plummeted right there with it, and the company now trades at a small fraction of its former self ($775 million as of late November 2018).

Major brands, heed this call. As fast as you think you are moving now, move faster. Study Red Bull. Yes, GoPro adds a note of caution. But, inaction is not an option. Experiment. Seek inspiration from the likes of Warner Bros.' and its brilliant 2017 marketing move with smash hit *Wonder Woman*. With the help of Intel, Warner Bros. literally brought motion picture marketing to dazzling new heights with the help of 300 perfectly synchronized drones in a revolutionary light show. You can bet that social media accounts worldwide lit up the Internet, just as those drones lit up the evening sky.

So, invest in Media 2.0. Significantly. Whether its bite-sized or super-sized, just get into the game. Right now.

Content, community, and commerce baby!

16

THE MAINSTREAMING OF
LIVE VIDEO STREAMING

INTERNET-DRIVEN live video streaming certainly is nothing new. I served as CEO of live video pioneer SightSpeed over 10 years ago *(Logitech acquired us)*, and we offered both high quality one-to-one and one-to-many live social video even back then – well before its mainstreaming via Skype video and Apple FaceTime.

While live broadcast streaming is nothing new, live one-to-many personal broadcasting at mass scale is relatively fresh. Our increasingly mobile-first world – and our increasingly robust networks to which they connect – take the live broadcast opportunity further downstream to each of us. We now can, and increasingly do, easily broadcast ourselves in high quality to our friends, our fans, and the world via our mobile phones. And, we promote these live streams through our social networks, which then play it forward (hence, the "social" in streaming).

What's particularly exciting here is that social streaming offers the potential to break down barriers between individual broadcasters – who are increasingly Media 2.0 personalities and "celebrities" – and their audiences. Now true artist-fan and fan-fan engagement is possible, is happening, and is potentially extremely lucrative, since fans are happy to directly support their favorite personalities. Brands increasingly turn to live streaming opportunities to reach the coveted young demographic and engage with them more deeply.

Here are some of the key enablers and players in the live broadcasting OTT video space, plus some newbie innovators you should know.

I. THE ENABLERS

BAMTECH

Major League Baseball, a long-time Media 2.0 innovator, developed its BAMTech platform years ago to live stream not only its own games, but also other major live events like the Olympics, Super Bowl and Coachella. BAMTech also serves as the backbone for on demand streaming. That's why Disney, in 2016, invested $1 billion for a 33% share in BAMTech and ultimately acquired 42% more in 2017 (thereby owning a 75% controlling stake at a $3.75 billion valuation). BAMTech now serves as the foundation for Disney's new premium OTT video ambitions.

Ever-observant competing media company Turner which, like Disney's ESPN, also places live sports front and center, followed Disney's lead and bought a majority stake in competing live streaming platform iStream-Planet. Turner had no desire to be beholden to a competitor's technology platform.

BULLDOG DM

Meanwhile, smaller fish also play big in this live streaming pond, as they focus on particular high impact use cases. With unique expertise and deep industry cred born over the course of several years, Bulldog DM ("DM" as in "digital media") is *the* innovator and trusted source for the live streaming of major music festivals like Bonnaroo, Governors Ball, Outside Lands, Afropunk, Pickathon, and Numberfest. Major brands (including AT&T, Samsung, American Express, Coca-Cola, Sony, Nestle, Snickers, Tiffany, Hilton, Nissan and Facebook) flock to Bulldog to reach and engage with the coveted youth audience that increasingly prioritizes "experiences" over "things." Facebook reports that users watch Bulldog DM's live streams 3X over on-demand streams, and those live streams garner 6X more engagement. Heady stuff. Particularly for marketers.

With its pole position in the burgeoning market for the streaming of live festivals and events, Bulldog DM looks to expand its vision significantly in 2019 and become the central home and brand for all things "festival." According to CEO John Petrocelli, *"The world by and large transitioned to an experience economy, especially for millennials and gen Z consumers. Their priority is shared experiences, and if they cannot attend, they still want to have collaborative, participatory, real time engagement on their device. Live streaming provides both that engagement and the amplification brands want from their experiential marketing strategies. We enable brands to present experiences to viewers and transform those viewers into delighted participants in the live streamed digital broadcast – creating a 'win win' for all stakeholders – brand, content owner, artist, promoter, fan, and platform."*

Bulldog is one important Indie to watch. It too will be swallowed up – for its deep expertise, its unique festival and brand relationships, and its ultimate strategic vision. No one does it better.

II. THE SOCIAL ANIMALS

FACEBOOK LIVE

Then there's Facebook Live, which stole a page from young upstart Meerkat. Remember them? Not so long ago – in 2015 to be exact – Meerkat unleashed social streaming's "broadcast yourself" possibilities *en masse* and became an instant Media 2.0 darling, attracting $12 million in blue chip venture capital cash in the process.

But, as is frequently the case in the world of Media 2.0, a much deeper-pocketed player – in this case Twitter – copied and soon eclipsed Meerkat with its own Periscope app. Subsequently, in yet another case of tech-driven survival-of-the-fittest where the strong prey on those beneath them in the food chain, Facebook stormed onto the social streaming scene with Facebook Live and dealt a significant blow to Twitter's pole position. Clever little Facebook even borrowed Twitter's original magic number and signed 140 celebrities and companies to create live content for its launch.

Facebook Live is now the live social streaming platform of choice, although Snapchat and Instagram aren't too far behind – particularly for teens and tweens.

TWITCH

One-to-many Internet-driven broadcast services like Twitch have catered to specific, frequently non-obvious live streaming use cases for quite some time as well. In Twitch's case, the service live streams gamer challenges and contests. So massive and valuable are Twitch and its young male audience that Amazon scooped up the service in 2014 for nearly $1 billion *(see, there's that stealthy, crafty, somewhat insidious Amazon again).* Could any of you reading this book have predicted that one?

Well, welcome to the mysterious, ever-changing and unexpected world of Media 2.0.

MOBCRUSH

LA-based Mobcrush caters to gamers as well, enabling them to "go live, get paid" by live streaming their gameplay on all major social platforms (Twitch, Facebook, YouTube, and Twitter), as well as its own. CEO Mike Wann boldly tells me that *"Mobcrush is leading the creator driven revolution."* He explains it this way. *"With the advent of the digital camera and integration into everything we own, and the social platforms now becoming where most consumers now consume their content, content popularity and distribution are now a true meritocracy. Mobcrush is helping creators reach all their audiences in real time across social platforms all at the same time."*

Mobcrush's live platform also enables its gamer creators to chat with each other and benefit from sponsorship and other monetization opportunities, thereby – in Wann's words – *"empowering creators to reach their true potential and help them turn their passion into their career."* Yes, you read that right. Gaming is now a career option.

In any event, who am I to disagree with Mike and his "Who's Who" of blue chip media/tech investors that include Kleiner Perkins, Evolution Media, CAA Ventures, Raine Ventures, BAM Ventures and Advancit Capital that have placed bets to the tune of $36 million?

CAFFEINE

Backed by a buzz-worthy $100 million Q3 2018 investment from 21st Century Fox, Caffeine is a new live social broadcasting platform that emulates

Amazon's Twitch. Fox executive chairman Lachlan Murdoch, who sits on Caffeine's board, explains the new platform's power this way. *"The combination of the Caffeine platform with a content studio that benefits from Fox Sports' expertise in live events and programming, will help position Caffeine to deliver compelling experiences in eSports, video gaming and entertainment."*

Caffeine aims to unite what it estimates to be more than one billion *(yes, billion!)* gamers, their frequently rabid fans, and streamers in general. *"We want to bring the world together around friends and live broadcasts,"* says CEO Ben Keighran.

COUNTLESS OTHERS

Other live streaming-focused newbies have come and gone. In 2016, leading karaoke app Musical.ly birthed Live.ly, giving our kids yet another way to broadcast themselves in order to receive the validation they apparently so desperately crave (despite it being so obvious to us). But, Musical.ly later shut it down, only to be swallowed up and spit out itself by Chinese media company Bytedance *(as discussed earlier)*.

We are still very much in the early innings of live one-to-many social broadcasting, but its reach into our daily lives just these past few years is impressive.

PART III, SECTION 3
TODAY'S STREAMING-FIRST MUSIC WORLD

APPLE fundamentally changed the music game with iTunes and its $.99 digital downloads 15 years ago. But, a funny thing happened in the past couple years. Digital downloads' dominance in the music industry – which, by definition, also meant Apple dominance – gave rise to a newly dominant OTT streaming model.

17

THE RISE & DOMINANCE OF MUSIC STREAMING

I anticipated Media 2.0's new streaming reality more than 15 years ago when I served as president & COO of Musicmatch, where we pioneered on demand streaming "back in the day" and were shockingly profitable doing it (Yahoo! ultimately acquired the company in 2004 for $160 million). I vividly recall virtually everyone in the music industry scoffing at the notion that consumers would ever leave their digital downloads behind for subscription streaming. Well, guess what, although it took a while, they did. The mass consumer market ultimately realized what we always believed – i.e., that "renting" and "owning" music makes no difference in a mobile-first, always-listening world.

In fact, so-called "renting" songs via on-demand subscriptions gives you "more taste" (Apple Music boasts access to 45 million songs) and is "less filling" (generally $9.99 per month for all those tracks instead of iTunes' $.99 per track rack rate or $20 for a single physical album). That's a truly amazing value proposition when you think about it, which gets even better for Amazon Prime customers who pay only $7.99 monthly for that unlimited music listening privilege.

We consumers now finally "get" the value, power and experience of streaming (both literally and figuratively). Music industry analyst Midia Research reported that the number of music streaming subscribers world-wide grew from 198.6 million to 229.5 million in the first half of 2018 alone – and an even more impressive 38% year-over-year. While Midia expects growth to slow in the U.S. and other developed markets in 2019, it expects continued hyper-growth in mid-tier markets like Mexico, Brazil, Japan and Germany (with emerging markets in Asia and Africa to follow, albeit under more challenged economics).

Streaming revenues surpassed digital downloads for the first time in 2015, and now account for a rather astounding 75% of the U.S. music indus-try's overall $4.6 billion in sales. That's up from total sales of $3.5 billion in 2016 and $4.2 billion in 2017, according to the Recording Industry As-sociation of America's ("RIAA") mid-year 2018 report. And, the RIAA's bullish report sees no end in sight, as paid subscription revenues grew 33% year-over-year to $2.55 billion and continue to accelerate. It wasn't all wine and roses in the eyes of the RIAA, of course, as the organization continued to lament that ad-supported on-demand revenues from ser-vices like YouTube and Vevo contributed only $369 million, representing a mere 11% of total streaming revenues.

(As a side note, for this fan of classic vinyl, it was inspiring to see that vinyl continued its overall resurgence, with U.S. sales up 13% year-over-year and surprisingly now accounting for 10% of overall industry revenues).

In any event, at least some semblance of optimism now permeates the overall music industry – a welcome break from the past two decades of universal (music group) misery. Not optimism from all players in the ecosystem, mind you. But, in the aggregate, generally yes. As it should. After all, Goldman Sachs expects streaming revenues to more than triple by 2030 and contribute $28 billion to a reborn $41 billion global music industry.

So, much-maligned streaming looks like it may become the industry's ultimate savior after all, also opening up other tantalizing revenue possibilities for artists in the process *(more on that in Chapter 20)*. And, to think that even Steve Jobs – the innovator amongst all innovators – once (in)famously (and somewhat arrogantly) proclaimed, *"The subscription model of buying music is bankrupt"* and couldn't be saved even by *"the Second Coming."*

Well, guess what's Coming in 1st place right now?

18

THE MUSIC INDUSTRY'S
YOUTUBE "PROBLEM"

D ESPITE now offering significant hope to Media 2.0 doubters, the music industry's newly dominant streaming reality still doesn't make too many in the business happy, with a few notable exceptions. In the minds of most music execs, as well as many highly respected artists, Apple iTunes economics were bad enough – stripping out singles from albums and selling them for, well, a song. A general refrain of devaluing content, denigrating artist integrity, and chilling overall artistic creativity filled the airwaves, especially in the early days of iTunes. But at least those downloads were easy to compartmentalize, track and pay.

Both ad-supported and subscription-based music streaming continue to be very different in most industry minds. Free ad-supported streaming radio services like Pandora classic – which give users no on-demand artist or song control – pay artists and labels a statutory per-stream royalty that represents a tiny fraction of a digital download royalty. On the other hand, paid subscription on-demand streaming services like Spotify – which give users full artist and song control – pay higher rates negotiated directly with the music labels and yield 6X the revenues of ad-supported streaming. Yet, even those higher rates generate pennies on the dollar in the minds of many traditionalists who already felt pummeled by digital down-loads.

The stark reality is that, aside from a few notable exceptions, virtually no one in the U.S. music industry – at least not yet – makes any real money on "just the music" anymore. Not the vast majority of artists. Not the labels. Not even Spotify and now SiriusXM-owned Pandora, the two streaming music services that arrived on the scene as pure-plays to challenge iTunes' digital dominance. Neither generates any ongoing profitability *(Pandora is no longer independent, so its calculus changes on a going-forward basis)*. In fact, long-term profitability always has been very much out of the their reach *(more on that in Chapter 19)*.

So, artists and labels understandably demand more in terms of royal-ties, and the pure-play streaming services understandably beg to pay less. Nothing pencils out. No long-term commercially sustainable stand-alone business model has been worked out yet. YouTube and tech-driven me-dia giants Apple and Amazon are glaring exceptions to this pessimism that continues to surround the streaming music business model.

Let's discuss YouTube first *(I discuss Apple and Amazon later in Chapter 19)*.

In a fact that may surprise you, YouTube is the number one music lis-tening platform for millennials, by far. Here's why. With the rise of smart phones, YouTube's video dominance also led to YouTube's music listening dominance, because the line that previously separated audio music expe-riences from pure music video experiences blurs in a mobile-first world. For millennials, it more like simply vanishes. Why pay for music when you can listen to it for free on YouTube? Video and the music within it are indistinguishable in an on-the-go smart phone environment. You simply don't watch it. That's why industry trade group The International Feder-ation of the Phonographic Industry (IFPI) reported in October 2018 that consumers spent nearly half of their time listening to on-demand music through YouTube.

And, here's the punch-line. Because of its video-first roots, YouTube's royalty structure is fundamentally different from all audio-first services. Whereas Spotify and other music-first streaming services pay a fixed royalty for every single stream no matter what, YouTube only pays on the basis of the ad revenues it collects. No ad revenues, no royalty payments – no matter how much music its users stream. That means that YouTube, unlike all others, makes money on the music itself. Every time. It always wins (*"just like a casino,"* in the words of one deeply knowledgeable label exec with whom I spoke, but preferred to remain anonymous).

Yes, you read that right. YouTube's video roots give it a fundamental advantage over all pure-play streaming music services. And, its bottom line shows it. YouTube's enviable business model is both endlessly scalable and profitable. Has been since the dawn of time (*Media 2.0 time, that is*). Spotify's ad business, on the other hand, results in a gross margin of -18% (as in, negative 18%). *And, that's its gross margin!* Think about what that means for its net margin. So, while 40+% of YouTube's video views are music-focused, some insiders say that YouTube only accounts for about 4% of the music industry's overall revenues. The RIAA openly acknowledged this inequity in its 2017 annual report, concluding that the current royalty system *"benefits platforms like YouTube and disadvantages companies like Spotify."*

In its own subsequent 2018 report, the IFPI went much further. The IFPI concluded that Spotify delivers $20 to every $1 contributed to the industry by YouTube, and called YouTube the single greatest threat to the renewed growth of the music industry. So, YouTube, the music industry's largest player (by far) receives highly preferential pricing treatment (by far).

You can only imagine how that makes others feel, and you'd be right (although let's not forget that the major music labels freely negotiated these deals with YouTube in the first place to create this state of affairs). Spotify used this un-level playing field to renegotiate more favorable royalties from the major labels in 2017, reportedly bringing down Universal Music Group's (the largest of the majors) royalty rates from 55% to 52%. Doesn't sound like much, but that 3% matters at Spotify's scale. It's a start at least, and others like Pandora hope to bring down their royalties as well to achieve at least a bit more balance. *"We won't get rid of minimum guarantees, but we'll be able to adjust them,"* says optimistic new CEO Roger Lynch.

Warner Music Group hopes to level the playing field a bit for itself as well. That's why it entered into an innovative new distribution arrangement for its videos in 2017 – and expanded that initiative in 2018 – with under-the-radar mobile-first video company Natcom Global *(discussed earlier in Chapter 13)*. Natcom gives Warner Music a major new platform that it can control and monetize more directly. Warner now incentivizes and steers music lovers to watch its videos across Natcom's global channels by offering exclusive valuable content (like behind-the-scenes footage) that is not available anywhere else. In other words, off YouTube, rather than on it.

In any event, you can bet YouTube has a good explanation for its uniquely favorable economics, and you'd be right. In a widely-circulated blog post mid-2016, YouTube's chief product officer Neil Mohan insisted that YouTube should be praised, rather than denigrated, because it had paid out over $3 billion to the music industry over time up to that point (including $1 billion in 2016 alone). Of course, Mohan failed to reveal how much YouTube had generated for itself in music-related ad revenues during that time. Perhaps that would have been an inconvenient truth.

Nonetheless, he unapologetically argued that YouTube single-handedly could be the music industry's savior, if the industry let it.

Mohan also pointed YouTube's finger at terrestrial radio as being the real culprit driving music industry angst. After all, because we all drive a lot, good old-fashioned radio remains a surprisingly deep music force in our lives. Nielsen reports that 93% of millennials still listen to AM/FM radio, although separately Cowen & Company confirmed that *"YouTube is the leading source of music for millennials."* In any event, importantly, terrestrial radio – like YouTube – plays by very different rules. It pays absolutely nothing directly to artists and labels, and instead keeps virtually all advertising revenues for itself. Mohan contended that the music industry's size would double *(yes, 2X!)* if just twenty percent of radio and television advertising revenues shifted online *(which, surprise surprise, certainly wouldn't hurt Google's advertising-driven bottom line either)*.

YouTube's head of music, long-time music industry mogul Lyor Cohen, later double-downed on Mohan's controversial analysis with his own high profile thoughts. Cohen argued first that YouTube actually pays higher royalty rates than other ad-supported free streaming services. He further proclaimed that YouTube should be applauded for creating more breakout artists than any other service – artists who then achieve visibility and monetize in myriad ways not traceable back to YouTube.

Not so fast, retorted the RIAA's CEO Cary Sherman, who immediately responded with a fiery post that asks, *"Why is YouTube paying so little?"* In it, Sherman wrote that YouTube pays music creators far less than 400 other digital music services on both a per-stream and per-user basis. And, Richard James Burgess, CEO of the American Association of Independent Music, piled on with language reminiscent of 2018's debates about our President's willingness to share equal blame with Russia over human rights abuses. Writing *"there is absolutely no moral equivalency between*

Spotify and YouTube," Burgess flat out rejected Cohen's assertions, countering that *"Spotify commits to pay creators with every play of their music,"* while YouTube *"chooses when they will pay, what they will pay, and the circumstances under which they will pay."* Touché!

Bottom line is that virtually no one outside YouTube buys its arguments.

Perhaps it's because the last tech titan(ic) music force that called itself the industry's savior also came from Silicon Valley. And, that purported redeemer completely shifted the industry's balance of power in its favor – dressed in a black turtleneck bought in Cupertino.

You can bet the music industry remembers.

19

MUSIC'S STREAMING WARS

(CAN ANY PURE-PLAY WIN AGAINST THE BEHEMOTHS?)

YOUTUBE, Spotify, Apple Music, Pandora, Amazon Music Unlimited, Tidal, SoundCloud – these are the main cast of characters in the global music streaming wars that now dominate the music industry. New players continuously enter the market, and many old ones leave. Amazon Music Unlimited launched in October 2016 to disrupt the entire U.S. streaming game and its long-established $9.99 monthly subscription price point, while Samsung quietly and downright sheepishly closed the door on its essentially-overlooked Milk Music service in 2016. And, then there's little-discussed (in the U.S., at least) China-based behemoth Tencent Music. Tencent Music planned a U.S. IPO in 2018 (*more, much more, on Tencent Music below*).

Market realities nearly pulled the plug on music darling SoundCloud in 2017 before media-focused private equity firm Raine Group and Singapore's sovereign wealth fund Temasek injected $169.5 million into the company at the 11th hour to keep the wheels on the bus. Others like iHeartRadio, Deezer, Slacker, and the second coming of Napster (*okay, maybe third, since this version is rebranded Rhapsody*) continue to languish in relative obscurity.

Nonetheless, 2018 brought its share of strategic moves to change that. iHeartRadio (previously Clear Channel) filed for bankruptcy and re-birth in order to restructure $20 billion of crushing debt *($20 billion!)*. Meanwhile, Warner Music Group's owner Access Industries and others injected a fresh $185 million into Deezer at a valuation of $1.16 billion. And little-known media company LiveXLive acquired Slacker for a surprisingly robust $50 million, before LiveXLive faced its own music by watching its market value plummet and then flat-line throughout the year.

Overall, in 2018, market sentiment in our tech-transformed, increasingly streaming-driven music space became decidedly more positive *(note to self – positive with a small "p")*, reversing its long downward-trending course.

Let's take a look at where things stand right now with the key players in this Media 2.0 music space in which YouTube *(as discussed in Chapter 18)* continues to be the dominant force for millennials – and in which analyst firm Midia Research reports that Spotify held #1 global market share for paid subs as Q3 2018 began (83 million subscribers), Apple Music at #2 (43.5 million), Amazon Prime Music & Amazon Music Unlimited #3 (27.9 million), and China-based Tencent Music #4 (17.6 million).

I. SPOTIFY & PANDORA – THE LEADING PURE-PLAYS

Spotify is the closest thing to holding Netflix-ian dominance amongst music streaming services. We all use it. As of Q4 2018, Spotify counts 87 million paying subscribers (of its total 191 million active user base) across 60+ countries for its $9.99 monthly on-demand streaming service. That's up from 62 million paying subs in Q4 2017. Spotify also offers ad-supported streaming. Spotify had a big year in 2018, finally successfully going public after years of anticipation.

We also likely listen to Pandora. Prior to 2017, Pandora offered only less-controlled radio-like streaming in two flavors – free ad-supported, or ad-free at $4.99 monthly. But, in a major strategic shift to significantly improve its overall challenged economics, Pandora launched its own "Spotify-Killer" on-demand service in 2017 at a now-familiar $9.99 monthly price point. Pandora announced big plans when it did, forecasting 6-9 million paying subscribers by end of 2017.

But, those lofty goals hit cold stark reality soon thereafter when the company reported that roughly only 5% had converted to paying subs by year's end. That's when Pandora needed a lifeline, and got one in the form of a $480 million investment from SiriusXM, which acquired a 19% stake in the company in the process.

Pandora's newly-constituted board later pressed "play" on a new executive team in 2018 to lead them to the promised land, and generally liked what it saw throughout the year. And, guess what? Unexpectedly, Pandora's paid subscriptions grew 49% year-over-year in Q3 2018 to 6.8 million and now drive 30% of overall revenues. That's the good news. The bad news is that Pandora began Q4 2018 with 5 million fewer active listeners than one year earlier (a total of 68.8 million), and its losses continued to mount ($15.5 million in Q3 2018 alone).

Spotify and Pandora (and Tidal, Napster, Deezer, and Slacker) are pure-plays like Netflix on the video side, exclusively monetizing just the music itself via ads, subscriptions, or both *(as mentioned earlier, that now changes for Pandora as a result of the SiriusXM acquisition)*. As a result, most continue to bleed cash. Spotify alone lost $1.5 billion in 2017 despite gargantuan revenues of $4.9 billion. Yes, its revenues reached $1.54 billion in Q3 2018 with narrower losses. But, they were significant losses, all the same. And we already know why. Pure-play music services face the same challenge – the same existential crisis – that Netflix confronts on the video side against multi-faceted behemoths Apple, Amazon, AT&T and YouTube. As discussed in Chapter 10, the business models of those tech behemoths differ fundamentally from those of stand-alone pure-play streaming services like Netflix and Spotify. For Apple, Amazon and YouTube, content (in this case music) is simply a means to an end. Not the end itself.

For all these reasons, I wrote the following passage last year in my book, *Media 2.0 (18)*:

"It certainly wouldn't surprise me – in fact, I fully expect – that neither Spotify nor Pandora will stand alone long-term as independents unless they achieve some kind of new monetization breakthrough. They will instead end up playing strategic roles in a much bigger machine. In the belly of one of the behemoths. For Pandora, the most obvious path is outright acquisition by SiriusXM, which already owns a minority share and can benefit most by extending its brand with the help of another's."

Well, fast forward to this past year when, as predicted, SiriusXM acquired 100% of Pandora for $3.5 billion. At the time, Pandora's active user base reached 71.4 million, 6 million of whom were paying subscribers. Adding that number to SiriusXM's 36 million paying subscribers, the combined companies projected $7 billion in revenues for 2018 and anointed themselves as being "the world's largest audio-entertainment company."

With Pandora now part of the SiriusXM family, what's next? Well, many pundits predict that SiriusXM will try to buy Live Nation and bring an off-line, physical world component to its overall music experience *(this may have already happened by the time you read this – that's how fast things go)*. For reasons I lay out in Chapter 26, I think that could be smart. Very smart.

II. THE BEHEMOTHS

Now it's time to discuss the music giants that have the luxury of being able to use music purely for marketing purposes as a means to achieve their ultimate individual ends.

APPLE

Let's first take Apple. Apple Music is one big advertisement for Apple hardware (iPhones, iPads, Macs). Content is its Trojan Horse. Apple Music succeeds even if Apple Music doesn't generate $1 of profit. But, that doesn't mean that Apple Music isn't strategic for Apple, because it most certainly is. Apple needed an on-demand music streaming service to counter its declining iTunes music download business and continue to drive the faithful into its kingdom of hardware delights. Unable to build it itself, Apple looked into the marketplace and found a kindred spirit in streaming service Beats, a company that shared Apple's DNA by operating primarily in the consumer electronics space with its headphones.

Apple Music offers two tiers of music streaming – monthly $9.99 or $14.99 for a family plan *(note to self – Apple also quietly offers a $99 annual plan that can be unearthed with some digging)*. In May 2018, Apple Music boasted over 50 million subscribers – about double its numbers from one year earlier. But, this number included free trials, and analyst firm Midia Research pegged the actual number of paying subs to be closer to 43.5 million as of September 2018. Still impressive – a feat driven by Apple's unique ability to bundle and headline Apple Music across all of its Apple products (and essentially dare us not to use it).

That kind of seamless integration is certainly a luxury that no pure-play has. And, that's why, as of Q3 2018, Apple Music has overtaken Spotify as counting the most paid subscribers in the U.S.

AMAZON

Amazon's multi-pronged business model is like Apple's, but also very different. Yes, Amazon too sells hardware, including the surprisingly successful Kindle and Alexa-driven Echo. But, unlike Apple, Amazon is not and never fundamentally will be a consumer electronics company. Amazon is all about commerce, pure and simple. Selling stuff. And lots of it. So, Amazon's Music Unlimited subscription service, like its companion Amazon Prime Video service, functions as an Apple-like gateway to Amazon's virtual mega-mall and its increasing focus on mobile shopping. Like Apple, Amazon doesn't need to profit from the music itself, and that gives it great business and competitive freedom.

Amazon flexed those threatening muscles big time when it launched Amazon Music Unlimited late 2016 with a disruptive new monthly price point $2 lower than the competition ($7.99 for Amazon Prime customers, $9.99 for everyone else). Amazon's royalty rates with the major music labels likely aren't any different than those of the pure-plays, but Amazon simply can "eat" that extra $2 and spread it across its overall financials.

Scary indeed for those that can't.

GOOGLE/YOUTUBE

Ahh yes, and then there's the biggest 800 pound Media 2.0 music gorilla of them all, YouTube – a very different animal altogether *(as I discussed at length in Chapter 18)*. We now already know that YouTube continues to feel virtually uniform industry wrath for the very different, highly advantageous economics that flow from its very different video-first DNA. Yet, YouTube nonetheless succeeded in negotiating new licensing deals with all major labels in 2017, because its strategic position in the overall music industry is now simply too cemented in millennial lives.

Google simplified its various confusing brands (out with YouTube Red and Google Play Music) and now operates its YouTube Music and YouTube Premium streaming services (the former at the now-industry standard $9.99 monthly price point, and the latter at a $11.99 monthly price which also gives ad-free YouTube videos plus Originals). But, both services pale in significance to music on YouTube itself, and together counted only 7 million subscribers as of August 2018. Google likely doesn't really care that much, however, because both services (whether separate or together) are all about driving Google's fundamental underlying and seemingly unlimited advertising-based cash machine. Its *raison d'etre* is to just keep its overall user base entertained amidst increasingly predatory competition.

That's quite a differentiator and competitive advantage.

TENCENT MUSIC

Too often in the U.S., media and tech execs forget that a whole world exists out there beyond our borders. And a much bigger one at that. Case in point, China's Tencent Music, which is majority owned by Tencent Holdings – owner of several other mammoth Media 2.0 services as well, including social mobile giant WeChat, instant messaging service QQ, and *League of Legends* developer Riot Games. Bold and brash Tencent Music (of which Spotify intriguingly owns 9.1%) planned to use its U.S. IPO billions to continue its own onslaught on the streaming world. And, Warner Music Group and Sony Music each purchased $200 million worth of shares to be part of that IPO, underscoring that the music industry certainly thinks Tencent Music is real.

Tencent Music is a fascinating success story. The service counts more than 600 million active users, which translates into about 80% of China's online music market. And, get this. Tencent Music is stand-alone profitable –

and, I mean, mega-profitable. Its IPO filings indicated that it expects its revenues to climb 72% in 2018 to $3.1 billion, with profits nearly doubling to $764 million. The company finished the first half of the year at $1.3 billion in revenues and $525 million in gross profits.

How does this "stand-alone" do it when all other major stand-alone music services like Spotify and Pandora can't? The answer isn't higher free-to-pay conversion rates. In fact, Tencent Music's conversions are significantly lower than Spotify's and Pandora's. Rather, several factors are at work. First, Tencent Music plays by very different copyright rules and payments than its Western-focused brethren. According to analyst BO-COM International, *"Some popular musicians in Europe or the U.S. may require royalty payment per play count, while the current practice in China is for companies to sign three-year contracts regardless of play count, so the economy of scale helps the platform's profit."* Here's another nice little benefit. Tencent Music owns more music copyrights in China than anyone else (17 million of them). No music licensing required. Western-focused stand-alones can't really compete with that.

But, it's not all about fundamentally different licensing realities. Tencent Music also does several things very differently – and better – than Spotify, Pandora and others. Most significantly, *"Social interaction is the main difference between Chinese music apps and Western music apps,"* according to Asian telecom and Internet research firm CLSA. And none other than U.S. music industry bible *Billboard* agrees, concluding that *"70.4% of Tencent Music's revenue comes from a unique ecosystem that no Western music streaming platform has effectively tapped into yet: a suite of value-added, monetizable interactions with music and its creators that Tencent calls 'social entertainment services.'"*

One prime example of these social services is the live broadcasting of karaoke, which Tencent Music monetizes by taking a commission on all tips and virtual gifts given to creators by their adoring fans. If this sounds more like the micro-payments you would expect to see in the world of free-to-play games like *Candy Crush Saga* or *League of Legends*, you'd be right. Tencent Music leverages the power of those types of game mechanics. In fact, much like in the world of games, a tiny percentage of Tencent Music users generate the vast majority of its revenues. 1% of Tencent Music's users account for 70% of its total revenues (whereas 10% of users generate 70% of revenues for the average mobile gaming app).

Tencent Music also sells a lot of music-related merchandise (including the microphones and headphones needed for karaoke) and virtual tickets for concerts streaming live on its platform. Bottom line is that it has successfully developed and scaled multiple revenue streams – a lesson that Western stand-alones should not only study, but actively emulate.

Ultimately, Tencent Music possesses something even more daunting – direct access to parent Tencent's massive online social communities of billions. *Billboard*, presumably predisposed to favor U.S.-centric music services, sums it up this way. Tencent Music *"has grander, more lucrative ambitions in shaping the future of entertainment and tech – encompassing more flexible digital revenue streams beyond monthly subscriptions, more direct-to-fan opportunities for creators, and tighter integration with existing social media platforms."* That last statement is important. Maybe Tencent Music's ultimate lesson is that stand-alone streaming success at scale can best be achieved by direct linkage to major social media platforms. And, the ultimate form of direct linkage is M&A. Ultimately, that could be Spotify's fate.

But, what company has the will and pocketbook to pull that off? How about our good friends at Facebook? We know that Facebook sees Tencent's great success and is feverishly developing its own native music service. Is it too much of a stretch to believe that Facebook may instead audaciously jump-start its music ambitions with Spotify and become music streaming's global leader with one stroke of the pen?

I certainly don't think so. Facebook + Spotify. I can both see and hear that as being a real possibility. Envious Facebook easily has the cash to make that deal happen, and the Street would love it.

III. So What Can the Pure-Plays Do About It?

Apple, Amazon and Google/YouTube also control massive marketing dollars outside the wildest dreams of the pure-plays. Apple continuously bombards us with Apple Music pitches in its own characteristic "sexy" way, with every breath you take and every move you make, across all of its platforms – both virtual (online) and physical (offline retail stores). There is no escape. And, to be absolutely sure, Apple features Apple Music natively on all Apple devices (iPhone, iPads, Macbooks). No app install is needed. That's immediate distribution and marquee positioning that Spotify and the others can't match.

The behemoths also certainly have the ability to invest significantly more deeply in artist exclusives – differentiated content that is increasingly important to these services in this aural battle royale (just like the strategic role Originals play in the Media 2.0 video world). Nonetheless, pure-plays must try to feature artist and song exclusives themselves, much like Tidal has done over and over with major artist releases. Content is king here in the music world too, and featuring big name artists may be more important to boosting paid subscriber numbers than adding yet another playlist feature. The trick, of course, is for the pure-plays to find a way to continuously incentivize artists and labels to work with them rather than with the deeper-pocketed big guys. Tidal got the job done by making Jay Z and a few other mega-artists part owners. So, that's one option.

But, to make that happen, it's critically important for pure-plays to be artist-friendly. Remember, Steve Jobs played to artist sensibilities from day 1, and Apple underscored the strategic nature of its heritage when it retained Jimmy Iovine and Dr. Dre as part of its Beats acquisition. Meanwhile YouTube, faced with mounting music industry pressure, smartly hired long-time music executive Lyor Cohen as its head of music in order to try to quell the music industry masses about YouTube's advantageous economics.

Spotify, on the other hand, seemingly bit the hand that feeds over the years and counted a very vocal and very bitter Taylor Swift and Radiohead – in addition to the labels themselves – as foes at various points. Sweden's Spotify – born a long, long way from the U.S.-based music industry – proudly celebrated its colder tech-based roots first and foremost in its early days, ignoring the music industry's more sunny soulful essence until it learned the hard way. The company finally atoned when it hired well-known, highly respected entrepreneur and artist manager Troy Carter (Lady Gaga, John Legend, among others) as its new global head of creator services in 2016 (Carter later left the company post Spotify's 2018 IPO). These kinds of gestures matter.

But, most fundamentally – nay, critically – Spotify and other pure-play music services must follow Tencent Music's lead and diversify their one-dimensional business models. Yes, everyone around the world uses Spotify, but that doesn't mean that its stand-alone economics are long-term sustainable. They're not. Conversion rates from free ad-supported music streaming to ad-free paid subscription streaming are simply too low. Even if they weren't, today's per-stream licensing realities and overall economics just don't pencil out. At least not right now. The more they make, the more they lose.

As discussed at length earlier in Chapter 12, one big bet for Spotify to change the order of things is our good old friend video Originals, a previously-abandoned strategy that it schizophrenically resurrected post-IPO in 2018. Pandora also announced major premium video plans in 2016, but nothing much has materialized since. Perhaps that will change now that it has a new plush home at SiriusXM. Tidal succeeded briefly on the video front when it debuted Beyonce's incredible long-form *Lemonade* video in 2016 and boosted its paid subscription numbers significantly in the process.

But, video game playing by Spotify and other pure-play services won't be easy. Their DNA is music, and we go to Spotify and the others to listen. It's not obvious that we will also go to watch when we already have so many other choices, and so little time. Pattern behavior, after all.

So what else can the pure-plays do to surmount their daunting challenges in the face of seemingly impenetrable behemoths? Why not follow Tencent Music's example and take their broader revenue-generating quest significantly further by engaging much more directly with their users who are massive and frequently rabid artist fans? Fan engagement means live events, compelling e-commerce (merchandise), and direct artist-fan and community engagement. Hey Spotify. Focus on deeply integrating those components into your overall customer experiences and, man, significant monetization (not to mention brand love, fandom and loyalty) may follow.

No music streaming service *(no, not even Tencent Music or the behemoths)* does that type of direct artist-fan engagement right. That's a massive opportunity. Music is unlike any other form of media in terms of its impact on our lives. Artists are our messiahs. Tap into that transformational human element, and man, that's where the magic happens *(more on this in Chapter 20)*. Fans will pay a lot for that direct connection, as well as for a direct link to others in the community who feel the same way about the artist as they do.

To expand its story, Spotify also announced a major new podcast initiative late 2018 "creatively" called Spotify for Podcasters, which enables podcasters to easily share their feeds with Spotify's gargantuan global audience. *Bloomberg* reports that 15% of U.S. individuals over age 12 listen to at least one podcast weekly (and nearly 25% of us at least one monthly). Podcast ad revenues skyrocketed 86% in 2017 to close at $314 million in the U.S. alone, and are forecast to top $650 million by 2020. That's some massive growth. And, importantly, podcasts don't come with music licensing royalties, which reportedly account for an EBITDA-killing 75% of Spotify's costs.

"Voice" is another new area of growth for Spotify, which now integrates with Google's Home smart speaker in its quest to enhance its monetization hopes and dreams. It has also been quietly striking direct licensing deals with a small number of Indie artists, thereby essentially acting as a music label (although CEO Daniel Ek protests – perhaps a bit too much – that *"licensing content does not make us a label, nor do we have any interest in becoming a label"*).

IV. PURE-PLAYS – FACING THE INEVITABLE?

Even so, however, the pure-play music existential crisis is unlikely to resolve itself in the face of behemoth superpowers, which means preordained M&A for most. After all, even if stand-alone economics don't pencil out, some of these services – especially Spotify – are extremely valuable. How many of us listen to streaming music services for hours each day? *(I know I do, virtually 24/7 – it keeps me sane as I continuously edit this book)*. That's some kind of reach. And, Goliath buyers can amortize the myopic and fundamentally challenged pure-play business model across all of their many revenue streams. They can simply throw those challenged financials into their marketing expense lines. So, in the immortal lyrics of one of my favorite 80's bands *Tears For Fears*, these Media 2.0 music realities inevitably will be *"sowing the seeds"* of M&A for Spotify and a host of others. Just like they did for Pandora and Slacker in 2018. And for Beats just a few years earlier.

Of course, that means fewer competitors in the music distribution game – certainly not the optimal reality for any supplier (in this case the music labels). The more competition, the better. More demand for the content that fuels that competition. More leverage in negotiations. More lucrative terms. Today's reality feels almost like those "big box" days of yore, when Walmart and Target used music as loss leaders to drive sales of paper towels. Don't forget, Amazon is kind of doing that now by charging its Prime members $2 less per month for Amazon Music Unlimited, so that they stay in its virtual store and buy more, well, paper towels (and all kinds of other stuff that most certainly is not music). That race-to-the-bottom pricing pressure and overall mentality ultimately killed the pure-play Tower Records and Virgin Megastores of the past.

Quite a different state of affairs, then, from what's happening in Media 2.0's video side of the house. On the music side, the number of streaming music players continues to shrink. The top four music subscription services account for 72% of the global subscriber count as they offer essentially the same catalog, frequently at the same cost. Meanwhile, it's "go, go, go" time in the world of streaming video, where we see a continuing string of new market entrants joining the long list of premium OTT players already in the game. All of these video gamers can be found kicking and screaming to find their own unique place in the crowd by creating as many Originals as possible (and significantly driving up video content prices in the process). That's why the video side is much less concentrated. The top 4 SVODs in the U.S. reportedly account for 54% of all subscribers.

Music and video. Both premium content. But, content that plays by very different rules of the game (because of the very different players who wrote them).

Which of the remaining pure-play streaming music services will stand alone at the end of 2019? Share your M&A playlist now.

20

A SPECIAL WORD TO MUSIC ARTISTS

("DON'T FEAR THE STREAMING REAPER")

MUSICIANS, how can you actually make money (monetize) in this brave, yet sometimes frightening, new digital world that has completely disrupted (more like shattered) longtime business models? We already know from Chapter 17 that streaming music services like YouTube, Spotify and Pandora drive significantly less direct revenues to artists, at least at this point. Right?

Yes, that's certainly true if streaming service revenues are considered in isolation. But, for the vast majority of musicians – all except the biggest names – it's not primarily about selling the music itself. Was that ever enough to support your calling anyhow? Instead, it's about touring. It's about getting out to your fans and making new ones by connecting and engaging directly with them. And, that's something that this brave new Media 2.0 world enables in a way that was never before possible. A new kind of direct-to-audience linkage is available to all musicians (established or not) anytime, anywhere, 24/7. The Internet has democratized overall opportunities available to musicians and significantly expanded opportunities for discovery, engagement and obsessive listening.

Let's take Instagram for example. As of October 2018, the social media app counted about 600 million active users – twice the population of the U.S. Of those voracious Instagrammers, nearly half followed 10 or more musicians. Instagram gives artists an easy way to humanize their listening profiles – to literally put a face on their streams. Streaming's potential, then, is to expand artist revenues by opening the door to new fans and deepening direct artist-fan engagement – and all of the myriad tantalizing new revenue opportunities that go with it. I call this a new "community-based" business model for artists in which each individual revenue stream today may be significantly less than streams of the past, but taken together, they ultimately hold the potential to drive greater overall revenues.

In this new community-based business model, the goal of artists should be to open as many legitimate doors as possible for fans to experience their songs. Yes, many fans may be reluctant to pay for content that they have been sadly conditioned to believe is "free." But, they are more than happy to fork over big cash to get closer to you, the artists and bands they love. Sprinkle in direct access for your fans to your daily life *(your hopes, your dreams, your shows, your world – yourselves!)* and you really begin to build something. "Things" you can monetize. Music fans will pay for that kind of access. Fan clubs have proven that. Fans also will pay extra (frequently significantly extra) for "experiences" that expand your live show's impact.

Here's one example. In 2015, oft-overlooked long-time streaming service Rhapsody (now resurrected in the guise of Napster 3.0) implemented a significant strategic partnership with artist-fan engagement service Band-Page to bring unique offers like VIP meet-and-greets into their overall streaming experiences. So, let's say you stream Beyonce. Now, you receive notifications for her upcoming shows, as well as potentially other "goodies." Here's another. Inspiring startup Seeds gives fans an ability to connect directly with their favorite artists and follow their ongoing creative journeys – including every person, place and sound featured in each song on the their next album. Think of it as a microscopic view into the artist's head and song's DNA. And fans may even have a chance to influence it. How cool is that?

It's up to artists, their representatives, and the services themselves to explore all tantalizing possibilities. To experiment. Seed's new direct fan engagement paradigm – and Napster's treasure trove of data with Band-Page's artist toolset – give hope to these new transformational possibilities. So does LA-based Repost Network, a music startup that identifies under-the-radar trending SoundCloud artists and adds its own kind of rocket fuel to get them noticed (and monetized). Repost is one to watch. It announced that it had collected over $12 million in revenues on behalf of its partners as of Q3 2018, doubling its revenues every 6 months and being profitable all along the way. Meanwhile, new innovators enter the market continuously, such as blockchain-based streaming service Audius, which scored a healthy $5.5 million Series A round of financing in Q3 2018 to become the "SoundCloud of the blockchain."

Musicians, listen up. Don't fear our new Media 2.0 streaming dominated world. Streaming is not the Blue Oyster Cult-ified grim reaper that you may think it is. Streaming, instead, may help you reap great rewards.

So, be entrepreneurial. Put yourselves out there. Use all available means to establish direct connections with your fans. Grant them access. Create unique experiences. Most importantly, experiment in this brave new Media 2.0 world. Throw caution to the wind and test the ever-increasing set of new artist-friendly programs offered by leading music streaming services that need you more and more each day as a result of feverish competition. Remember, those services can't be kings in this streaming game without you and your songs. Your experiments today may lead you to the promised land of actually being able to afford your music career. Perhaps even thrive.

Imagine that. Because I absolutely believe that is possible.

PART III, SECTION 4
OUR IMMERSIVE NEW MEDIA 2.0 WORLD
OF XR – VR, AR & MR

VIDEO in our Media 2.0 world. Check. Music. Check. Now it's time to explore Media 2.0's immersive new world of extended reality (XR) – an umbrella term that encompasses virtual reality (VR), augmented reality (AR), and so-called mixed reality (MR).

21

THE XR MARKET – AN OVERVIEW

2016 marked the year when both VR and AR broke out into the Media 2.0 mainstream. VR, as expected. AR, not so much *(okay, not at all – it took the long overlooked and somewhat mocked world of Pokemon to make that happen)*. Analyst firm IDC pegs the combined immersive market opportunity to reach $143.3 billion by 2020. Meanwhile Goldman Sachs predicts sales of VR and AR headsets alone to reach over $95 billion and overtake TV sales by 2025. AR is ultimately expected to dwarf the overall VR market by about 4 to 1, and Digi-Capital projects over 1 billion AR users and $83 billion in mobile AR revenues alone by 2021.

It's easy to see why. We can go about our daily lives and actively engage with others in an AR world, because AR overlays digital content and data on a real world that we fully see. We can't do that in a fully-immersed, completely virtual and more solitary VR world, where you are literally blind to everything not in your headset. MR differs slightly from AR by layering synthetic, virtual content over our actual realities, sometimes even without a headset or handheld device. Disney wowed the world in 2017 with its *Magic Bench* "walk-up-and-play" MR experiment that enabled multiple users to *feel* the presence of CGI characters and interact with them.

Another fascinating and related immersive storytelling concept is "volumetric filmmaking" – think holographic characters that you can view from any angle at any moment in time. How will that work? Who knows, but many are trying, including Paramount's futurist Ted Schilowitz *(yes, that's his title)*, who also doubles as co-founder of HypeVR. Ted's company offers what he calls "spatial" technology that goes beyond immersive to give *"six degrees of freedom"* – i.e., media experiences that know where you are in space and react to you accordingly.

Meanwhile, Metastage opened its doors in Culver City, California in 2018 to be a new kind of studio for volumetric VR and AR production and holographic development. LA-based VNTANA also promotes holograms, enabling us to interact with "live" *(well, kind of)* personalities in real-world settings (theme parks, sporting events, retail). LA-based innovator BASE Hologram hopes to do the same, and plans to bring back legendary (but deceased) artist Amy Winehouse for one final world tour.

And, then someone needs to tie it all together – full-body style. This is what LA-based MAP Lab uniquely does. MAP builds immersive cross-platform technology that ushers in a paradigm shift in how consumers relate to themselves and the world at large. How about that for ambition? MAP utilizes proprietary innovation in gesture, body-tracking, personal data integration, and experiential learning, thereby creating an ecosystem of experiences that compel individuals to become their most engaged, creative and healthy selves. And some of the world's biggest brands – Nike, Lululemon, Microsoft – have taken notice and seek out MAP to engage in transformational new ways with consumers (including in the tantalizing realm of immersive entertainment).

The media and entertainment world is fascinated by these immersive technologies, as it should be. XR technologies hold tremendous promise to expand the connection to, and impact of, content over time. And, the sheer numbers involved are staggering. Just think of all the content needed to fuel the coming onslaught of immersive technology.

Notice a recurring theme here creators? You should. Yes, that's right. Content is king, and our newly-immersive world of Media 2.0 not only craves it, it demands it in order to fulfill its ultimate promise.

22

VR – THE VIRTUAL GETS VERY REAL

FOR many leading media/tech insiders, like Paramount's futurist Ted Schilowitz, VR is nothing less than game-changing. Geek standout publication Wired effusively agrees, heralding VR as "creating the next evolution of the Internet – an Internet of experiences." VR, in all of its manifestations, is important to understand, follow closely, and experiment in.

VR's most obvious "here and now" Media 2.0 promise is in the world of games, a market that few doubt will be massive. The fact that VR headset pricing has dropped dramatically in a short period of time certainly doesn't hurt. In Q3 2018, Facebook announced a $399 Oculus Quest stand-alone headset that, notably, requires no PC or mobile phone to run VR games and other experiences.

But, VR-driven live-action entertainment and location-based entertainment immersive experiences are expanding rapidly too. And smart, forward-thinking media and entertainment companies are actively experimenting and placing their bets in this space.

I. Live Action VR

First, let's talk about live action VR. Fox has been amongst the most aggressive to date. Fox immersed itself completely in VR in 2017 when it launched an entirely new VR unit called FoxNet and partnered with the likes of VR innovator Chris Milk and his company Within (discussed below) to produce Planet of the Apes experiences, among others. Sony also has been relatively aggressive in VR. In June 2017, Sony announced a new Breaking Bad VR project with that iconic show's creator, Vince Gilligan. Imagine what it will feel like to "break bad" spherically? Who needs Breaking Bad's drugs when you are already fully immersed? That may actually freak you out more than the drugs themselves. And then there's Sky in the UK – which has developed several new VR film projects. Meanwhile, Verizon's AOL created a new team focused on VR and AR to bring immersive stories to life for major legacy brands like Sports Illustrated.

And, just like in the OTT video and music streaming world, *"It's the content, stupid."* Content drives successful adoption and overall success. If media/tech companies build compelling immersive experiences, more and more consumers most certainly will come. VR and immersive experiences in general represent a rare opportunity to build an entirely new transformational media and entertainment kingdom.

But how? How do creators solve VR's trickiest dilemma of transforming headset-laden solitary experiences into more social shared experiences? Even more fundamentally, how do creators even develop and produce live action VR stories? Imagine trying to direct a fully-immersive live action VR experience, choreographing all actions at once in a 360 degree spherical setting. How do you direct talent, or focus an audience on one particular element, in those spherical settings? Storytellers must first develop an entirely new language of "experience" – a new lexicon for VR, if you will, to address these foundational mind-bending challenges. That's what

Chris Milk and others are trying to invent. So, consider these to be live action VR entertainment's early days, much like the early days of cinema a century before.

Immersed in this background, here are some key players in the burgeoning world of live action VR.

KEY LIVE ACTION VR PLAYERS

JAUNT

Jaunt singlehandedly sums up the perils of writing a book about the ever-changing Media 2.0 world. Just when I thought it was safe to discuss this VR pioneer in this section, lock down my final draft, and go to print … POOF! There goes Jaunt! Late 2018, seemingly out of nowhere, Jaunt announced that it was laying off "a significant portion" of its team to refocus exclusively on AR and volumetric capture technology. All pending VR projects would be wound down.

How did this happen? After all, blue chip investors like Google Ventures flocked to immerse $100 million in cash into this Bay Area-based VR company when it launched in 2013 to develop and commercialize a revolutionary 360-degree live action VR camera *(I demo'd it in its early days at Jaunt's Silicon Valley office, and was blown away at my first fully-immersive experience)*. Yes, Jaunt later changed course to focus on VR content and distribution (and set up its own LA-based VR production studio in 2015), but VR remained the name of its game. Jaunt ventured into high-end live VR experiences that ranged from steamy (a Fifty Shades of Grey immersive experience … I know, I know, say no more) to supernatural (Invisible, a series directed by Bourne Identity director Doug Liman).

But, warning signs surfaced throughout Jaunt's non-linear journey. Most glaringly, in 2018, Jaunt's board replaced its CEO for the second time in

221

two years. Then, in October, the other shoe dropped. VR "out," AR "in" *(while I grabbed aspirin and scrambled to revise this section)*. Jaunt – a very expensive fully-immersive experiment gone awry. Yet another Media 2.0 cautionary tale of how fortunes can change seemingly overnight.

NextVR

NextVR remains a live action VR market leader last time I checked *(who knows anymore?)*, and it too has attracted investment of well over $100 million. Traditional media, including the venture arms of Comcast and Time Warner (which means AT&T at this point), immersed the company with that cash. NextVR's focus is to bring live events and sports to life, and its client list is impressive. It plays with the likes of the NBA, Live Nation, and the WWE.

Here Be Dragons/Within

From the innovative and iconoclastic mind of Chris Milk, one of the immersive space's most respected creative visionaries, we have two related companies – Here Be Dragons (formerly VRSE) and Within. Here Be Dragons is a VR-driven content studio through and through – no hardware in sight. Discovery Communications fueled it with a $10 million cash injection in 2017.

Meanwhile, Within is both a distributor of Here Be Dragons content and a content/experience creator itself. The company's investors include the likes of diverse A-players Fox, WPP, WME, Raine Ventures and Andreessen Horowitz to fuel what it calls "spherical filmmaking." Within also now focuses extensively on AR *(which I discuss more broadly in Chapter 23)*, and the company released its Wonderscope app for children late

2018 that uses mobile AR to superimpose characters, scenes and stories onto mobile and tablet views. According to Milk, Wonderscope is *"like a lens for invisible magical things that you couldn't see with your naked eye."*

WEVR

Wevr is another SoCal-based VR startup. Its mission is to be the premier home and community for the most innovative immersive creators and storytellers and to foster groundbreaking content. Wevr provides a platform for VR creators to showcase their work, build their audience, and encourage engagement between the two.

Wevr also immersed itself in cash, including $10 million from consumer electronics giant HTC. In addition to serving as a distribution platform for its VR creators, Wevr produces its own live action VR experiences and counts Lionsgate as one of its major Hollywood partners.

EMBLEMATIC

Emblematic is yet another SoCal-based immersive company you should know (see the pattern here – much of this immersive innovation comes from LA). The company developed the first VR documentary, Hunger, which premiered at Sundance in 2012 – downright ages ago in the world of Media 2.0. Emblematic's self-proclaimed mission is to be the home of the world's foremost visionaries to create "fully immersive environments that place the user inside the scene, allowing them to move through, interact, and play with the story." In other words, to fully develop, flesh out and realize VR's live action entertainment possibilities.

EMERGE

One more worth mentioning is super-stealth immersive company Emerge, which is tucked away in a quiet corner of Marina del Rey, California. Emerge calls itself "a *teleportation* company." Yes, you heard me right.

The company's first product is a tabletop device that, in the words of Emerge's marketing materials, *"transmits our sense of touch from a distance"* by mapping *"a tactile interface onto digital 3D objects/holograms in real time, allowing you to physically feel and interact with your bare hands in a shared co-located or telepresence experience."* In other words, just imagine playing with virtual objects – and actually "feeling" those objects – without the need for any type of wearable.

I did. Mind blown. Check.

INTERNATIONAL LIVE ACTION VR PLAYERS

As in any nascent market, the list of live action-focused VR players goes on and on and, of course, includes major international players. Usual suspects include China's BAT companies Baidu, Alibaba and Tencent, each of which is already all-in amidst a Chinese consumer market that buys 40% of the world's VR headsets. Baidu, via its iQIYI streaming video service, intends to build the world's largest Chinese language VR service. The company is investing massively to produce compelling VR content to fuel that consumption. Tencent is also investing "big-ly" in live action VR content, including fully-immersive VR movies and music concert experiences. Meanwhile Alibaba, not surprisingly, focuses first on delivering VR shopping experiences to its hundreds of millions of customers. It fueled adoption of its new form of immersive commerce by giving away Google Cardboard VR glasses, making it easy *(maybe too easy!)* for VR-laden shoppers to pay for goods with a simple nod of their heads.

II. VR-DRIVEN LOCATION-BASED ENTERTAINMENT

And then there's VR-driven location-based entertainment (LBE), which takes the live action VR experience out of the home and into the real, physical world where users can "experience" together and interact with actual physical objects. Think of this as being a much less solitary form of total immersion. These experiences frequently offer guests haptic jackets or other wearables to add the dimension of actual touch and feel.

These are some of the leading innovators in the VR-driven LBE space.

THE VOID

The Void is perhaps best known in this burgeoning category. Think of The Void as being a VR-driven theme park that takes traditional Disney and Universal Studios experiences to an entirely new, fully-immersive level – way beyond the physical. In fact, The Void enjoyed a stint within the Disney Accelerator, so mouse DNA impacts its moves. The company hopes to capture significant share of the $40 billion plus global theme park market and even broader LBE market. After all, once The Void develops VR experiences, it can easily replicate them across other high traffic areas. Imagine your very own theme park "in a box," because that's precisely what "it" is.

You can find The Void's first immersive zones in Downtown Disney Anaheim and Orlando, featuring the "Star Wars: Secrets of the Empire" experience. The company plans to populate the globe with similar highly sophisticated and pricey experiences in its quest for world domination.

The Void, at least partially, has cleverly solved two of VR's greatest challenges – movement and shared, social experiences. The Void participants walk freely, untethered, in its open spaces, wearing vests that carry batteries and processing power and sensors that deliver 4D vibrations timed in synch with the action to deepen the trickery on your mind and body. Guests can virtually "see" each other via avatars as they engage, thereby making The Void's experiences much more social than sitting at home in solitary confinement.

IMAX

The Void is the most high profile player in the VR-driven LBE space, but certainly is not alone. Not surprisingly, semi-immersive film pioneer IMAX also pushed hard to open fully-immersive VR-driven "experiences" in big cities across the globe. But, faced with a dearth of compelling content, IMAX shuttered two of its flagship VR centers during the dog days of summer 2018, effectively killing off its entire immersive ambitions.

IMAX pulled the plug even before the VR-driven LBE opportunity truly began. Wouldn't surprise me, though, if IMAX comes back with a VR-driven acquisition in tow (perhaps with one of the companies I discuss below).

The opportunity is simply too great.

TYFFON

Like The Void, Tyffon graduated from the Disney Accelerator and is another player worth knowing in the VR-driven LBE space. Tyffon's haunted house-themed immersive experience is its first and operates out of two separate "Tyffonium" centers in Tokyo. Tyler Halstead, who works in global business development for Sony in LA, tells me this after his first Tyffonium experience. *"I felt like I was in a haunted house, not in a virtual reality environment, which was a huge game-changer."* I agree. I experienced it myself, and it is impressive. And, Tyffon's haunted house experience is just the first of many.

Tyffon's ultimate goal is to be both more humble and more practical than The Void. It plans to operate and scale its immersive "boxes" across the globe far more cost-effectively, on smaller physical footprints and with significantly lower capital costs. Tyffon will open its first U.S. Tyffonium in 2019.

First stop, LA of course – where much of immersive innovation is happening.

NOMADIC

Silicon Valley-based Nomadic, like Tyffon, plans to extend its immersive environments across the nation in significantly larger and more scalable numbers than The Void. Nomadic planned to open its first VR zone in Orlando, Florida late 2018 with an adaptation of *Arizona Sunshine,* a zombie VR shooter game that already has been popular in VR arcades and individual VR units. According to CEO Doug Griffin, *"When you can reach out and touch things, that really is the magical moment."*

Like Tyffon, Nomadic also plans to expand its VR destinations to Los Angeles in 2019. It's definitely land grab time. Worth knowing this one as well.

TWO BIT CIRCUS

From the minds of co-founders Eric Gradman and Chuck E. Cheese DNA'd Brent Bushnell (Bushnell is son of Chuck E's creator Nolan Bushnell), this new "funhouse on steroids" packs it all in. It's one part old style carnival, two parts VR, and three parts immersive theater. Speaking like a Media 2.0 P.T. Barnum, Gradman boasts, *"We can make the entire park feel like it itself is a story with a narrative to be experienced."*

Two Bit Circus's first location is in the newly-trendy LA warehouse district, in which guests can choose to either play good old-fashioned Skee Ball, or enjoy separate VR-enhanced escape room-like experiences (sipping their very real, trendy and expensive cocktails all along the way to further enhance their immersive experience).

THE RIFT

The Rift, based in Malaysia, is another major player in the VR-driven LBE space and already operates multiple attractions outside the U.S. One senior U.S. LBE insider recently experienced one of The Rift's, well, "experiences" overseas and came back impressed. Immersive experiences are universal, after all, and VR-driven LBE is very much a global arms race.

Stakes are high. Very. But the overall VR-driven immersive market opportunity is even higher. It requires action. Fearless action.

I discuss another – very different – "flavor" of live immersive entertainment in Chapter 27. That one requires no headset or other wearable, and is even more social.

Intrigued? Well, read on.

23

AR – Significantly Augmenting its Early Success

AR surprised virtually all of us in 2016 – especially after Google's clumsy Glass experiment – when it became a mass cultural phenomenon and everyday reality years ahead of its expected time due to our good old friend Pikachu. *Pokemon Go* became the world's collective *"AHA!"* AR moment, and we downloaded our new little friend 750 million times in its first year. *Pokemon Go* served as the media and entertainment world's early AM *(I mean, AR)* wake-up call.

To virtually all of us, *Pokemon Go* arrived out of the blue. And when it did, the befuddled huddled masses were so obsessed and overwhelmed that two of them actually fell off a cliff experiencing it. *(That happened here in my backyard of San Diego where, thankfully, both young men survived with non-life threatening physical injuries, although they likely will continue to suffer deep emotional scars from the very real taunts that will continue to dog them).*

Ultimately, *Pokemon Go* was yet another powerful Media 2.0 wake-up call to action. To not just copy, but experiment, innovate and create new experiences. And, to invest heavily in R&D.

MEDIA 2.0'S KEY AR/MR PLAYERS

Research firm Digi-Capital sees AR's mass adoption coming in four major waves that I will use to frame this discussion: (1) mobile AR software; (2) mobile AR hardware; (3) tethered smart glasses; and (4) stand-alone smart glasses. Using this semi-immersive framework, here are some leading players driving today's semi-immersive AR and MR revolution.

NIANTIC

Pokemon Go's creator gets the top spot on this list, because Niantic first revealed AR's mass market, highly commercial potential in 2016. But, what has Niantic done for us lately?

You may think, not much. But, *Pokemon Go* continues to, well, "go." Strongly. It is no mere fad. More than 13 million users continue to play on a monthly basis in the U.S. alone as of July 2018 (likely including some of you reading this). To put things into perspective, all of Activision Blizzard's hit games reportedly add up to 41 million monthly users.

Still, what will be Niantic's next act, er, app?

In 2017, Niantic announced an intriguing new partnership with the Knight Foundation to drive more of us outside into the real world and into our cities via customized *Pokemon Go*-like experiences (SoCal-based AR startup Animate Objects is an innovator doing similar things and plays with even more sophistication). In the words of Knight Foundation VP Sam Gill, *"We were excited to see someone who had seemingly cracked the code of how to use this device we're all carrying around to go out and interact with each other."*

230

Just ponder that last statement for a minute. Quite incredible, really. Gill talks about using AR to fuel real world interactivity – in other words, the original "AR." Reality itself. *(Why not just step outside and talk?)*

Yes, parents, that's the world we live in.

APPLE

If mobile AR software represents the first giant wave of mass global AR adoption, then Apple is one of its biggest players with its ARKit iOS platform. That's why it's second on this list. Even before Apple unveiled its latest double-sided glass iPhone XS and XR, hundreds of millions of devices were ARKit-compatible and ready to amaze us semi-immersively. Apple also is widely reported to be testing its wearable AR Glasses that it plans to unveil in 2019.

Leading immersive industry analysts, including Robert Scoble and Tim Merel of Digi-Capital, are betting big on Apple ultimately becoming the single most dominant AR force in the world. Merel puts it this way, *"Apple's end-to-end ecosystem of hardware, software, app store, developers and retail are natural advantages that can't be beaten."*

That's a damn good argument for AR being Apple's "next big thing."

GOOGLE

Of course Google is a major player in this nascent game of AR. Its big AR software bet versus Apple's ARKit is ARCore, its new platform for Android phones. Unlike Apple, which operates alone in its own closed hardware/software ecosystem, Google gets a little help from its friends (its hardware partners) to succeed – just as it does with Android. Thankfully for Google, it has a lot of friends.

Google, like Apple, is also focused on AR glasses, which isn't surprising since it invented the widely-mocked v1 Google Glasses in the first place and now hopes to redeem itself. Google's new Google Lens essentially is image search in reverse, empowering users to identify the details of (and data behind) virtually everything they see. Kind of like the *Six Million Dollar Man* or *Terminator (take your pick whether you want to be good guy Steve Austin or bad guy "Ahnold")*.

FACEBOOK

Of course Facebook is here too, just like every behemoth. It sees a pile of cash and can't resist jumping in. Oculus's proud owner naturally is already a leading player, rolling out yet another ARKit competitor – its AR software kit Camera Effects Platform *(hmm … not sure about that name)* that it distributes to billions of Facebook Messenger and WhatsApp users.

Facebook, of course, is also hard at work developing its own pair of futuristic glasses that enable you to see virtual objects in the real world. And, you can bet this ain't no mere hobby. After all, Mark Zuckerberg has boldly anointed immersive technologies as being the next major revolutionary computing platform – capable of replacing our smartphones and computers.

So, maybe don't go out and buy that iPhone just yet!

MICROSOFT

Fellow behemoth Microsoft also plays in the AR space of course, although perhaps a bit more quietly and un-sexily than the others (it is Microsoft after all). Microsoft's main AR contender is HoloLens, an untethered wearable computer that gives users an ability to freely roam about as they experience. Non-flashy Microsoft – the tech world's punching bag for years –

wants to conquer both the enterprise and consumer AR markets. Its Development Edition unit is priced at $3,000, making it mostly enterprise-focused at this point. HoloLens proudly proclaims that it enables "human understanding," which it defines as being the ability to *create and shape holograms with gestures, communicate with apps using your voice and navigate with a glance.* HoloLens also delivers "spatial sound," which enables users to hear holograms from anywhere in the room.

Make no mistake, like Facebook, Microsoft believes that AR will ultimately render all PCs, Macs, laptops, tablets and phones "obsolete" *(yes, that's its words from its own marketing materials).* And, Microsoft certainly has plenty of cash in its quest to takeover the immersive market much the same way it became the dominant operating system for PCs.

So don't *(scratch that, never!)* count Redmond out. Microsoft is Media 2.0's "Sidler." Remember that *Jerry Seinfeld* character? When you least expect it, Microsoft sidles up next to you and is just "there."

MAGIC LEAP

And then there's privately-held unicorn Magic Leap, perhaps AR's most enigmatic company, tucked away in Florida about as far away as possible from Hollywood and Silicon Valley. The company has raised an astounding $2.3 billion to date, including a fresh $461 million in 2018 from the Kingdom of Saudi Arabia's investment arm (among others) at a new valuation that undoubtedly exceeds 2017's mind-boggling $6 billion. Insane, right? Reason overtaken by AR hype? A sign of a coming tech meltdown and apocalypse?

An increasing number of incredulous doubters materialized over the course of the past couple years, demanding that Magic Leap reveal the goods. And, at long last, Magic Leap finally did in August 2018 at a price-tag of $2,295 and to largely rave reviews. Many believe that Magic Leap's semi-immersive MR technology holds the potential to enable entirely new media and entertainment experiences that far surpass VR. That's why *Lord of the Rings* director Peter Jackson jumped on board *(literally, on Magic Leap's advisory board)*.

In any event, with its massive funding, Magic Leap, well, leaps over all other privately financed AR players. How can other startups compete against those virtually unlimited resources? Mega-rounds of capital don't guarantee success, of course, but they certainly don't hurt. That kind of money enables Magic Leap to grab the land in this AR arms race and hold on tight. It also affords long-term experimentation and patience to "get it right," or at least get noticed in the process. Magic Leap certainly gets noticed. Perhaps more than any other player in the semi-immersive world of XR.

And, look at the pedigree and diversity of Magic Leap's private billionaires' club of strategic investors. It represents a veritable "Who's Who" of media and technology. Alibaba, Google, Qualcomm, Warner Brothers, J.P. Morgan and now even the Kingdom of Saudi Arabia all joined the investor party. Respectively, those represent behemoths in (i) international e-commerce and social media, (ii) search and video, (iii) mobile, (iv) content and media, (v) finance, and (vi) even government. That's a pretty well-rounded, global blue chip cast of characters. And, this A-team, with its collective reach and influence, is committed to freezing out others to drive mass success across all consumer and enterprise channels.

Formidable.

Ultimately, it wouldn't surprise me if one or more of Magic Leap's giant investors make a play to buy out the entire company. *"Try before you buy,"* remember? Magic Leap is certainly a helluva try – about as audacious as you can get.

My best guess of which one it could be? Alibaba.

META

And then there's privately-held Meta based in the heart of Silicon Valley. Like Magic Leap, Meta makes both AR hardware and software. Its self-proclaimed goal is to develop *"a new generation of natural machines that are poised to become a healthy, vital extension of how people create, collaborate and communicate."* But, Meta is trying to accomplish those lofty goals on a comparatively shoestring budget. The company has raised a "mere" $85 million to date, including $50 million from Comcast Ventures and Chinese media-tech giant Tencent. Meta is first focusing on enterprise applications. It claims a wider viewing area than HoloLens and more natural interaction with holographic images.

But, we all know that "best" doesn't always win. Meta is a David immersed in a sea of Goliaths.

METAVERSE

San Diego-based Metaverse (not to be confused with Meta above) empowers anyone to easily create and share sophisticated interactive content, including AR experiences and games. Metaverse essentially does for interactive content what YouTube did for video – i.e., simplifies it, democratizes it, and scales it. Not surprising, given that Metaverse comes from the visionary mind of founder & CEO Dmitry Shapiro, who was the first to conjure up YouTube-ian UGC video experiences even before YouTube launched *(as discussed earlier)*. Investors funded Dmitry second that time to create Veoh (which was second only to YouTube back in the day), but they don't plan to miss the boat this time. Like Magic Leap, the company's early investors include a veritable "Who's Who" in media and tech, including Michael Eisner and Marc Pincus.

In explaining his vision for Metaverse, Shapiro takes me on a Media 2.0 journey. *"The capabilities of average people to create and publish content continue to evolve. GeoCities, launched in Nov 1994, was the first service that made it easy for anyone to publish a personal website. Over the years, many services have continued to expand on that capability. FlickR, which launched February 2004, was the first major photo sharing service that made it easy for anyone to share photos. Since then, many services have expanded on the capability, and we find ourselves in the world of Instagram. YouTube revolutionized the world by democratizing video publishing and creating a new generation of content creators that would have never existed in the old media world. So what's next? New platforms are making it possible for all of us to create interactive content. Whether you want to create games, interactive marketing collateral, interactive ads, interactive books, interactive memes, whatever – all of these are now possible to create and distribute without having to write complex code."*

That's where Metaverse lives. And, it's a damn compelling place to be. Be prepared to be wowed!

8i

8i, which describes itself as a holographic company, was a promising new startup in 2017. Its Holo app turns your smart phones into holographic devices that bring your favorite characters to full 360-degree life (a la Princess Leia when she beseeches Obi Wan Kenobi to help her because he is her *"only hope"*). This LA-based startup raised $41 million from an international cast of very real and powerful strategic characters to pursue its vision, including Time Warner (now WarnerMedia), Baidu, Hearst and Verizon.

But, even with a little help from those very big friends, 2018 proved to be tough – and 8i shed a significant number from its team as it pivoted to focus on creating a low cost, high quality stage that creates pre-recorded and real-time XR content. Newly-installed CEO Hayes Mackaman remains undaunted. He sees *"significant opportunity to create 3D stories with major influencers – creating an entirely new market for user generated and brand sponsored content."*

BLIPPAR

Another AR innovator worth mentioning is Blippar, backed by none other than mobile global kingpin Qualcomm, among others. It too has a massive cash hoard – in its case $100 million-plus. Blippar started its life as a marketing agency, but later pivoted in a big way to leverage its image recognition capabilities to create a visual search engine for the physical world. One year ago, CEO Ambariash Mitra aspired for Blippar to be a *"complete visual browser,"* with its app recognizing anything a user views with his or her phone.

But, Blippar's vision sounded a lot like the vision of virtually all the behemoths discussed above, especially Google Lens. So, even with all its cash and big brother Qualcomm behind it, the company faced an uphill battle. Apparently, this reality set in this past year, and Blippar appears to have reverted to its original more down to earth marketing roots. It now operates an AR studio through which it creates next-gen semi-immersive experiences for major brands, and also recently launched its own DIY Metaverse-esque AR tool called BlippBuilder.

No universal visual browser in sight.

Ubiquity6

Ubiquity6 is one of a handful of startups focused on back-end features to accelerate overall AR growth. This innovator's technology enables users to create a cloud-based AR copy of the physical world (3D mesh maps of public areas) in order to enable dynamic multiplayer experiences. Notably, Ubiquity6 raised an additional $27 million from A-list investors Benchmark and Index Ventures in 2018, bringing its total financing haul to $37 million.

Other Behemoths

Like all other Media 2.0 opportunities, AR is a global phenomenon, and this chapter only scratches the surface. As examples, China's Tencent is very much focused both on AR's software layer and AR-friendly entertainment. Alibaba, on the other hand, invests massively to become China's immersive e-commerce leader.

Bottom line is that we are still very early in the AR game. Mobile analytics firm App Annie reported in June 2018 that users downloaded 1.25 million copies of the top 500 AR iPhone apps. While impressive, that number pales in comparison to the 500+ million iPhone downloads in the U.S. alone that month.

You can bet that rapid experimentation and bold innovation – not to mention billions in investment dollars – will massively accelerate AR's growth over the next five years. The behemoths are betting big on this semi-immersive industry. And if they build it (which they are), we most certainly will come – to experience incredible things that we can't even fathom right now.

Chapter 24 offers some tantalizing clues.

24

VR, AR & The Great Unknown

TOGETHER, as we have seen in Chapters 22 and 23, VR and AR virtual experiences already deliver meaningful actual realities in our Media 2.0 world. And, much is written about the incredible power and promise of immersive technologies for all of us, including those of us in the worlds of media and entertainment. They ultimately will take us places, and enable us to *experience* things, that we can't even fathom right now.

Much less is written in the Media 2.0 industry press about the known and, even more importantly, unknown risks associated with full (or even partial) sensory immersion. These are VR's and AR's great unknowns.

Yes, VR is another way for creators to reach consumers with compelling content. But, it's so much more than "seeing." VR, in fact, is not really a visual medium at all. It is an "experiential" one, and that's not just marketing hype. We aren't so much watching or listening to stories. We are immersed directly in them. VR, unlike purely visual media, generates very real deep physiological and biological impacts – your mind and body actually believe you are experiencing a particular non-virtual reality moment right here, right now. No separation from reality exists. You are simply "present." Presence, in fact, is a concept fundamental to total immersion.

Many tantalizing positives flow from all this, of course.

Enhanced entertainment is an obvious one. You can now actually *be* Obi-Wan Kenobi or Darth Vader inside *Star Wars* (take your pick). Or, even better, really emotionally *feel* for those in the experience itself. VR can transport you to anywhere in the world, enable and empower you to get a real sense of what it feels like to be "there" at that particular moment and time. And, that can potentially drive mass empathy and real social impact.

Case in point *Carne y Arena* (flesh and sand), an immersive experience created by Academy Award winning director Alejandro Inarritu (*Birdman*), which became the first VR project to be officially selected by the Cannes Film Festival. *Carne y Arena* utilizes VR to place us in the middle of the Sonoran Desert, being one amidst a group of immigrants who reach the U.S. border only to be stopped by the border patrol. In this new kind of reality, those "Trumped up" anonymous immigrant stories transform into real understanding of harrowing lives and emotional pain that drive that migration. The immigrants' daunting, frightening journey becomes more personal, more tangible, and, therefore, more real. That's when real emotions take hold. Real empathy. Empathy that holds real power and potential to drive real understanding. Perhaps our President should experience a demo.

Here's another breakthrough example. VR pioneer Chris Milk *(whom I have already mentioned several times ... no, I am not his publicist)* created *Clouds Over Sidra,* an immersive experience that places you directly in the middle of a Syrian refugee camp, through which you are guided by a 12-year old girl named Sidra. As you experience a day in her life, no longer is being a refugee in some far away land just some mere abstract concept. Now, due to VR's immersive power, Sidra's daunting challenges come to life both in your mind and body in a way that simply "is." Again, real emotions take hold. Real empathy. Empathy that holds real power and potential to drive real change. To take real action to better the lives of Sidra and others like her around the world.

Imagine journalists taking that VR-driven empathy machine to cover tragic and catastrophic global events like 2018's horrific, endless string of California wildfires and the U.S.'s relentless, devastating hurricanes. Who can doubt that our charitable donations and overall mindfulness would substantially increase as a result of being immersed in those otherwise unfathomable scenes and suffering *(even as climate deniers turn their heads away from undeniable climate change realities and the devastation that flows from them)*.

Let's take VR's teleportation power a different direction. Global travel. Think of that power for the elderly, the physically-challenged, the under-privileged – those for whom the luxury of travel is simply out of reach. Now all can see the world. Scratch that, *be* in that world. Imagine your kid's next field trip. The Travel Channel indeed! Here's one small, but notable, example. Google (via its little-known Google Arts & Culture site) enables all of us, right now, to immerse ourselves in over 1,000 of the world's greatest museums, all from the comfort of our own homes. For free. We can "walk" and experience these museums in full 360 degrees. Now, those arts and educational opportunities are available to entire societies, not just the privileged few.

Beyond media and entertainment, but still in the realm of content, imagine experiences for the treatment of health and psychological issues. First-hand Technology (previously DeepStreamVR) is a VR startup that helps children burn victims cope with pain by immersing them in a VR world of snow, refocusing their bodies and minds. That VR-induced trickery is reported to directly result in pain reductions comparable to that of opiates. Incredible.

241

Spanish startup Psious is another interesting VR startup changing lives for the better. Its immersive technology develops an exposure therapy tool that helps people cope with debilitating fears of all kind – fear of flying, fear of heights *(perhaps even fear of where Media 2.0 takes us next!)*. The company has found that if its patients (for lack of a better word) can experience their particular fears in a controlled environment, they can learn to overcome them.

These examples demonstrate VR's revolutionary potential to enhance quality of life.

But, as with any new technology that holds great promise, serious known – and unknown – risks exist.

In the realm of entertainment, VR takes already-intense horror experiences several extremely scary steps further. Now, you aren't just watching the gore, knowing all the way that you are divorced from it. Outside of it. Now your mind and body actually feel the bloodbath. That you are inside of it. I've been there. When I first demoed a VR zombie apocalypse experience, my body instinctively recoiled with horror after a ghoul approached me from behind to attack *(okay, I admit it – I actually kind of screamed out loud)*. And, that was just a zombie experience. Imagine that power and impact in the hands of horror-meister Jason Blum.

Take that even further. Imagine gamer-beloved *Call of Duty*, VR style. You aren't just playing war amidst all of its death and destruction. Your body now feels as if it is at war. The prospect of very real trauma becomes very real indeed. Researchers already study the potential post-traumatic stress disorder impacts of VR. And, some experts believe fully-immersive VR experiences may cause actual – even permanent – psychological damage. That's why Alex Schwartz, CEO of leading Google-owned VR game developer Owlchemy Labs (developer of popular VR title *Job Simulator*), concludes that VR-driven scares *"are borderline immoral."* And, that's why many in the industry now push for new content standards for this brave new immersive world.

So, does that mean we have some kind of moral obligation in terms of how we develop, distribute and experience these immersive possibilities? After all, we simply don't yet even come close to understanding the full implications here. We just know that serious questions exist.

Talk amongst yourselves.

PART III, SECTION 5
GAMES & ESPORTS

PART III, Section 5 gives a brief overview of the massive overall games market and the surprising rise of the related Media 2.0 industry known as eSports.

25

ESPORTS & E-THLETES

A s massive as the theatrical motion picture business is with global box office approaching $40 billion in 2017 ($11.1 billion of which came from North America), it pales next to the global games market that reached nearly $100 billion that same year. In the movie business, a $100-$200 million box office opening weekend signals a blockbuster. Multiply that by 10, and you have the game industry's largest opening. In 2013, *Grand Theft Auto V* grossed $800 million in its first 24 hours and hit the $1 billion mark in just three days – and now, according to analyst firm Cowen, is the highest grossing work of entertainment *ever*. Period.

Media and entertainment companies (and storytellers in general) benefit from this relentlessly lucrative market, of course, via lucrative licensing deals. Gamers are hard-core super-users – generally young and male – who certainly aren't afraid to spend money (at least for the games they love). They engage deeply with content and with each other, and obsessively watch other gamers in action *(hence the Twitch phenomenon I discussed earlier in Chapter 16)*. Gamers love to watch a good, live head to head challenge, even if they watch it virtually, online. You may not "get" that. But, beauty is in the eye of the beholder. And, gaming and playing guitar exhibit similar "twitch" behaviors. There is an art to it all.

In any event, these head-to-head gamer battles on epic games like *Call of Duty* and *League of Legends* spawned a surprisingly massive new industry known as eSports, which is projected to generate billions of dollars worldwide over the next few years. eSports is already far bigger than you may think. Game market analyst Research and Markets expects the eSports market to have grown more than $250 million in 2018 to $926.3 million (38% of which flows from North America). And, the firm forecasts global eSports revenues to reach $2.17 billion by 2023. For several years *(yes, years)*, eSports have already attracted more young male viewers than the World Series or NBA finals. And, analyst firm Activate forecasts that eSports will exceed 10 percent of all U.S. sports viewing and reach 500 million fans worldwide by 2020, significantly more than major traditional sports like NBA basketball.

Just like any real world traditional sport, eSports feature teams of players who compete with each other and become celebrities in their own right with massive social followings, of course. Leading players, like their more traditional star athlete counterparts, become LeBron-like superstars to a digital-native millennial audience that finds them to be more directly relatable. *League of Legends* superstar Faker, for example *(yes, that's his Prince-like one word name)*, makes $2 million-plus annually, excluding sponsorship revenues *(yes, "excluding" – you heard me right)*. In fact, it was reported that SK Telecom offered him $2.5 million to re-sign with its T1 eSports team after the team won its third straight *League of Legends* championship. Faker and other super-"e"thletes *(like that one?)* are increasingly repped by a new breed of management firm like LA-based Cloud9, which raised at least $28 million from WWE, among others. So, it's starting to look a lot like traditional sports.

It shouldn't surprise you, then, that head to head team competitions now regularly take place in large-scale arenas filled to capacity with tens of thousands of fanboys. PricewaterhouseCoopers projects that eSports will continue to pack them in over the next several years, forecasting tickets sales for eSports events to rise massively at a CAGR of 21.1% through 2022.

"But, should eSports really be considered to be a new 'real' category of sports?" You be the judge. Where "real" sports go, gambling always follows. And, market research firm Eilers projects fans to bet $23.5 billion on eSports by 2020. That seems real to me.

Brands and advertisers agree and increasingly think of eSports as simply being a new class of sports for a new millennial generation (just like Whistle Sports is a new kind of sports-focused media company for a new digital and social native audience). All the big brand names you know and love, especially highly-caffeinated ones like Red Bull and Coca-Cola, already spend significant sums to sponsor individual e-thletes, teams and events. That's why eSports sponsorship revenues are expected to nearly quadruple to $2.5 billion by 2020.

Smart, bold traditional media and entertainment companies see these unmistakable trends and are moving aggressively into eSports to reach this valuable millennial audience that is increasingly glued to their screens (eSports fans reportedly spend twice their time playing and watching video games than watching TV). In 2017, even Media 2.0-challenged Viacom invested in Super League Gaming, a company known for hosting eSports competitions in movie theaters, as well as online. And, in another notable and more aggressive move one year earlier, Turner Broadcasting partnered with mega-agency WME-IMG to create the first eSports league appropriately called ELeague. Think of it, aspirationally at least, as being the NFL of eSports. Turner now broadcasts eSports events from its ELeague on its very traditional cable channel TBS.

Not to be outdone on its gaming home turf, behemoth Activision Blizzard joined the party, buying live eSports event organizer Major League

Gaming in 2016 for $46 million and creating its own eSports league called Overwatch. Activision's stated quest is to become the "ESPN of eSports." Sound familiar? Meanwhile, ESPN embarked on its own quest to be, well, the ESPN of eSports, by launching its own dedicated eSports channel online and broadcasting tournaments offline. And, underscoring the global and borderless nature of eSports and all of these Media 2.0 opportunities, Chinese behemoth Tencent in 2017 committed to invest $15 billion on eSports over the next five years.

Clearly, the virtual has become very real big business that generates very real cash. Lots of it.

And, eSports is not just for existing giants either. You can bet that a long list of startups are also in the game, and you'd be right. LA-based Scopely is perhaps most intriguing. This eSports wunderkind has raised boatloads of very real cash from a "Who's Who" of leading media/tech venture capitalists. Another worth knowing is Riot Games. But, those are just two of the most notable from a long list of others that include SLIVER.tv (a NorCal company that has raised $16 million from Samsung NEXT, Sony Innovation Fund, and leading talent agency CAA to develop a platform to record, view, and stream eSports in fully immersive cinematic VR), Dojo Madness (a Berlin-based startup with $12.8 million from The Raine Group, 500 Startups and others to offer a virtual coaching app for competitive gamers that leverages machine learning), Smash.gg (another Nor-Cal-based company with $11 million from Accel Partners and Horizon Ventures to host online gaming tournaments), Gamer Sensei (a startup that is headquartered in Boston, has raised $6.3 million from Advancit Capital, Greycroft Partners and others to offer an online platform that uses algorithms to match competitive video gamers with "coaches"), and LA-based Fanai (which has raised nearly $2 million from Greycroft Partners and others to optimize fan and brand engagement in eSports via an AI-driven monetization platform).

eSports already is a major new Media 2.0 force, and it is still very much in its early e-nnings *(yes, forgive me)*. Don't think of it as being a fad, because it isn't. And, its hockey stick-like rise will be fueled further by the mainstreaming of VR and AR which, in turn, will further accelerate growth of the already-massive overall games industry that underpins it.

PART III, SECTION 6
OFFLINE, LIVE REAL WORLD EXPERIENCES

THIS book focuses on our increasingly tech-driven online virtual world of media and entertainment, not so much on the offline physical world of live entertainment experiences. But, in an interesting paradox, our increasingly virtual, disconnected lives generate a very human counter-reaction – an accelerating human desire for *real* connection, physical interaction, and lasting "experiences."

These forces are too frequently overlooked in our Media 2.0 world, but absolutely should be actively considered and implemented in any fully-formed multi-platform strategy.

26

LIVE EXPERIENCES – THE OFT-FORGOTTEN MULTI-PLATFORM PLANK

(& THE ONLINE/OFFLINE VIRTUOUS CYCLE)

WE still go to the movies, don't we? We still fight traffic and the throngs, and still pay for expensive popcorn when we can watch from the quiet solitude of our own homes. Why? Precisely because we are social creatures, and we don't always want quiet solitude. Have you experienced watching a thriller like 2017's blockbuster *It* in a theater and, then, the same thriller at home? "It's" *(yes, pun intended)* an entirely different experience due to the entirely different energy generated in the big communal room versus your smaller private room. It's simply more thrilling to watch a thriller with others who gasp when you gasp and jump when you jump (or even trigger your jumps in the first place).

The virtual and physical worlds absolutely can (and should) be connected in this increasingly disconnected digital world in which we all "communicate" with each other more, but frequently question how meaningful that communication is and whether we are part of any real community. Remember *Pokemon Go* from Chapter 23? That's what I'm talking about. And, that's just one rather small possibility. Let's think much bigger.

Disney is perhaps the single most multi-platform media company on the planet. The Mouse House practically invented offline real-world brand engagement with its theme parks, and now plans to take its vision significantly further. Disney – soon-to-be Netflix's new SVOD arch-nemesis – announced in 2017 that it would open immersive *Star Wars* hotels where each guest gets his or her own storyline. Talk about a truly multi-platform experience. Now, *The Force* can be with you anywhere you are – online, in movie theaters, in merchandising, in virtual reality, in theme parks, and now in hotels where the line between where your guest status ends and your active participation begins, blurs.

And, how about Amazon? As I discuss over and over in this book, this new Media 2.0 juggernaut thinks anything but small. Amazon constantly amazes, especially in its understanding of, and increasingly aggressive action in, delivering a full 360-degree multi-platform branded experience that increasingly incorporates offline live, real-world experiences and brand engagement.

Amazon debuts its motion picture Originals, including Academy Award-winning movie *Manchester By the Sea,* in movie theaters (not online). In another fascinating example of counter-programming, Amazon increasingly builds out and operates Amazon "book" stores across major U.S. shopping malls, while others tear them down. And, in its most audacious multi-platform move to date, Amazon acquired Whole Foods in 2017 for $13.4 billion to humanize its overall brand and engage more directly with us on the daily. Don't think for a moment that Whole Foods is just about groceries. Amazon undoubtedly will market all of its produce – especially Prime memberships – across its stores, offer us special Whole Foods incentives to sign up for Prime, lure us into shopping more online, and gather even more data about us and our shopping habits all along the way. Think of it as being your very own 360-degree Amazonian journey that brings new meaning to the term "super"-market.

No surprise, then, that Amazon's brick-and-mortar ambitions don't end there. In August 2018, *Bloomberg* reported that Amazon was eyeing leading Indie movie theater chain Landmark Theatres. Just imagine receiving the full Amazon treatment on your date nights. Amazon will offer Prime members discount tickets and tasty Whole Foods at its theaters. Amazon undoubtedly will strategically program the films we see (not mention the ads we see before they begin) – particularly during the awards season – in order to supercharge its hype machine and get us to help build Oscar buzz for its features. Even more audaciously, ever-crafty Amazon reportedly will open up to 3,000 more brick-and-mortar stores by 2021.

Not surprisingly, visionary (yet now apparently sleep-deprived) Elon Musk absolutely thinks this way. He, of course, is already "out there" multi-platform-izing in the most audacious and fearless ways – with his Earth-connected Teslas, rocket-lifted SpaceX's and particle-fueled Hyperloops *(which, according to some visionaries whom I trust, are closer than we think in terms of becoming reality and undoubtedly will fully immerse us in content as we travel in "pods" when they are).* Reports have swirled for years that Tesla's very own new in-car music and media streaming services may be coming to your Model S(oon). Perhaps Apple, which stopped development of its own autonomous cars in 2017, should finally just buy Tesla and merge their shared stylized hardware/software, offline /online innovation-driven DNA.

Could this really happen? Yes, I really think so. In fact, I predicted this all the way back in 2013 and have the blog post to prove it.

All these examples demonstrate that what we have here, ladies and gentlemen, is a virtuous cycle of increasingly online/virtual social interaction that fuels the growing movement of offline/physical and downright tribal live real-world engagement. That, in turn, fuels more ongoing online social interaction, action and impact – and then back again. Welcome to our new truly multi-platform Media 2.0 virtuous cycle and overall *Zeitgeist*. Welcome to holistic, 360-degree storytelling.

Let's first take the business of music where, as we saw in Chapters 17-19, disruption rules the day and traditional revenue streams wither. All doom and gloom, right? Wrong. PricewaterhouseCoopers forecasts global live music revenues to continue to rise sharply over the next five years, reaching $30 billion in 2022. Music festivals sprout up everywhere *(I am obsessed with them)*. Why? Because these festivals become so much more than the music itself. The music draws you in, but the real magic comes from the like-minded community and shared immersive experience created during that moment in time. "Experience" is the key word (and result) here. Experiences and shared humanity are lasting.

Rick Farman, co-founder of Superfly (producers of Bonnaroo and Outside Lands, two of the largest U.S. music festivals) strongly agrees. In my conversation with him, Farman describes the need for actual live physical connection as being *"the thirst for high-touch, authentic real-world experiences as people increasingly immerse themselves in the digital world." You have a symbiotic relationship here,"* says Farman. *"Social media helps drive the communal aspects of these very social events, and mobile takes it to another level and amplifies it – driving the whole phenomenon of FOMO."*

Live Earth co-founder and executive producer Kevin Wall, an intensely creative media visionary and activist who has created and produced many of the largest live events the world has seen, adamantly agrees. *"Festivals use digital as a driver, but they are anti-digital in what they represent,"* he tells me.

So, how many digitally-driven content companies get it right and fully embrace their physical alter-ego? Not many.

On the music side, we now know that Spotify's and Pandora's challenges are daunting (to say the least), and that they must either significantly diversify their businesses or be acquired to survive *(Pandora smartly chose the latter in 2018)*. One part of that solution may be to bring their online customer engagement into the physical world of music festivals. Expand their brand into the real world in order to expand their overall connection (brand love) with their otherwise rather anonymous customers. Deepen them. Create a real differentiated and fully realized community. How about the Pandora *Unboxed* Music Festival? *"Gold Jerry, Gold!"* Again, the online virtual community drives more offline participation and success which, in turn, drives more (and more continuous) online brand engagement and success.

Young upstarts, like new Asian youth-focused and music-heavy 88rising *(discussed earlier in Chapter 13)*, point the way. 88rising has fast become a major new lifestyle brand that started online with some of Asia's most popular influencers, but increasingly focuses on offline engagement as well to deepen its brand's personal connection with fans and the creators they support. 88rising's Double Happiness tour boasted several sold-out shows, and the young upstart also held its first major LA-based festival in Q3 2018 (the Head in the Clouds Music & Arts Festival). Given that 88rising could gauge exactly what its audience wanted based on online engagement, it was not at all surprising that Head in the Clouds quickly sold out.

It goes the other way too. Hey, music festivals, harness the energy from your magical weekends that typically dissipates when the weekend is over. Mobilize that passionate community you created. Continue its life and extend that energy online and on all platforms. Continue the conversation and almost-tribal sense of community beyond the physical venue itself via ongoing virtual interaction and social media. You'll be glad you did. So will your investors. You have the new Media 2.0 tools to drive success like never before.

Instagram is one such increasingly critical tool. Remember, in the words of Ray Winkler who designed Beyonce and Jay-Z's 2018 *On the Run* tour, *"A show no longer starts when the curtain rises. The show starts the moment the first person takes a picture of it."* Those Instagram moments are lasting. They extend the brand. KAABOO, the major music festival that just completed its successful fourth year in my backyard of San Diego (and is now expanding into Dallas and the Cayman Islands), smartly thinks this way. It increasingly seeks to extend KAABOO brand engagement throughout the year.

Now let's take video. How about Netflix, the granddaddy of the OTT video space? Yes, Netflix is the category leader. But, as I discuss throughout this book, it too faces its own existential business model challenges. Netflix's customer experience is all virtual. Why shouldn't Netflix try to differentiate itself from its increasing list of behemoth competitors (like Amazon, Google/YouTube, AT&T and Apple) that have fundamentally more diverse business models? Why not bring the Netflix brand and experience into the physical world much like Apple did with its stores – and Amazon now smartly does with its new "book stores" and Whole Foods?

That may mean differentiated Netflix stores. But, it also may include Netflix-driven theater experiences (again, Amazon is already there), Netflix-branded community screenings, film festivals. Myriad possibilities exist. After all, online video services like Netflix gather deep user data of like-minded viewers in cities across the country. If any of these premium video services successfully create physical communities under their individual banners, then they can leverage these new offline experiences to drive further and magnified success online. Netflix apparently now "gets" this, after first resisting the urge. After mocking Amazon in 2017 for its strategy of releasing its feature films first in theaters, Netflix announced in 2018 that it would do the same.

Traditionalist Viacom signaled its recognition of these new online/offline possibilities in 2018 when it first made a surprising move to buy VidCon, the premier industry conference dedicated to online video and its creator community. Viacom undoubtedly will shower all of us attendees with its online brands throughout our very real experiences as it seeks to expand its VidCon vision globally. But Viacom didn't stop there. As year-end approached, Viacom's MTV bought the SnowGlobe Music Festival in order to directly link the critical live, experiential element to the overall MTV music experience. When announcing the deal, MTV explained that SnowGlobe represents an important next step in MTV's *"resurgence by expanding deeper into live events."* Kudos to Viacom. Well played.

And, let's certainly not forget the sports world, which exhibits perhaps the deepest and most personal type of fan/brand engagement. I am proof positive of that. As go my Minnesota Vikings, so goes my mood (*just ask my wife and two kids who frequently avoid watching with me on any given Sunday out of fear for what may happen next*). Our wide world of sports frequently now leads on the Media 2.0 online/offline virtuous cycle front, as we watch increasingly powerful "smart stadiums" being built in which we can simultaneously engage and experience both actually (with our family and friends at the game) and virtually (with our friends online watching from home). Just think of the data our favorite teams, and the brands that support them, increasingly collect all along the way.

These are just some ideas and concepts that hold the potential to be transformational. Perhaps these concepts spark some ideas of your own in your own personal quest to be fearless.

Action, remember? Not merely reaction. Or, even worse no action at all.

I'll say it again. Go out there and be fearless!

27

INNOVATORS IN IMMERSIVE LIVE EXPERIENCES

("THERE'S NO PLACE LIKE DOME")

WANT a truly immersive experience? One that is highly social and deVOID of headsets and other wearables? Then try the oldest new platform – live, live, live – and jump into the wonderful world of domes. Domes offer a welcome respite from frequently isolating hardware-driven live immersive experiences. If done right, dome experiences tie multiple Media 2.0 strands together to create unforgettable and transformational impact and "community VR."

Here are two innovators in this 360-degree spherical space.

THE MADISON SQUARE GARDEN COMPANY

Immersive experiences come in many different flavors. One of the most audacious – and a personal favorite – is the MSG Sphere project by The Madison Square Garden Company (MSG). In 2018, MSG's CEO Jim Dolan and partner Irving Azoff announced its first two massive MSG Sphere projects – in Las Vegas (of course) and London. The MSG Sphere is, well, a near-fully spherical venue that seats 15,000-20,000, every inch of which (both internally and externally) is covered by programmable, wraparound LED lighting. That's technology capable of displaying 250 million pixels – more than 100 times clearer than today's HD TV technology.

But, that's not all. The MSG Sphere also innovates at a grand scale on sound, offering a revolutionary new so-called "beam-forming" acoustic technology that customizes its sound to each individual in the audience (as if they were wearing their own pair of headphones). Wait. There's more! The MSG Sphere will add an infrared haptic flooring system so that guests actually "feel" their experience via bass emanating from the floor. Still not convinced? Well, the good people at MSG also plan to add the fourth dimension of smell to enhance things further.

MSG's audacious goal is nothing less than to reinvent the venue and live event experience. Love it. That's why I named MSG one of my "Fearless Five" Media 2.0 companies of 2018.

VORTEX IMMERSION MEDIA

MSG's Sphere project certainly isn't the only dome in town, even if it is the most audacious. Whereas MSG goes for broke with a limited number of massive 360-degree experiences worldwide, Vortex Immersion Media seeks to take its revolutionary dome technology across the globe in smaller packages without reducing overall immersive impact. As one example, Vortex enabled innovative pop superstar Childish Gambino (Donald Glover) to create an entirely new music experience dubbed *Pharos* in the Joshua Tree Desert. *Pharos* enabled the fortunate few to experience music together in an entirely new immersive way. *Billboard* called Vortex's dome *"the highlight of the night"* that *"provided a glimpse into how fans might consume music in the future – and the bar has been set high."*

Vortex's founder Ed Lantz, a former aerospace engineer, pioneered immersion domes in the late 1990's. Now over 1,500 digital domes operate in science centers, planetariums and theme parks around the world. Vortex envisions its new far more sophisticated class of domes as being *the* next-gen out-of-home immersive entertainment venues, not just for cinema but also for live entertainment, eSports, and a host of other applications. Lantz asks, *"Who wants to go out on the town with friends and opaque out the world (and their friends) with a VR headset? Headsets are great for arcade experiences or as VR home theater, but are not suitable for long-form concerts or theater experiences. People go out of the home to connect with others, often enjoying entertainment over drinks or food. 'Generation VR' will demand more immersive experiences in their leisure entertainment without the encumbrance of glasses, goggles or head gear."*

Vortex's immersion domes are not just venues for 360-degree entertainment. The company's bold vision is to create group immersive portals into cyberspace (and vice versa). Imagine putting on a headset at home, taking control of an avatar, and joining a global dance party in London. Partiers in London look up and see hundreds of avatars dancing along with them in the dome. Vortex plans to seamlessly merge real worlds and virtual worlds with machine learning and a strong social media component. With domes, we can also immerse large audiences in virtual environments that feature live performers who further enhance audience impact. Unlike theater or *Cirque* performances, these performers are not limited to the laws of physics. Literally anything becomes possible.

Brands crave these radical (yet "here and now") possibilities to deepen consumer engagement and impact. Not surprising, then, that Vortex creates compelling dome experiences for the likes of Nike, IBM, Nokia, AT&T and Microsoft. For Nike, Vortex created a 360-degree interactive experience in a 60 foot dome in the Philippines for Nike's *We Run* woman's marathon. Nearly 10,000 marathon runners finished their races inside the dome with an RFID tag that uniquely identified them and pulled their personal data (photo, run-time, signature and personal quote) and automatically incorporated those elements into the immersive experience itself.

Vortex refreshingly also brings a sense of social awareness to the overall immersive conversation. CEO Mark Laisure understands the psychological power of immersive media *(discussed earlier in Chapter 24)* and feels a deep need to use it responsibly. *"Watching a violent scene on film or television has nowhere near the impact of immersive media because the brain registers 360 programming as 'real,'"* Mark tells me. *"Vortex is focusing on programming with positive, life-affirming content and impact. We are passionate about creating awe-inspiring experiences and compelling stories that inspire a deeper connection within ourselves, our communities, our families. This is the future of entertainment and a path to a happier world."*

I love that idealism. We need more of it.

Laisure sees a bright future for Vortex. *"We are poised to scale rapidly. We hope to have at least 30 Vortex Dome immersive performing arts centers and DomePlex immersive entertainment centers operating interactively within the next 5 years."* That's bold, audacious and fearless. The Media 2.0 trifecta! Love it.

Obviously, I am a believer in Vortex and in the unique power and impact of the experiences these innovators create. The Vortex team thinks, dreams, and produces "big." In the words of Vortex producer and head of creative development Kate McCallum, *"This new, exciting era of emerging immersive media technologies is providing artists, content creators, philosophers, educators, businesses, and all of humanity with yet more tools for experiencing alternative perceptions of reality. New ways of creating and sharing our stories, visions, and experiences through frameless walls of light and sound, and colors and meaning. We are on the cusp of an evolution of expanding the frame of media reality that will surround us naturally, more like we perceive with our own senses."*

Now *that* is what I'm talking about!

Immersive domes are a "next big thing."

PART III, SECTION 7
SOCIAL IMPACT
– THE STEALTH PLANK, RISING ...

OKAY, I've now essentially covered all main individual "planks" that, together, build a holistic, fully fleshed-out 360-degree Media 2.0 vision and strategy.

But now, as we move forward into 2019 and beyond, it's time for a very different and more ethereal plank – Media 2.0's unprecedented power and potential to reach, activate and motivate us to do "good." To generate real positive social impact on a mass global scale. This discussion nicely piggybacks on the thoughts of Vortex's Mark Laisure that closed the previous chapter.

Now, we take them further.

28

MEDIA 2.0'S UNPRECEDENTED POWER
TO MOBILIZE & DO "GOOD"

ONSIDER social impact a "stealthy" plank that can be overlaid on top of all the others discussed in this book, and hearkens back to themes from decades past that are making a comeback. And, if you use this one right then, man, you really have something! A virtuous – truly virtuous – cycle of online/offline/connection and impact. *This* is when your multi-platform vision becomes fully realized in the deepest sense.

That is precisely what renown global music event producer Kevin Wall *(discussed earlier in Chapter 26)* had in mind with *Live Earth 2* in 2015 – to mobilize one billion voices, all committed to urging world leaders to take real action to address climate change. How? Wall created a 360-degree campaign that inspired and activated millennials around the world to leverage their collective reach, power and virtual might via all available channels (social, mobile) to connect with each other and send messages directly to world leaders and influencers. The actual physical *Live Earth 2* festival served as the climax to a mostly online campaign that was, of course, televised to a global audience *(traditional platform, activated)*.

And, you know what? It worked! Wall's ambitious, audacious campaign not only achieved its goals, that overwhelming wave of Media 2.0-enabled mobilization also served as a clarion wake-up call to global leaders, reminding them that the world's youth were watching. That global microscope, in turn, motivated essentially every single global leader to finally take action and sign the unprecedented Paris Climate Accord. Media 2.0 enabled this collective action. Media 2.0 fueled it. Media 2.0 empowered the people.

And then the Trump happened ....

Well, let's take that back *(the mid-term elections may have been a start).* Do any of you reading this really doubt that 2018's California wildfires and the nation's cataclysmic hurricanes are a direct result of climate change? Let's build a wall! No, not that kind of wall. Rather, a new Kevin Wall-inspired *Live Earth 3* movement that refuses to accept denials and deniers. And, let's use all of Media 2.0's planks to get us there.

Or, how about this? Several of Media 2.0's top young creators and influencers – including Lilly Singh and Lizzie Velasquez *(both properly honored at The Streamy's inspiring 2017 inaugural "Purpose Awards" that I was fortunate to attend)* – use their massive global social platforms to educate their tens of millions of millennial followers about global causes and crises and to motivate them to take real action and be part of the solution. To volunteer. Contribute. Be aware. Inclusive. Or, just plain be positive, respectful and "good." You know, basic human elements of decency too often missing in the course of our everyday discourse *(especially from 1600 Pennsylvania Avenue).*

And those positive actions breed more positive actions that, in turn, seep into and transform society's overall DNA. That's happening right now. I see it everywhere. Doing "good." Standing up (or kneeling down) for what's right. Those have become central priorities for our younger generations that, studies show, carry real significant dollar value (as in, earning less money, but achieving more lasting fulfillment).

That's the power of Media 2.0 storytelling. A compelling message can reach virtually all of us at any given moment in time, and just about anywhere on this planet. We can now, for the first time, take immediate action from our phones. We are moved by a video or immersive experience (like Chapter 24's *Carne y Arena*) and then, with a few taps on our phone, we can immediately donate to a cause, sign up to volunteer to ease suffering, or sign an online petition demanding more immediate government action. We can even create our own stories and immediately inject them into the global conversation. Now that's democracy in action! That's precisely the vision of crowd-funding platform GoFundMe, which established a new video production studio late 2017 to mobilize action and giving via stories of empathy and compassion.

These are the transformational themes that serve as the very foundation of the *Life is Beautiful* music, arts and education festival in Las Vegas (themes that will never die in Vegas, or anywhere else, despite unthinkable attempts to snuff them out). That was the mission of Media 2.0 startup Good Amplified, a multi-platform media company dedicated to showcasing and promoting non-profits, foundations, and these overall ideals. And, similarly impactful (yet still highly commercial) themes drive the mission of Uproar, the new media company focused on wildlife and conservation that I profiled in Chapter 13.

Just three examples of a growing movement in Media 2.0's new world order.

In the words of Nobel Prize winning poet Bob Dylan, *"The times, they are a changin'...."*

PART IV

2019 & BEYOND
– WHERE MEDIA 2.0 IS GOING

PART I laid out Media 2.0's headline stories for 2018 to give you a dose of instant gratification. Part II then took us on a journey that set the stage for today's digitally-transformed world of media and entertainment. We arrived at our Media 2.0 destination in Part III – the state of play and leading players in today's brave new world of video, music, immersive media, eSports and live entertainment.

Now, Part IV looks forward, crystal-balling where Media 2.0 is going in 2019 and beyond.

First stop, my annual "Top 10 Media 2.0 Predictions" – this time, for 2019 and into 2020. Stop #2 features predictions – backed by real dollars – of leading venture capitalists investing in the Media 2.0 space.

29

MY TOP 10 MEDIA 2.0 PREDICTIONS FOR 2019

Now onto my Top 10 Media 2.0 Predictions for the coming year and into 2020. This is where I put myself out there, after synthesizing the various strands of what I have seen and heard throughout the year – including from top executives, entrepreneurs, creators, and influencers in the Media 2.0 world.

Drumroll please!

PREDICTION #1

Blood continues to spill in the relentless battle amongst premium OTT video giants, as Apple and Disney join the subscription video fray and add to the epic collective assault on Netflix. In the midst of it all, smaller "niche" players either find their singular voices that attract "fandom" and broader monetization, or risk being marginalized and swallowed up by their strategic investors (for a fraction of what they would have commanded a couple years back).

Originals continue to be the primary weapon used in the premium subscription streaming video battlefront, extending Media 2.0's new "Golden

Age" for creators and further skyrocketing content-related development and production costs (including the price tags for A-list marquee talent). Fierce premium OTT video competitors increasingly use content both offensively and defensively, like Disney withholding its crown jewels from Netflix (*Star Wars*, Pixar, Marvel, Princesses, *X-Men, Avatar*). Netflix feels the heat, as will its investors, as the collective crew of "Netflix-Killers" put increasing pressure on its pure-play business model.

Meanwhile, the newly expanded list of virtual MVPDs fix their initial flaws, offer consumers real competitive choice, and hasten consumer cord-cutting even further. Whereas we started 2016 with 2-3 real, viable mainstream choices in the U.S. for live television, as of 2019, consumers now can access nearly 10 (cable, satellite, Hulu Live, YouTube TV, DirecTV Now, Sling TV, PlayStation Vue, fuboTV, etc.). And, even in these nationalistic times, let's not forget about massive international players like Tencent, Alibaba or Baidu's iQIYI, which went public in the U.S. markets this past year.

Amidst this battle of video giants, several smaller so-called "niche" or segment-focused video players either expeditiously find their uniquely compelling voice and build a fandom-fueled multi-pronged monetizing brand around it, or simply get lost in the noise.

PREDICTION #2

Media 2.0-driven M&A continues to rule the day in all segments. On the video side, both traditional media companies and undercapitalized and underperforming privately-held new media companies languish in this beyond-crowded OTT video space and become logical M&A targets.

M&A is a hallmark of Media 2.0's overall digital, multi-platform tech-infused transformation of the media and entertainment business. Just like

AT&T closed its acquisition of storied traditional (yet slow-moving) Time Warner ($85 billion), Disney beat back Comcast to acquire Fox's entertainment assets in 2018 ($71.3 billion), Comcast struck back and acquired Sky ($39 billion), and SiriusXM acquired the remaining 81% of Pandora it didn't already own ($3.5 billion), expect more massive deals in 2019, together with a number of smaller, yet still significant ones. Viacom/CBS is one likely candidate.

And don't just look within U.S. borders. No virtual wall exists in our borderless Media 2.0 world, which means that M&A's pace will accelerate internationally as well. Remember, the Comcast/Sky deal represents a U.S. behemoth's ambitions to significantly expand its footprint into multiple European territories. Lots of mega-companies around the globe desperately hope to expand their footprints to places where, up to now, they have never been.

To be clear, not all M&A will flow from weakness. Sometimes the numbers offered simply will be too high to reject. But make no mistake. Weakness will abound amidst hyper-competition, and winners will swallow up losers in an environment of accelerating M&A. Many of the so-called niche-focused OTT video services still primarily rely upon ad dollars (especially the younger ones), but remember, Google and Facebook already own about 2/3 of that global digital advertising market. That means that most pure-play OTT video players simply cannot succeed on ad dollars alone. And, for most, other means of monetization will be beyond their reach, as they fail to deliver a sufficiently compelling, differentiated and emotionally connected media experience. So, much like Uproxx did this past year when Warner Music Group acquired it (likely for a song), expect several of the new media players I discuss in Chapter 13 to lose their Indie status.

PREDICTION #3

The music industry's streaming-driven turnaround continues and streaming revenues accelerate, but pure-play music services led by Spotify continue to hemorrhage money as losses mount. Meanwhile, the giant "big box" retailers of the day – Apple, Amazon and YouTube (particularly YouTube) – brazenly march on, indifferent to that suffering with their fundamentally different underlying marketing-driven business models.

Yes, Spotify boasts massive scale. Yet, scale alone does not financial success make. In fact, pure-play growth success leads to higher and higher losses due to sobering industry economics these pure-plays can't stomach, but the behemoths can due to their multi-pronged business models. These harsh realities mean that investors of many pure-play streaming music services will take a hard look at themselves in 2019 as they contemplate their next strategic next steps. Many will realize that they can't go it alone. And that leads to more M&A, much like we saw this past year with SiriusXM buying Pandora and LiveXLive buying Slacker. Spotify is not immune here. Unless it successfully expands its business model and drives major new revenue streams, it too could be bought. Facebook anyone?

PREDICTION #4

Tech-driven media companies thrive and increasingly dominate the entertainment world by using data to their advantage. They use AI, voice and machine learning to dominate further and even more broadly infiltrate our lives and impact our media and entertainment experiences.

Netflix, Amazon and Facebook increasingly mine their deep data about all of our hopes and dreams to maximize "hits" and minimize "misses" as compared to traditional media companies. In many respects, the studios simply can't compete. Faced with that reality, the quest for data – and the services that provide, analyze and inform – takes on new urgency. Further, the Hollywood establishment and creative community still have yet to understand – at least in large numbers – the power of new cost-effective Media 2.0-related ways to test and measure new characters, stories and engagement in order to more smartly and efficiently place their big expensive bets.

Meanwhile, the new tech-driven media giants hope to increase their overall Media 2.0 dominance through the soothing voices of Alexa and Siri *(sorry Google, yours is a little less so)* and the overall AI/machine learning revolution. "Virtual assistants," "smart speakers" (or whatever you want to call them) increasingly dominate our home conversations, improve significantly over time, and serve up our favorite content via "intelligent" recommendations (as well as increasingly targeted and smarter incentives, promotions, ads and goods). 71% of us already use voice assistants at least once per day (most frequently for selecting the music we like to hear), so voice most definitely is here to stay.

More exotically, and perhaps somewhat alarmingly, AI also increasingly drives so-called "intelligent" creation. AI already develops movie trailers that some believe approach the impact of their human-generated counterparts. You be the judge – check out the first AI-produced movie trailer, care of IBM's Watson, for the fittingly AI-themed 2016 motion picture thriller *Morgan*. And, just imagine how much AI has advanced in just these past two years since then. Can AI screenwriters be far behind? Gong Yu, founder and CEO of China's leading streaming platform iQUIYI certainly doesn't think so. In his words, AI *"will reshape the entertainment industry over the next 10-15 years, much more so than the Internet did over the past three decades."* Just chew on that for a bit.

So, AI may become a real threat even to creative pursuits that, up to this point, most in Hollywood believe are untouchable by computers, bots, and robots. Tesla maven and global futurist Elon Musk is downright dystopian and takes things even further, warning that AI may be an ultimate global threat to us all. Musk tweeted in 2017 that *"competition for AI superiority at national level most likely cause of WW3."* Those were his precise words, so that was either Musk's particular form of Twitter-speak, or his mind had become a bit hazy during one of his notorious cannabis-fueled interviews!

PREDICTION #5

Behemoths Apple, Google and Facebook, together with other Media 2.0 giants and deep-pocketed financiers from around the world, increase their already-massive investments in immersive technologies and accelerate mainstream adoption of AR.

AR's gold rush means continued growth in the related wearables market and consumer adoption of AR-driven eyewear. Investors of all stripes also continue to throw boatloads of cash into the overall immersive space to fuel the development of experiences (including real world live entertainment and storytelling, not only games) to feed these new platforms. Expect significant investment in content *(much to the delight of the companies I profile in Part III)*. The immersive market opportunity is still so nascent, yet its ultimate promise is so great, that the money working to capture it in 2019 and beyond will seem endless. And, when so much money chases a market, that market becomes our consumer reality.

The onset of 5G wireless networks will only hasten the growth of extended reality (XR) in all its forms. Speaking of 5G …

PREDICTION #6

5G Networks launch, reveal their early Media 2.0 promise and possibilities, and begin to transform our media and entertainment experiences (as well as the overall ecosystem that supports them).

5G networks are critical for media experiences that require low latency, including AR, VR, and eSports. For AR, 5G reduces the size of consumer headsets, because processing is now done on the network itself rather than on the device. That makes wearables increasingly user-friendly and fuels further innovation and adoption. 5G also accelerates more high quality video consumption on our mobile phones, thereby pushing purveyors of premium OTT video like Netflix to increasingly focus on mobile-first content experiences.

Quibi certainly saw this train coming, and jumped on first.

PREDICTION #7

The oft-overlooked, yet potentially game-changing, live entertainment and event plank increasingly finds itself in multi-platform Media 2.0 strategies, deepening overall brand engagement and monetization possibilities. Expect more significant "offline"-related experiments, initiatives and M&A by Media 2.0 companies.

Call this the "Amazon Effect," as players across the Media 2.0 ecosystem stop scratching their heads about Amazon's direct-to-theater film releases, brick and mortar retail expansion, and Whole Foods superstore operations – and, instead, increasingly study, respect and emulate them. Netflix certainly did in 2018. After trashing Amazon one year earlier for releasing its features first in theaters, Netflix announced it would begin to do the same.

Amazon understands what most still haven't even considered – that direct, non-virtual offline consumer engagement may be the most impactful plank of them all, driving online engagement into the real world (and then back again) to create a virtual cycle of daily brand engagement and consumer monetization every step of the way. Even traditional media company Viacom now shows signs of understanding these online/offline brand synergies. It bought both youth-focused video industry conference VidCon and music festival SnowGlobe in 2018.

So, while MoviePass *(my #1 most "fearless" company of the year)* may go the way of the Dodo bird in 2019, movie theaters themselves will not die. They simply will be re-imagined. We humans, after all, are social creatures. We like to get out, and we won't be satisfied binging on Netflix alone. Movie theater subscription services most definitely are here to stay, and Amazon will offer one soon for Prime members. After all, in a fun fact that may surprise you, more museums populate the planet – significantly more – than McDonald's. See, there is hope!

But, there's more. In reaction to significant and pervasive negative forces that permeated much of 2018, Media 2.0 innovators take things even further and begin to infuse their offline efforts with social impact, an inspirational and motivational element that is demonstrably proven to also be commercially smart. These fully-realized efforts hold the tantalizing power to transform Media 2.0's virtual cycle into a fully-realized multi-platform cycle that is downright *virtuous*. Double bottom-line – profitable both commercially and societally.

Hey, Media 2.0 companies. Don't underestimate the power of humanizing your efforts with a healthy dose of offline "soul." More and more of you will in 2019 and beyond. Both, because it's good. And, because it's good for business.

PREDICTION #8

The #MeToo Movement continues to transform the face (and faces) of both old and new media. And, new faces will invest new industry dollars in new (and frequently very different) content choices, bringing us new (and frequently different) stories and transforming our media and entertainment experiences.

Revelations aren't over. Abuse was simply far too pervasive. Old players are gone. New, frequently younger, Media 2.0 savvy faces get a seat at the Media 2.0 table. They change the game of "what" and "how" we experience content.

Ultimately, #MeToo both cleanses the Media 2.0 industry, and fills our plates with very different media and entertainment choices.

PREDICTION #9

Fake news, fraud and breaches of privacy continue unabated and accelerate, as does marketing concern for "brand safety." These seemingly unstoppable negative forces continue to place downward pressure on ad-dependent open Media 2.0 platforms.

Make no mistake, we are in the midst of hacking wars, the likes of which we've never seen. This "good versus evil" reality is here to stay, and players across the Media 2.0 ecosystem either significantly increase their investments in counter-measures and related PR, or risk the wrath of consumers and the overall ad market (much like Facebook did this past year).

Twitter housecleaned 70 million fake and automated accounts in a two month span last year (and 1 million more daily), Instagram conceded that over 50% of engagements on its posts tagged as #sponsored are fake, Spotify similarly conceded prevalent ad fraud and decreased its total reported content hours streamed by hundreds of millions of hours, and competing music service Tidal faced accusations that it had falsified tens of millions of streams. Just a few examples of how pervasive fraud and audience manipulation has become in our Media 2.0 world. These fake accounts create, in the words of *Variety*, "*a shadow army of followers that has comparatively little monetary effect. But perform the same manipulation with music streams, and it constitutes fraud.*"

PREDICTION #10

Blockchain technology and crypto-currency-fueled investment and experimentation, already over-hyped and under-performing, continues apace. Yet, once again, there will be little to show for it in the world of media and entertainment. At least for now.

Early blockchain leaders continue to be irrationally overvalued, which is always the case with any nascent market. But, on a happier note, the voice of blockchain technology – heard thus far mostly in investment circles with promises of "instant millions" (or even billions) – becomes increasingly heard for its more positive potential for the world of media and entertainment. Blockchain technology conceptually holds revolutionary industry-transforming new offensive and defensive power. On the offensive front, blockchain enables new ways to monetize content via micropayments and direct creator-to-consumer distribution *sans* today's leading middlemen. These possibilities begin to reveal themselves in 2019. On the defensive front, blockchain promises to eradicate piracy, but that happens in years, not this coming year.

THE BOTTOM LINE

2019 certainly will push 2018's Media 2.0 boundaries noticeably further, driven by these and other industry meta-forces. But, these changes will be barely noticeable compared to the seismic shifts to follow in the next ten years.

I close with Paramount futurist Ted Schilowitz's perspective on all of this. In our conversation, Ted points to two phenomena – the first of which he calls *"the known unknown,"* and the second he calls *"the ten year curve."* *"The known unknown"* refers to what he calls the *"scary"* fact that we all know that massive tech-driven change is coming, but we don't know the *"twists and turns that get us there."* Meanwhile, *"the ten year curve"* refers to *"big dynamic change waves"* that follow ten-year cycles. In Ted's view, we just recently finished the YouTube and iPhone 10-year cycles, and now essentially everyone around the globe participates in those dual phenomena.

So, what's "the next big thing?" Ted calls it the *"the evolution of the screen"* – so-called "visual computing" via new forms of eyewear (wearables) that replace our smartphones. Think *Minority Report*-like data and content interaction, and you get the general idea. *"Surprisingly little has changed with human/screen interaction in the past 30 years,"* Ted points out. He reminds me that while user interfaces have become more sophisticated, actual screen interaction is not massively different – comparing interaction on Mac screens 30 years ago and on iPhones today.

That is all changing right now – as you sit, read and soak in Ted's thoughts either in print, or more likely on your own v.2019 screen. According to Ted, we are only about 3.5 years into this 10-year visual computing cycle. *"In 2013-2014, we saw the first idea of commercializing a track-able screen, a spatial screen. That is a massive change. We will fundamentally change how we use our screens. I see a very distinct future where these things will emerge from their cocoon and replace the iPhone, laptop, etc. You will notice an evolution of 30 minutes per day, then one hour, then two hours, etc."*

Think that overstates things a bit? Well, Ted cautions you this way. *"It's the exact same paradigm shift we saw with mobile phones decades ago. Just imagine back then that you would – decades later (i.e., today) – carry a device with you almost every waking moment of your waking life. Even Bill Gates would have said that is ridiculous."*

Yet, here we are. Today. In that "unimaginable" world. That's how fast it goes.

Ted is adamant about this inevitable "evolution of the screen" reality, and he is convincing. *"I know the next evolution is coming. All of these experiments today are on their way to something really, really significant. 2019 will be very subtle in this revolution. Still for the early adopter, because none of these head mounted immersive devices today will replace our smart phones. But the constant and continuous evolution of this tech is happening."*

With less sophistication, I simply predict that AI and machine learning will begin to completely freak us out in all areas of our lives, including in the realm of content creation, development and production. No doubt, I will call the coming sea change "Media 3.0."

We can't anticipate where all of this will take us, of course. Just like we couldn't have predicted the journey that took us to today's Media 2.0 world *(which I laid out earlier in Part II)*. But, given the frenetic pace of today's tech-driven media and entertainment revolution, these changes no doubt will disrupt and transform yet again. Continuously. Many of today's leading and seemingly invincible Media 2.0 players, like the Blockbusters of the past, will be marginalized or simply gone. Could it happen to Netflix? AT&T? Apple? You may think, *"of course not!"* But, then again, even "wealthiest person in the world" Jeff Bezos acknowledged that Amazon – one of my "Fearless Five" companies – could be one of them. In a remarkable year-end statement to his troops, he tempered any potential corporate complacency with the words, *"I predict one day Amazon will fail."*

And, you know what? He meant it, and he is absolutely right.

New massive players will rise up from nowhere, inject themselves into our daily lives, and disrupt today's Media 2.0 order of things. They will create *Media 3.0.*

And, looking back at it all, much of it will seem so very obvious – like it does now as we look back at the long and winding road that led us to where we are today.

30

VC Predictions — Follow the Money

(Where Media & Tech Investors are Placing Their Bets)

Okay, those were my predictions for the world of Media 2.0 in 2019 and beyond. But, where are venture capitalists (VCs) placing their bets? After all, VCs back up their predictions of which media/tech sectors are hot (or not) with cold hard cash.

I asked a diverse set of VCs whom I respect to share their bets, and the wisdom behind them. I run my own high impact seed and pre-seed stage venture fund, SAM CREATV Ventures, so I too will add my "two cents" and finish with a few overarching themes.

So listen up cash-hungry Media 2.0 entrepreneurs and startups! Now's the time to really pay attention. Pop open that can of Red Bull, pull out that yellow highlighter, and digest the wisdom (and realities) below. Carefully. These breadcrumbs may lead you to your very own financing promised land.

Let's first begin with LA-based VCs, because SoCal has become the center of the universe for Media 2.0 investing.

MUCKER CAPITAL

Leading LA-based VC firm Mucker Capital also focuses on seed and pre-seed investment, particularly in innovative media-tech startups based in Los Angeles. Managing partner Erik Rannala starts us off on a positive Media 2.0 note for the coming year. *"While I believe we might very well be in for a financial market correction in 2019, I still fundamentally believe what I wrote in early 2017 when everyone was talking about being in a big 'tech bubble.' I don't believe we are in a bubble, but that software and information technology are fundamentally changing the economy."*

THIRD WAVE DIGITAL

Media 2.0 pioneer Allen DeBevoise is one of LA's leading early-stage investors through his Third Wave Digital fund, with a particular focus on video over the years. He is a founding father of most of the leading digital-first video companies discussed earlier, including Jukin Media, 88rising, Mitu, All Def Digital, izo, Tastemade, StyleHaul and Pluto.TV. He has since expanded his focus with investments in Drone Racing League and VR-driven Wevr, among a host of others.

Allen tells me that this is where he sees opportunity for video. *"My main focus for digital video businesses is to see a diversified revenue model focusing on the lines of business that are growing and showing traction on digital platforms — most notably social commerce and music streaming and possible a freemium model to specific content franchises. Yield optimize the engagement with short form programming on the viral super-platforms — advertising (media, native), social commerce, music streaming, transactional video on demand, freemium content, etc. Brands should think about a 360 degree approach to their audience — monetization via short form, events, etc. Go deep with your audience via a diversified business model and points of engagement."*

Touchdown Ventures

Long-time VC Scott Lenet operates a different kind of fund out of LA. Touchdown Ventures establishes and operates corporate VC funds for a diverse set of Fortune 1000 companies. In Media 2.0 land, these include Fox and Tegna. Scott tells me, *"We will continue to see an inevitable march toward personalization and 1:1 targeting in digital media, but tempered by consumer demand for responsible use of personal information. In many ways, Seth Godin's 'Permission Marketing,' written two decades ago, may finally find its era."*

Luma Launch

Luma Launch is another LA-based fund that invests in high impact, early-stage startups. Its investments include Catalog, a platform for small to large brands to find highly curated, high quality and individualized content faster and cheaper.

I asked managing partner Laurent Grill his "take" about overall Media 2.0 industry dynamics, and this is what he tells me. *"The media/tech industry is shifting drastically with CPMs going down and the traditional ad structure fading away. Content businesses are having a much harder time monetizing and needing to be more creative to survive, let alone thrive. The transition into SVOD is becoming more and more necessary for any venture-backed content business to have a chance of massive success. Unfortunately, there are only so many dollars on the consumer side, so competition for these dollars has heated up."*

Laurent is bearish on the opportunity to establish new social media platforms. *"In terms of the social media landscape, it has become very clear that the days of the next Facebook, Instagram, or Snap are going away. These incumbents will continue to bring users to their platform, but starting any-thing new has become increasingly challenging."* He is, however, bullish on messaging *"Messaging (iMessage, WhatsApp, Telegram) has emerged as a leader in the future of social. The younger generation is seeking personaliza-tion, and brands/artists/influencers are seeking engagement. The messaging platforms will serve as a conduit to this new wave. We have an investment in a business addressing this change, Digits, and we continue to be excited to see how this industry evolves."*

NEXT 10 VENTURES

Next 10 Ventures is a new LA-based VC firm focused on the creator econ-omy. As an operating and investment company, Next 10 Ventures in-cubates and accelerates new businesses, content, products, and services. Former Google executive and founder Ben Grubbs tells me that his firm's mission *"is to enrich, inspire, and entertain kids and young adults through the investments and partnerships we establish with artists, entrepreneurs, educators, and opinion leaders. We believe that by encouraging children and young adults to discover new subjects and topics to study, we can in-spire a lifelong appreciation for learning."*

And inspire, Next 10 does. The firm launched a global EduCreator In-cubator in Q4 2018, its first step in expanding the playing field for global digital learning. This first of its kind one-year program seeks to support emerging video creators who produce education and learning content holistically – with seed investments of $25,000 to $75,000, programmatic support, and mentorship.

As for 2019 and where the world of Media 2.0 is going, Ben adds an inter-national flair and focus. *"We will continue to see strong audience growth from international markets such as India and Indonesia that are bringing millions of new users online for the first time. As these users access the Internet on their mobile phone, they will turn to services such as YouTube and Instagram for short-form video. Investments in e-commerce and mobile payment will bring monetization opportunities for creators outside of platform advertising and brand sponsorships. This is good for creators based in these international markets, as well as creators based in markets like the U.S. that draw a substantial audience from international markets."*

EXPONENTIAL CREATIVITY VENTURES

Now let's go over to the other coast. NYC-based evergreen fund Exponential Creativity Ventures – true to its name – focuses on frontier tech, tools, platforms, networks and marketplaces that fuel creativity and impact. Managing partner Adam Huttler lays out his fund's focus for 2019 this way. *"Virtual reality and augmented reality are starting to break into the mainstream, but we think they're still 3-5 years off from being ubiquitous. The best opportunities in 2019, for both areas, relate to basic infrastructure: platforms, protocols, and other core technologies that provide a foundation for the content that will drive mainstream adoption."* That's good news for startups like interactive content pioneer Metaverse, discussed earlier. In fact, Adam is a recent investor in the company.

Adam further tells me, *"Meanwhile, in the land of traditional media, the dust still hasn't settled from the havoc unleashed by Netflix and Amazon Prime. We're seeing a lot of great founders building streaming platforms for niche (demographic or psychographic) content and audiences, but the economics of bundling (which benefit the biggest content aggregators) create a powerful headwind. That said, we anticipate that someone will break through with a streaming service that attracts a passionate community willing to pay another monthly subscription for exclusive content – and 2019-2020 is a reasonable guess for when the winner(s) will emerge.*

Finally, we're seeing a lot of innovation and opportunity in music tech. The most exciting companies in 2019 are (1) those working on artificial intelligence and machine learning approaches to A&R and recommendation engines, and (2) those working to solve the (massive) problem of unpaid royalties."

PLUS EIGHT EQUITY PARTNERS

NYC-based Plus Eight Equity Partners agrees with Adam, and focuses exclusively on music-tech. While other investors frequently shy away from early stage music-driven venture opportunities, this VC shines a spotlight on them.

Co-founder and managing partner Rishi Patel tells me why. *"For years, the music industry did an incredible job of marginalizing itself in the wake of the complexities of music publishing and the consolidated power held by the major labels. At the turn of the century, the digital revolution paved the way for those analog dollars to implode into digital pennies, causing the industry to spiral into years of restructuring and forcing it to reactively formulate a digital strategy."*

But now, Rishi underscores, the music industry has been fundamentally transformed. And, that leads to new opportunity. *"After over a decade of adjustment, the music industry is now finding itself in a new era of power held by DSPs who seek to become the new labels, whilst those digital pennies begin to grow into nickels and dimes. These new financial opportunities are rooted in products and services driven by a focus on consumer experiences (like SubPac, a wearable technology that converts sound into high fidelity vibrations) and revenue streams for artists previously unknown (like Splice, which enables musicians to find sounds, get gear, and connect with each other). There is a new paradigm for investing in the media industry and music is the new frontier."*

Music, as a sector for investment, is certainly hotter than it has been for years.

ADVANCIT CAPITAL

Let's stick with a New York state of mind. Advancit Capital, also based in New York, was founded by Shari Redstone (Viacom vice chairperson) and Jon Miller (former CEO of AOL), and focuses on the tech-fueled transformation of media and communications. Recent investments include sports journalism-focused TheAthletic, podcast company Wondery, and eSports team 100 Thieves. Miller tells me that he thinks about future investments this way. *"As all enterprises need to persistently interact with their users and customers, we see companies deploying media in ever-more sophisticated and mission critical ways."* In other words, content used to fuel ongoing engagement, brand loyalty, and fandom – all of which leads to deeper monetization possibilities. Aspirationally, think about mega-platforms Amazon and Alibaba here.

THE ACTIVIST FUND

Bicoastal The Activist Fund was launched by Greg Suess and Bernie Cahill, founders of Activist Artists Management, together with Activist partner Tony Khan, owner of the NFL's Jacksonville Jaguars and the English Premiere League's Fulham F.C. Activist's fund sits directly in the heart of Media 2.0 and leverages the deal flow and industry knowledge of its partners, who were involved in mega-deals with Richard Branson and Spotify, among others. Recent investments include Epic Games (participating in its $1.2 billion financing, together with Smash Ventures) and Lyft (injecting Activist into the world of autonomous driving and in-car entertainment, trends the partners see as continuing to gain significant momentum in 2019 and beyond).

Regarding the fund's investment focus for 2019, founding partner Greg Suess tells me this. *"We will continue to focus on areas where we see industry disruption through the lens of our management business. For example, the upcoming roll out and revolution of 5G is expected to have a meaningful impact on the current disintermediation of the television, gaming and music industries. The consumer will have more capability in their pockets than ever before, and that will impact how, when and from whom content is consumed."*

Interestingly, Activist – true to its name – also brings an impact component to its focus. Greg tells me that the United Nations' Intergovernmental Panel on Climate Change deeply impacted him and his partners and colored their way of thinking. *"The partners anticipate that key entertainment industry stakeholders will get behind consumer friendly food tech and other environmental related initiatives that show a positive environmental impact. This is something the consumer is demanding and changes are inevitable. The best operators of movie theaters, music venues, theme parks, interactive multiplayer entertainment centers and other forms of out of home entertainment will start to integrate these new products and technologies into their businesses."* In other words, the *virtuous* circle that I discussed earlier.

From a macro standpoint, Greg and his partners *"see a greater need to identify and align with strong managerial leadership, which is essential when there is disruption and dislocation in the market, particularly as the venture cycle and availability of venture finance is impacted by the return of volatility and rising rates."*

7 GLOBAL CAPITAL

Now, let's go global. 7 Global Capital is a cross border growth fund focused on investing in the next generation of global Internet category leaders. The fund was founded by former KKR and international growth investors and is based in San Francisco and Berlin. The fund's limited partner base is comprised exclusively of European multi-billion dollar companies that include German media giant ProSiebenSat1 (hence the "7" in the its name, since "sieben" means 7 in Deutsch). The fund's investors serve as distribution partners for portfolio companies across twelve industries. Investments to date include new media darlings Cheddar and The Young Turks, as well as a diverse set of disruptive companies like Bird, Capsule, Opendoor, Oscar, Acorns, TheRealReal, and hims. Diverse indeed!

Founding partner Jack Leeney tells me this. *"We invest predominantly in the U.S. in businesses with $10-50 million in revenues with considerable growth, which have yet to expand abroad, yet have high visibility for global leadership."* Reflecting upon the diversity of the firm's investments, Jack explains, *"In Cheddar, we saw the evolution of both content creation and alternative distribution models to reach a digitally native audience with high quality live news as the world moves away from linear cable bundles. Our most recent investments in hims and Capsule are representative of evolution we see in the consumer healthcare space where the diagnosis, supply chain management and delivery methods in prescription drug fulfillment are fundamentally broken."*

7 Global Capital also continues to look for opportunity in what it calls "offline industries," where consumer and enterprise tools and interfaces enable entirely new business models and margin structures. Not surprisingly given some of the earlier chapters, I like this expanded focus. Jack expands his thoughts about the ultimate objective of these investments. *"This from the ground up process has the ability to dis-intermediate the old*

way of doing things in everything from media, real estate, shipping/logistics, commerce, and finance among other structural shifts across major industries."

MODERN TIMES GROUP

Staying with a globalist perspective, Nordic-based media conglomerate Modern Times Group (MTG) operates its own very active corporate venture fund. Scott Rupp, based in San Francisco, is its U.S. managing director and also doubles as a partner in BITKRAFT Esports Ventures. MTG's recent notable investments include Metaverse (the YouTube-ian interactive content creation app that I discussed earlier), Apponboard (a disruptive app discovery technology that powers the "try before you" install button in the Google Play store), Phoenix Labs (a group of former Riot executives disrupting the monster hunter genre with a free-to-play cross platform title), Nomadic (a leader in premium, gamified VR-driven location-based entertainment experiences that I discussed earlier), and Volley (the leading voice game developer for Amazon and now on Google). Meanwhile, BITKRAFT's portfolio includes a diverse set of 17 seed company investments across the entire eSports ecosystem, including H4X (a gaming fashion and apparel brand), Runtime (a performance nutrition company for gamers), Dojo Madness (the world's leading eSports big data company), and Epics (a blockchain-based mobile digital collectibles platform).

Scott describes his investment focus for 2019 this way. *"Looking ahead, I am interested in investing in the next great eSports games, where considerable room remains for genre and viewability innovations. I also believe there are numerous opportunities around genre innovation in story-driven games and interactive fiction, and new platforms empowering the creation of interactive content. Fundamentally, we are long-term bulls on games and eSports, as we see numerous catalysts in the years ahead, including continued demographic and behavioral tail winds; platform convergence/ true cross platform games; better and bigger mobile devices; 5G connectivity; game streaming that reduces hardware requirements and expands content availability; emerging markets now better able to afford PCs; next genera- tion interactive spectating experiences; eSports betting to drive engagement, monetization and new audiences; and next-gen eSports experiences made possible with AR and VR."*

"MY TAKE"?

What can we take away from these VC prognostications? Does consen- sus or do any patterns emerge? Perhaps not from these individual VC thoughts. After all, the overall Media 2.0 market opportunity is multi- platform and inherently diverse.

But, based on what I see and in my own investing experience, I think it's safe to point out four overarching Media 2.0-related investment themes. First, general video-centric new media companies are in disfavor, but identity-driven, fandom-focused media companies can be compelling – particularly those like 88rising and Uproar *(both discussed earlier in Chap- ter 13)* that are cross-platform and drive multiple revenue streams. Sec- ond, the XR/immersive sector is attractive, which is good news for com- panies like platform-transforming Metaverse and MAP Lab *(discussed in Chapters 21 and 23, respectively)* and experience-creating LBE companies like Tyffon and Vortex Immersion Media *(discussed in Chapters 19 and 24, respectively).* Third, eSports continues to be top of mind and of great inter- est. And, fourth, companies that facilitate new forms of monetization are very much in favor, like San Diego-based alternative payments platform Jib Technologies and LA-based influencer-driven marketing and brand- ing firm Bent Pixels.

In any event, the dollars driving continued innovation and transformation will continue to flow. The Media 2.0 market opportunities are simply too great.

PART V

HOW TO ACT FEARLESSLY IN 2019 AND BEYOND

A⊤ the beginning of this book – which ultimately is a journey through the disruptive and transformational new world of Media 2.0 (and the possibilities and pitfalls that go with it) – I defined my main goal as giving you a firm foundation and framework to understand the forces that drive that change. And, then to motivate you, your teams, your companies and your organizations to get into the game! To act on those forces and fully leverage Media 2.0's power and potential to your advantage. To spot never-before opportunities. And, then seize them. Boldly. Fearlessly!

Now that you've reached these final pages *(whew!)*, hopefully you fully embrace this call to arms and are ready to take action.

But, you also may be asking, *"how?"* and *"where do I begin?"*

Well, read on. I'm here to help (at least, that's my hope).

MEDIA 2.0'S TOP 10 LESSONS & STRATEGIES

Now, it's time to dig in. Get granular. Specific. Time to take all of the learning and lessons from the earlier pages and convert them into real, concrete, focused and impactful action. This chapter is meant to do just that. To guide you in your own Media 2.0 pursuits. To lead you to *your* promised land.

Because we now live in a technology-infused BuzzFeed-ian world of short attention spans and "listicles," here are my Top 10 lessons learned from our Media 2.0 journey – and, importantly, the concrete strategies that flow directly from them and may help you take your own fearless actions. Smartly. These may be especially important to those of you in traditional media who need to fundamentally transform your way of thinking amidst Media 2.0 realities.

In true David Letterman fashion *(one of my Media 1.0 heroes who now actively plays in the Media 2.0 world on Netflix at a price tag of $2 million per episode)*, I start with lesson and resulting strategy #10, and work my way down to the single most important lesson of them all (which should now be obvious).

Cue the drumroll, please.

LESSON/STRATEGY #10

The Internet and technology have changed everything about engaging with an audience – content development, content marketing, content distribution, and content monetization.   Hey, traditionalists. This means you need to rethink essentially everything about your media business … and then rethink it again.

Heed these sage words spoken by Disney Chairman & CEO Bob Iger to an audience of analysts in 2017. *"I think the most important thing one has to do when they're contending with change is to admit that it's occurring and to assess very carefully what the impact of the change is on all the businesses."* Amen to that.

And, that kind of re-thinking includes who is actually doing the thinking for you. Do they have the right background and digital DNA? After all, it all starts with people *(yes, even in our increasingly AI world).*

So, hire young, hungry new Media 2.0 talent – including social media and data mining experts – and bolster them with the right experienced advisors to accelerate your company's learning.

LESSON/STRATEGY #9

The speed of change and technological advancement is only accelerating. That means you should increasingly invest in studying it (including the key players and what they are doing) and immersing yourself in it.

Challenge yourself to stay ahead of the curve, as well as the competition that is increasingly trying to do the same. Get out of your offices and into the field. Attend industry events. Meet key Media 2.0 startups, innovators, execs. Task your digital transformation team and top advisors to identify the most relevant leading innovators and most promising Media 2.0 companies. Conduct pilot programs with them. Demo days. Trust me, those innovators will be thrilled to be in business with you and likely won't even charge you for it.

Or, identify some of the most compelling Media 2.0 companies before your competitors do and strategically invest in them in order to get your feet wet and learn, learn, learn. Even bolder, start a digital/tech-focused incubator internally – essentially an R&D lab with innovative companies that apply to be part of it. Fox did just that with the Fox Innovation Lab, Disney did it with its Disney Accelerator, and innovative media/tech law firm Stubbs, Alderton & Markiles did it with its highly respected seed-stage Preccelerator *(Well done Stubbs!)*. To the rest of you, if lawyers can do it, you can too *(no slam on lawyers, since I too was once a member of that club)*. If nothing else, those kinds of moves send an important message to your company, employees, investors and the world that you take the disruptive Media 2.0 forces that engulf you seriously and are taking real, concrete action to use them to your game-changing advantage.

And, one more important thing. Don't forget to study what the kids are doing. Watch them. Listen to them *(yes, actually listen to them – don't assume you know)*. They are the best Petri dish to discover and understand new technologies, new services, new ways to engage that are gaining traction with coveted young audiences. So, start a focus group program to formally inject this priority into your company's DNA. Or at least just spend some real time at the dinner table with your kids. They'll tell you what's happening out there. I certainly have learned a lot from my two teens *(who, I often joke, serve as a key part of my R&D team)*. And, you'll get closer to them by prioritizing that precious and fleeting family time (an important old school lesson amidst all the new school forces that increasingly rock our worlds). Remember what Brian Robbins' kids did for him? They led him to create AwesomenessTV, which he later sold for

$115 million less than three years later. What have your kids done for you lately?

LESSON/STRATEGY #8

Data matters, is incredibly valuable, and can be a game-changer for you. If you aren't extensively collecting and harnessing the full power of data right now and constantly investing in the latest Media 2.0 technology and services to do it, then you are leaving money on the table. Likely piles of it.

Data represents more than a mere Media 2.0 opportunity. It's an outright necessity that can yield immediate ROI. You will also likely be surprised by the enlightening information you see – critical data that was always available, but simply masked by preconceived traditional Media 1.0 notions. Internet and technology-driven market intelligence should inform your strategies, decisions and customer engagement like never before (and can also add a critical feedback loop).

For video creators and digital-first media companies, emulate Netflix and other leading Media 2.0 giants. Use data extensively to drive your content development and distribution strategies. That doesn't mean that you should use a soul-less "paint by numbers" approach to development of your Originals. No, that's not what Netflix does. Rather, Netflix, Amazon, Facebook, Snapchat and others smartly use data to inform certain elements of their development decisions (what genres, who directs, who stars). You know, just like traditional media uses box office metrics. After all, philosophically at least, are those two approaches really that different? One is simply much more precise than the other.

LESSON/STRATEGY #7

The Internet has made the world truly borderless and connected. Go global and partner! The opportunity to expand and monetize your reach is here and now. Seize it, and don't feel the need to go it alone.

Partner with like-minded international media companies and technology innovators to speed your path. Conduct a deep, thorough overall market and competitive landscape market assessment to identify the right ones. And then connect efficiently.

Aggressively and smartly pursue international opportunities to significantly expand your marketing, distribution and monetization possibilities. But, don't forget that successful international pursuit means recognition and respect for different, diverse cultures. That's why virtually all leading Media 2.0 players set up offices across the globe and seek out like-minded local partners. Global partners help navigate the complexities of operating in a foreign land, and also add critical localized content that speaks uniquely to that particular culture and language.

HOOQ, mentioned earlier, is one example, bringing SingTel, Sony Pictures Entertainment and Warner Bros. together to beat back Netflix in Southeast Asia. Netflix, on the other hand, initially failed to penetrate China on its own, because it failed to establish close partnerships with Chinese companies that know how to navigate that coveted territory's highly complex local systems. Netflix later saw the light and changed course. Two examples of two very different approaches and with two very different results.

LESSON/STRATEGY #6

New platforms demand new stories and new ways to tell those stories. Creators, know your distribution platform! Mobile has become the sin-

gle most important screen and universal connection point in our multi-platform Media 2.0 world.

Embrace this reality – and massive potential opportunity – and craft your strategies of engagement with mobile top of mind. That's why, as we saw earlier, NBCUniversal and WarnerMedia now smartly develop entirely new content for Snapchat's Shows service. That's why DirecTV Now features very different premium mobile-focused Originals than AT&T's millennial-focused fan-centric Otter Media child. And that's why traditionally formatted Warner Music Group music videos performed poorly on Snapchat's Discover at launch. Standard traditional music videos simply didn't make the cut.

As a corollary, media companies can and should use mobile-first Media 2.0 platforms like Snapchat and Instagram as "farm clubs" – entry points to migrate and better monetize a significant number of digital natives who otherwise may never be exposed to traditional programming. Experiment efficiently with new digital-first characters and stories, and then take core elements from the most successful ones to develop related expanded stories for more traditional highly monetizable platforms.

Remember Crypt TV? That's what I'm talking about. Take Wattpad as another example. A 15-year old's teen romantic comedy story on its platform, *The Kissing Booth,* graduated to the big leagues in the form of a Netflix original movie in 2018. Or, how about podcast company Gimlet? That ambitious young upstart created a "traditional" media arm (Gimlet Media) early 2018 to develop features and television based on its podcast franchises (one of which, *Alex, Inc.,* was featured on ABC). Highly visual, comics-driven multi-platform "motion book" start-up Madefire is another company worth watching. And, check out Yarn, an LA-based startup that creates bite-sized, mobile-friendly episodic text narratives for our 2-minute snackable moments throughout the day. Even text can be powerful here.

LESSON/STRATEGY #5

Media 2.0's multi-platform world gives creators, brands, and all voices new power to reach, engage and impact consumers. Seize on a holistic overall approach to your storytelling. Take core elements on a continuing unified journey across all planks.

This lesson is related to the previous one. Creators, start your journeys small and social (mobile). Extend them into more traditional platforms (television, movies). Continue that journey of engagement into perhaps less obvious platforms (offline into the real world of live entertainment that I discussed earlier in Chapter 26, or even into brave new worlds like VR and AR which I discuss in Chapters 22 and 23). And then, bring the journey back home to its initial mobile, social roots.

Otter Media's Crunchyroll is a good example here as we have seen earlier. Video content is just the first step to build overall brand loyalty and "love" that it can then take to (and monetize on) other platforms, including live events, retail merchandise, and now in games. And, then there's Disney and Amazon – the two most multi-platform Media 2.0 companies on the planet. Study what they are doing. Closely. And, be inspired by them.

LESSON/STRATEGY #4

All media is (or at least has the potential to be) social, particularly in our always-on mobile-first world. So, invest deeply in social. And remember, if your audience finds your content compelling, they will be your most effective marketing channel.

Make active social engagement, sharing and community central elements in your video marketing, distribution and monetization strategies. Empower your audience to do the heavy lifting for you. Thrill them with your content, make it easy for them to share it, and offer ways to gather around it and communicate directly with both the creators and with each other. Don't forget to add the live social streaming element to make it even more personal and instantly actionable. Don't worry. You don't need to do this alone.

Again, it all starts with people. Invest in them. Hire young, hungry social media mavens, agencies, and experienced advisors to craft your new positioning and execute an effective social media strategy that is fully integrated into your overall multi-platform marketing and engagement efforts. And, be authentic to your brand. Gotta be true to your voice. Audiences are savvy and getting savvier.

LESSON/STRATEGY #3

Media 2.0 is hyper-competitive and unforgiving. The playing field is incredibly crowded, and its frenetic pace will only accelerate. No company, not even today's market leaders, is immune to these forces (and certainly not invincible). Emphasize brand "fandom," focused execution, and multi-pronged monetization to break-out, drive success and optimize long-term viability amidst the market noise.

"Focus is your friend" in any business, and the Media 2.0 world is no different. Let's take the world of video. Rather than try to be all things to all people like Netflix, Amazon or Hulu, new video players should instead build a brand that targets specific passionate and frequently underserved so-called "niche" audiences (think of Crypt TV in the horror genre or Uproar for wildlife and conservation). If the newbie's content is compelling and its voice is authentic, those otherwise-neglected audiences may bite and spread the word. That's how most of the leading digital-first media companies discussed in Chapter 13 broke out.

Underserved "niche" audiences more actively seek out and engage with these more targeted brands (and the content they serve) and, therefore, more passionately support them. That leads to the magic ingredient of fandom, which drives deeper monetization possibilities. So, move your business model beyond pure-play or advertising-only "one-trick-pony" status. Fandom and the "brand love" it generates can diversify your risk and drive monetization across multiple revenue streams – extending into the world of subscriptions, licensing, merchandise, e-commerce and even live events.

LESSON/STRATEGY #2

History does repeat. New technologies have always disrupted the media and entertainment industry's status quo – television disrupting radio, the Betamax later threatening television and the movies (you know the drill). But the overall business of media and entertainment evolves and always comes out significantly stronger and more deeply engrained, albeit transformed.

Despite the significant pain felt by many to date as a result of our Media 2.0 revolution, the overall media and entertainment ecosystem's pie will grow. Massively.

Remember, the U.S. recorded music industry just enjoyed yet another period of double-digit growth at the hands of streaming. And, Goldman Sachs now forecasts the overall global music marketplace to balloon from $15.7 billion to $40 billion by 2030. Premium OTT video streaming services proliferate worldwide and DTC distribution points are "always open." That means ever-more opportunities to engage. And, as discussed throughout this book, we have only begun to leverage Media 2.0's transformational possibilities.

So, don't be blind to this history. Learn the language and heed the lessons of Media 2.0. Believe deeply that Media 2.0 will follow this path. Communicate your newly-transformed lexicon, confidence and overall priority across your teams to set the overall tone. I can't stress enough how critical it is to do this. Better to be positive than negative in any event, because you certainly won't stop this train. It's going with or without you. So, where do you want to be?

LESSON/STRATEGY #1

It is time for action! Not reaction. Don't reject the obvious forces around you – like a slow-down or steady decline in your traditional business, or increased competition that is cannibalizing your opportunities – simply for fear of not doing it right or disruption to your long-standing business model.

Financial projections not penciling out? Maybe your traditional assumptions just don't work in today's Media 2.0 world. Remember, no one has it all figured out. Few, if any, have defined the perfect business model.

But, you absolutely must be in the game – boldly! Experiment with new distribution models, marketing and monetization strategies. Iterate. Partner. Buy. Aggressively hire the right Media 2.0 executives and advisors to chart the course. Establish Media 2.0's new rules of the game. Don't be dictated by the rules of others. They're making them up too.

And, heed the cautionary tales and ghosts of Media 2.0 past – the Blockbusters, AOLs and Yahoo!'s of the world – that failed to internalize and act upon these lessons (especially this Lesson #1). Tremendous opportunities await, but you must put yourself out there and actively seize them.

Boldly. Tenaciously. Relentlessly.

FEARLESSLY!

That's what this book is all about.

EPILOGUE

A PERSONAL NOTE FOR OUR INCREASINGLY DIGITAL, VIRTUAL AGE

So, there you have it. Everything you need to know about Media 2.0, but have been afraid to ask. With your new found – or significantly expanded – wisdom, fear no more!

But first, indulge me one last time. Time for a bit of good old-fashioned self-reflection and soul ….

My family and I have watched the John Cusack movie *"High Fidelity"* several times *(I just did again last night, in fact)*. Classic movie for any music lover for many reasons – not the least of which is that it unleashed hilarious Jack Black into the world. In the film, Cusack plays the owner of a vintage record shop who is part slacker, part hopeless romantic, and part simply confused by life – but a 100 percent believer in the power of music and compelling content in general *(something I wholeheartedly share)*.

Cusack recounts the "Top 10" romantic breakups of his life, and essentially sets each one to music. He is an avid creator of mix tapes *(remember those?)* and agonizes over every single individual track he adds to create the most impactful and meaningful "whole." He literally caresses the vinyl and plucks out tracks he deems worthy to establish the perfect overall vibe of what he experienced in that particular moment in his life, and with that particular romantic entanglement.

And, that got me thinking about that old mix tape. I vividly recall those days when I too spent hours with my vinyl creating that perfect mix tape that was meaningful to me and hopefully someone else. So much effort was put into this process. So much thought. So much nurturing. You see, it wasn't easy to make them. You needed to manually select the right album, pull out the vinyl, select the right tracks, and place the needle down onto the vinyl on the perfect spot, meld track to track, fade them in and out to the next one, write the name of each track on the cassette's sleeve, and, then, ultimately *(and the crescendo to the entire process)* come up with the perfect title for that mix tape.

That perfect title was particularly critical if your mix tape was intended to be given to someone else, because the goal was to make an impact. This all was time-consuming both physically – and frequently emotionally. You sweat the details. Why? Because each individual mix tape mattered. You couldn't simply churn them out one after another. Volumes were low, as in number of personalized tapes – not in the sound itself, which you frequently cranked to a Spinal Tap-ian 11. But, the "love for the game" was high.

And, here's the thing. The person to whom you gave your beloved mix tape – be it a friend, or your girlfriend or boyfriend at the time – knew it. They knew how hard you worked to make that tape. They inherently understood all of the steps involved. All that care and feeding. And that's why it made such a deep impact on them. It was meaningful. And, that was the point.

Fast forward to today and to the Media 2.0 world that I love – and in which I have deeply immersed myself both professionally and personally *(hence, this book, which itself comes in two flavors – eBook for sure, but good old-fashioned print as well so that you can actually feel the pages and my mom can place it on her actual bookshelf).* Yes, digital gives us so much power. Yes, digital gives us so much access. So much discovery. So much control. Sometimes, maybe too much?

Think about today's digital music playlists that we share. Yes, of course, we frequently give them some thought. Perhaps many of you give some of them much thought. But, the amount of effort, the amount of expenditure of time, and the amount of care and feeding are entirely different. Digital is comparatively easy. We can simply find and select individual tracks in rapid fire and churn out playlist after playlist, and then share them not only individually, but also with the entire world with one swipe of our smart phone.

It is precisely that mass volume. That mass sharing. And, that physical ease and fractional time commitment that make each playlist less impactful. Less impactful to you as the playlist creator, and less impactful to any one person with whom you share it.

This "lost art of the playlist" serves as an allegory of life in a sense. Digital is incredibly powerful. Sharing your musical tastes with the world is cool, very cool, indeed. But, something also is left behind unless there is pause, reflection, and dedication to seeking out some kind of "soul" to augment that power. To disconnect. Get away from the virtual. To get into the "real" and feel – literally, *feel*, something tangible.

That's why vinyl is making a comeback. That's why Amoeba Records in Los Angeles and other remaining labor of love "mom and pop" record stores have staged a small, but growing, revival. According to last year's RIAA mid-year report, vinyl continued its upward trajectory in 2018, now comprising 10% of total U.S. music sales – its highest market share since the mid-1980's when CDs began to take over. Something special and impactful happens when you actually dive into those stacks of vinyl records and sift through them. Time almost stands still. Hours go by. I've seen it with my own teen kids. They feel at home with that vinyl. At peace *(as metaphysical as that sounds)*. My daughter, now at USC and majoring in the music industry *(surprise, surprise)*, regularly finds solace and inspiration at Amoeba.

To be clear, this is not an indictment of digital. Not at all. Digital's power is real. Digital's opportunities are massive. I respect it. Generally love it *(in fact, I am streaming music as I write this)*.

But, for me, and for my "experiences," digital is frequently just the beginning. The introduction. My experiences need to be augmented with more. With effort. With dedication. With "soul." Taken outside into the physical world. With real *non*-virtual human connection and interaction. It takes a lot of work and commitment to prepare for, attend, and endure a music festival. But, boy is it worth it! My family and I will never forget our day-long journey literally across Iceland's frozen tundra to experience a DJ spinning deep down inside a glacier as part of 2016's "Secret Solstice" festival. Those kinds of experiences last a lifetime. And my family is so much closer because of them.

And, for me, that's what "It" is all ultimately about.

Vinyl and mix tapes represent that same kind of dedication. That's why you gotta watch *(re-watch?) High Fidelity*. Be inspired by it. Finding it certainly won't be difficult in our Media 2.0 world, that's for sure. You can stream it on demand right now from any one of your favorite OTT services and on any one of your multiple devices.

"And one more thing!," I say in an obvious Media 2.0 homage to Mr. Jobs. Go outside and watch the sunset tonight.

The real thing far surpasses the digital version that your friend just posted on Facebook last night.

Appendix
Media 2.0 Law School
(News You Can Use)

THIS Appendix identifies and analyzes important issues that surround two topics of great importance to many, if not most, Media 2.0 creators, entrepreneurs and companies: (1) music (the soundtrack to most every Media 2.0 project); and (2) financing (the green stuff needed to fund all creation).

Here, I enlist the minds of two leading lawyers. They offer their unique expertise and insights to you *pro bono*. No hourly billing here. Just buy them a drink next time you see them.

APPENDIX 1
CREATORS – "MUST KNOW" LEGAL ISSUES WHEN USING MUSIC

BY JORDAN BROMLEY, PARTNER, MANATT PHELPS & PHILLIPS

So, you want to add music to your videos, games, immersive experiences or other works? How do you properly "clear" it? Many don't understand that there is no "safe harbor" for use of music in a video or any other work. No matter how short, no matter how limited the views, no matter how you credit the creators, if you use music and you don't clear it, you are an infringer. Bottom line – this is something you must do.

Here are some tips to do things right.

(1) THERE ARE TWO "SIDES" TO EVERY SONG – THE MUSICAL COMPOSITION AND THE MASTER RECORDING.

Think of the composition as the sheet music, the song that you sing. Think of the master as the recording of that song. The composition is eternal, and the master is the recorded moment where you perform that eternal work. You must "clear" both.

(2) The relevant clearance is called a "synchronization license" ("synch license" for short) since you are synchronizing the audio to the video.

Boiled down, you need a synchronization license from both the composition owner(s) and the master owner(s), each of which can be several people if more than one collaborated in writing the composition or own the master. Generally speaking, however, there is normally one person or entity that owns or controls the master. And, you must get these before you share your video, game, immersive experience, or any other audiovisual work with the world. It doesn't matter if you're making money or not, and it doesn't matter how little of the composition and master you use. If you use any recognizable part of the composition or master recording, don't take the risk. Clear it.

If a song is popular, you can bet that companies control each "side." Music publishers control the musical composition, and record labels generally control the master recording. Not to belabor the issue, but even if the writer or recording artist says they are okay with your use, you still need an official clearance from each of the relevant company stakeholders. Seasoned clearance companies first issue a quote for any proposed use, and then require longer form license agreements once there is actual use.

In an interesting related side-note, Facebook faced a significant dilemma when it launched its new "Watch" video service in summer 2017. Watch included a massive number of UGC videos that incorporated music without the necessary clearances. Because Facebook had not yet developed a YouTube-like Content ID-like system, Facebook was reported to have offered the major record labels "hundreds of millions of dollars" so that they wouldn't need to take-down those infringing videos – and to enable Facebook users to upload their frequently music-infringing UGC content on a going-forward basis.

(3) Become familiar with the concept of "Most Favored Nations" (or "MFN" for short).

MFN clauses in license agreements are a way for the various music owners to make sure no owner is earning more on the license than any other owner. They are also a way to legally "game" the clearance system. If you can find one sympathetic owner to grant a less expensive or "gratis" license, you can then try to use that friendly agreement to get all other owners to play nice on an MFN basis with the first licensor. As you can imagine, this requires great finesse and knowledge of the major publishers and labels that own a majority of the world's musical content.

(4) You don't need a license from every co-owner of the composition or master.

A more complicated way exists to get around a stubborn songwriter, publisher or record label in the rare instances that involve co-owned masters. Put simply, under the real property concept of joint tenancy, one owner can grant a non-exclusive license for 100 percent of the work, provided that the other owners are paid their respective portion of the income made from the license. Of course, the co-owner needs to know of, and approve, the fact that they are clearing 100 percent of the work.

But, note that this is a particularly hot-button issue with songwriters right now. Without getting too granular, the largest performance rights organizations in the U.S. *(more on these below)* are fighting with the U.S. Department of Justice over whether they must issue 100 percent licenses, rather than the previous standard of licensing only individual shares. Long story short, if you attempt to use the strategy discussed above, you may run into more roadblocks at this point based on the current state of affairs.

(5) DON'T FORGET ABOUT PUBLIC PERFORMANCE LICENSES!

If you're exhibiting your music-laden video or other work on your own website, you need to obtain a public performance license in addition to the synch license. This separate license gives you the right to play the music in a public venue (which, in this case, is your public-facing website). Public performance licenses are generally issued by performance rights organizations ("PROs"). ASCAP and BMI are the two largest PROs and are bound by a consent decree with the Department of Justice, which means they must grant you this type of license if you request it – even if you disagree on the relevant fee.

What happens if you never agree on a fee? The dispute then goes to what is called "rate court" and a judge decides for you. Note that this comes with significant legal costs.

(6) CONSULT AN EXPERT.

If you're serious about your project, it makes sense to spend a little money to talk to an expert in this field. There are many clearance companies who can help you clear music in your video, game, immersive project or other work for reasonable flat fees. Look into it and hire one. At the very least, it will save you countless hours of figuring out who to contact and what to say.

Music rights are incredibly complex and messy. You don't want to run into costly legal issues – or, even worse, an order to "cease and desist" – once your video or other creation starts to gain traction.

Do the right thing now.

Appendix 2
Media 2.0 Investment and M&A (Key Issues to Consider from Both Sides of the Table)

by Greg Akselrud,
Partner, Stubbs Alderton & Markiles
and SAM CREATV Ventures

THROUGHOUT this book, Peter identifies strategic investment and M&A as being two weapons in Media 2.0's "fearless" arsenal that companies frequently use to take bold transformational action in order to achieve game-changing and game-winning results.

That kind of strategic activity frequently is based in L.A. And with the accelerating pace of that kind of strategic and venture capital investment – and with a similarly accelerating number of Media 2.0-related M&A exits that include mega-deals AT&T/Time Warner ($85 billion), Apple/Beats ($3 billion), Facebook/Oculus ($2 billion), and Disney/Maker Studios ($675 million) – we thought it was time to consider those deal-related issues.

Ladies and gentlemen, it's time for "news you can use," deal edition!

I. Investments – Justifying Value

In the ever-changing landscape that is Media 2.0, media and technology companies and investors continue to endlessly debate and negotiate value and valuations – how much is a company "worth." For investors, the formerly frothy investment bubbles have come and gone and fewer unicorns can be found. They thus push for the lowest valuation possible in order to get a larger stake in the company. Founders, on the other hand, of course negotiate for the highest valuation possible – to preserve control, limit dilution and set a baseline value for their idea. The question always arises – how do you justify value?

Without revenue, cash flow or EBITDA *(a widely-used acronym-ian measure of profitability that stands for "earnings before interest taxes depreciation and amortization")* – and many times without projections or even a revenue generating business model – value cannot be calculated based on numbers alone. Accordingly, the key characteristics that justify value end up being: (i) the strength of the management team; (ii) the disruptive nature of the company's business; (iii) market comparables (if they exist); and (iv) investor demand and scarcity. The more experienced the team (having one or more significant exits), the more disruptive the technology, the higher the valuations of other related or comparable market participants, and the more investors desire to invest and feel that they may lose out – the higher the valuation. Conversely, an inexperienced team with little investor demand, even in a strong environment for market participants, will end up with a lower valuation.

Take for example the anonymous messaging app "Whisper." In 2014, the company had drawn comparisons to Snapchat, Yik Yak, and other fast-growing communications apps. As a result, it drew a $200-million valuation and more than $60 million in funding, including from prominent Silicon Valley venture capital firms Sequoia, Lightspeed Venture Partners, and Shasta Ventures. Whisper was able to justify its lofty valuation based on, among other things, the extraordinary value of other key market participants, a then-growing trend in anonymous messaging, and the experience of at least one of its founders, Brad Brooks (who serves as the Chairman of Whisper and the CEO of TigerText). However, in 2017, even with

30 million monthly unnamed users, Whisper authorized a financing at a value that was flat to its earlier 2014 round – demonstrating the changing market landscape and confidence in Whisper's execution.

No matter what, I always advise my company clients that it is better to have a majority of "something" versus 100% of "nothing," which is to say – negotiate the valuation as best you can and stand firm to your vision and perception of value. But at the end of the day, take the best deal you can and give your business a chance to succeed, without over-worrying about how much extra dilution it will cost you.

II. Investments from Strategics

When looking for potential investors, companies tend to always seek out the usual suspects – friends and family, accelerators, angel investors, and venture capital firms. One target group that is often ignored is strategic investors. Strategic investors are typically larger participants in the target market that, in many cases, operate investment arms that look to make strategic investments in companies. While founders frequently consider these market participants for potential revenue-generating deals like co-marketing, co-branding and distribution – all of which are great – they many times ignore the fact that these strategics may often be in a position to offer so much more via direct investment.

While revenue-generating deals can add significant strategic value as well, they may not actually generate the revenue needed for the company to grow (at least in the short term). That makes the need for investment just as critical, whether from the strategic investor or someone else. Some great examples of strategic investment include Tencent's investment and ultimate acquisition of Riot Games, HTC's original investment in Beats Electronics, ITV's investment in New Form Digital, and WPP's investment in 88 Rising (a company in which my fund SAM CREATV Ventures is also an investor).

A. Advantages

In many cases, strategic investors add significantly more value over traditional investors, so long as founders are able to capture some of that value through typical business arrangements – distribution, marketing, and revenue-generation. The value is obvious. First, having a big name strategic investor on the capitalization table (the document that identifies all company shareholders) provides validation for your company/business/idea. It demonstrates to the broader market that this strategic investor has done its due diligence and believes there is adequate value in your company to invest its own money.

Operationally, strategic investors are in most cases larger, well-capitalized, multi-national companies that are able to bring resources to the early stage company (office space, headcount, legal and business affairs, tax planning, etc.). Strategics also are generally able to facilitate broader marketing initiatives and drive more significant distribution and revenue due to platforms and market access that early stage start-ups can't match with their own resources. In fact, in many territories outside the United States, it is extraordinarily difficult to enter a market without a local partner. In those markets, a strategic investor can help open doors, initiating international market expansion that would have been otherwise unachievable or at a minimum, cost prohibitive.

B. Disadvantages

With all of these advantages, there are of course disadvantages. Strategic investors willing to invest in an early stage company want something too. They see the value that the founders have created and want to take advantage. The "asks" by a strategic investor will always vary, but they will most times relate to the following: (i) preemptive rights to invest (essentially the right to invest more and, therefore, increase their ownership percentage in the company before others); (ii) exclusive distribution or advertising rights, or at a minimum, a "first look" or other right of first negotiation on distribution and advertising; and (iii) in some cases, the right of first negotiation to buy the whole company. All of these items are disadvantages because they limit the company's later strategic alternatives.

So, even if it may make sense to involve a big name venture capital fund in a later financing, a strategic investor's preemptive right to invest could eliminate that opportunity. Similarly, the strategic investor may not have the best distribution platform in Latin America, for example. But, if that strategic has an exclusive right to distribute internationally, then the company is stuck with that option. In some cases, even the very existence of a strategic investor on the company's capitalization table is a disadvantage, because it either prohibits the strategic investor's competitors from investing or doing business with the company, or scares off those competitors that may believe a nemesis has already poisoned the well.

In most cases, however, the advantages of having a strategic investor far outweigh the disadvantages, especially if a related commercial business deal is structured to consider and give more flexibility to the company's later-stage strategic alternatives.

As such, it makes a lot of sense for founders to look for these types of investors.

III. CONVERTIBLE SECURITIES – SAFES VS. CONVERTIBLE NOTES

The collective use of convertible securities (or "SAFEs" – simple agreement for future equity) and convertible promissory notes has grown in the early stage start-up investment market, and in some cases, in later investment rounds as well. In many cases, these instruments make sense for both companies and investors. They allow the company to accept investment capital without having to determine and agree upon its current valuation, and they give investors a benefit for making an early investment – essentially a conversion right into the next preferred equity financing at a discounted valuation or a fixed rate of return on a "change of control" (most typically, a company sale). The key difference between these two kinds of structured investments is downside protection. Convertible securities (SAFEs) have no downside protection for the investor, while convertible notes, being traditional debt instruments, do.

A. BENEFITS OF BOTH STRUCTURES

Several important benefits flow from these structures. First, they are much less complicated than a preferred stock financing, while still providing some benefit to the early investor over a straight common stock investment. A preferred equity financing involves adopting an entirely new class of preferred stock, thinking about what rights it should have, and signing 1-4 additional agreements depending on the complexity and sophistication of the round. All of that takes time and incurs legal cost – both of which the company simply may not have.

Second, from a business perspective, the company and investors in many cases either don't know what the valuation for the company should be at the time of investment, or cannot agree on that valuation. In both cases, the parties may still want to get the deal done because they understand that the company may need the money immediately. So these types of structures provide that necessary stop-gap between a basic common stock financing and a more complicated preferred stock financing.

B. COMMON FEATURES

So what do these investment structures have in common? They both provide a structure for an investor to invest now, with the right to receive some benefit in the future – either in the next preferred equity round of financing or in a change of control, whichever comes first.

For the next investment round, these structures typically provide a mandatory conversion provision that requires the principal amount invested in the SAFE or convertible note and interest (if any) to convert into the shares issued in the company's next preferred equity financing (sometimes preferred and common stock) at a discount to the next round, typically between 10-30%.

So as a basic example, (1) if an investor invests $100,000 in the SAFE or convertible note and (2) the discount provided in the SAFE or convertible note is 20% and (3) the next round's preferred equity is being sold at $1.00 per share, then (4) the investor's $100,000 investment would convert into the preferred shares being issued in the next round at a price per share of $0.80. In effect, the investor gets more shares in the preferred equity round as a benefit for having made the earlier investment.

The discount presents itself in mainly two ways – either as a straight discount as described above, or in the form of a "valuation cap" which states that the SAFE or convertible note will not convert at a price per share that is higher than the price per share inferred by that valuation cap (i.e., an agreed maximum valuation for the company divided by the number of shares outstanding immediately prior to the financing). If that number is lower than the price per share derived by the straight discount in the example above, then the investor would be entitled to that lower price per share. This mandatory conversion provision is only triggered if the company raises some minimum amount of money in the next preferred investment round, and that minimum is typically agreed by the company and the investor in advance.

In a change of control, both structures typically provide that the investment amount can convert prior to the change of control at some baseline valuation (usually the valuation cap) or, at the option of the investor, that investor can choose to be repaid some minimum amount which is often 2X the amount invested.

C. KEY DIFFERENCES

The differences between these two structures are straightforward. While the convertible note is a basic debt instrument that accrues interest and requires repayment at an agreed maturity date, a SAFE is a piece of paper, literally. SAFE documents typically do not incur interest and do not contain a maturity date. So, if a company never raises the next preferred equity financing and if there never is a change of control, then the investor in the SAFE will not receive anything and will remain stuck in its SAFE investment indefinitely. While in most cases that result means the company failed, it could also mean that the company had become moderately successful – never having to take in additional investment – but also not worthy of an acquisition.

On the other hand, convertible notes accrue interest and must be repaid at some point. That obligation to repay essentially keeps founders' "feet to the fire," requiring them to find alternatives to raise capital, seek a change of control, or potentially simply just repay the convertible notes.

Companies typically prefer SAFEs/convertible securities, and investors typically prefer convertible notes. But, both structures provide a great path to accomplish a financing.

IV. M&A – Bridging the Valuation Gap With an Earnout

In M&A transactions, like in equity investment transactions, there is always negotiation on valuation. The seller company, like the company in an investment transaction, wants the highest valuation possible. On the other hand, the buyer/acquirer, like the investor in an investment transaction, wants the lowest valuation possible – to either purchase the selling company for less or to hold a larger stake. While transactions can take many forms (a merger, sale of assets or sale of stock) and can involve different forms of consideration (cash, debt or equity), the underlying valuation is always the most important part of the negotiation.

A. Valuation Models

M&A participants use different valuation models to arrive at a mutually agreed valuation. Valuation models include: (i) multiples of EBITDA; (ii) multiples of revenues; and (iii) an analysis of discounted cash flow (i.e., the present value of future cash flow). In some cases where a target seller has not yet achieved revenues or EBITDA – or where preparing accurate projections may be difficult – buyers and sellers do the same thing as companies and investors in investment transactions. They look at the target seller's most important performance metrics (like number of users, market leadership, strength of the management team, etc.), as well as comparable transactions in the market and relative buyer demand.

In entertainment and digital media, typical multiples for production companies and other market participants are generally in the range of 4-8X EBITDA, while revenue multiples vary significantly between as much as 2X and 10X (and sometimes even greater). All of these multiples are unfortunately not formulaic and depend on a host of other factors. For example, a company that mostly offers services that are dependent upon the services of a few individuals may yield a lower valuation multiple than a company that manages a robust technology platform or library of content or other intellectual property.

B. EARNOUT DEFINED

In order to bridge the gap between the valuation desired by a seller and the price that the buyer is willing to pay, buyers and sellers frequently structure what is commonly called an "earnout." An earnout is essentially a contingent part of the purchase price in an M&A transaction and is only paid out if certain performance milestones are achieved. In plain terms, the buyer is essentially saying to the seller, "*You say your business is worth X and I think it is worth Y, but if the business performs over the next 1-3 years and hits various agreed milestones, I am willing to agree with you and pay X, and if not, I am only willing to pay Y.*"

Typical milestones for earnouts include the achievement of EBITDA thresholds, revenue thresholds, end user thresholds, product deliveries and sometimes just plain passage of time.

C. STRUCTURING TIPS

Because earnouts have a high probability of leading to future disputes, it's important to structure them in a way that best achieves relative certainty for both parties. For sellers, it's important that they retain adequate control of the post-closing operations and are employed and empowered by the buyer in order to have the best chance at achieving their earnout milestones. If they are not employed by the buyer – or even if they are employed but don't have adequate control of the post-closing operations – sellers will have a very difficult time ensuring that the earnout is achieved.

For both parties, it is important that the earnout thresholds are objective – easily determinable by a calculation or observation that can be made by a neutral third party. Introducing any subjectivity only leads to disputes. Of course, extremes also exist. I have seen cases where the buyer's leverage is so strong that the seller's earnout is structured such that its achievement (or failure) was to be determined by the buyer's board of directors in "good faith." Without a dispute resolution mechanism in place, that kind of earnout was essentially left to the discretion of the buyer – which meant that it was potentially completely meaningless.

Earnouts form an important part of the purchase price in an M&A transaction when bridging a valuation gap is not otherwise possible, but ultimately must be structured properly to avoid dispute and capture the value intended to be achieved by both parties.

V. QUICK TIPS

Here are some "quick tips" related to a few other key deal-related topics that literally could warrant their own chapters.

A. INVESTMENTS IN LLCS

Many investments in digital media and entertainment – and even some in technology – are structured through investments in limited liability companies (or "LLCs"). While technology investments have become formulaic (either following typical convertible security or convertible note terms, or following the NVCA [National Venture Capital Association] form of investment documents), investments in LLCs are the opposite. There are no model forms or industry accepted practices for LLCs. While some general issues have become somewhat customary, overall there is no governing model set of documents.

Because of this dynamic in LLC investments, it's important for companies and investors to make sure to cover all aspects of the investment relationship in the Limited Liability Company Agreement (or Operating Agreement). This kind of agreement governs the entirety of the parties' relationship. These documents can be very simple, or they can be extraordinarily complicated – reaching in excess of 100 pages! What's important is that the parties cover a number of critical areas in order to avoid later dispute. These include: (i) management (how the company will be managed and whether there will be any minority approvals); (ii) contribution requirements; (iii) operational matters; (iv) distributions; (v) transfer restrictions (including rights of first refusal, tag-along rights, and drag-along rights … *don't worry about those last two yet*); (vi) buy-sell arrangements in the event the parties desire to exit the relationship; and (vii) what happens in case of liquidation.

B. LIMITATIONS OF LIABILITY IN M&A

In M&A transactions, as in investment deals, the selling company (like the company seeking investment) gives representations and warranties about its business. This is the traditional way in which buyers and sellers allocate risks relating to the seller's business as it stands on the date of closing. A basic representation regarding a party's intellectual property may say, for example, that none of the seller's intellectual property ("IP") infringes the IP of any third party. Another example of this same kind of representation may instead say that *"to the seller's knowledge,"* none of the seller's IP infringes the IP rights of others. In the first example, the seller bares all of the risk in the event that its IP actually infringes the IP of a third party on the date of closing. In the second example, the seller only bares that risk if it actually knows of any such infringement and fails to disclose it to the buyer (which failure in and of itself could be viewed as fraud in addition to a breach of a representation and warranty!).

What happens in these representations and warranties is that the seller and the buyer negotiate them until they are both happy – or both mutually unhappy – and the result ends up shifting risk to one or the other.

The way in which parties limit their overall liability for breaches of representations and warranties is by adopting a standard set of provisions that typically limit the time period after closing for parties to bring a claim for breach, and by also adopting "baskets," "mini-baskets" and "caps." I will cover those briefly here:

"**Survival**" – Survival provisions for representations and warranties provide that those provisions will survive for a certain exact period of time and, after that time, no claims can be made for breaches of those representations and warranties. Typical time periods for survival of most representations and warranties are 1-2 years, with the exception of certain so-called "fundamental" representations and warranties like "due authorization," "good title to assets," "capitalization" and representations relating to taxes, all of which typically survive until the expiration of the applicable statute of limitations.

"**Baskets**" – Baskets act as a baseline of minimum damages that a buyer must first incur before they can bring claims against the seller for breaches of representations and warranties. Baskets can be structured as a "tipping basket," which means that if a buyer experiences damages exceeding some threshold amount, it can come back and bring claims against the seller all the way back to the first dollar of damages. Baskets can also be structured as a "deductible," which acts exactly like it sounds and is commonly understood in insurance terms. This kind of deductible means that if a buyer experiences damages exceeding some threshold amount, it can only bring claims against the seller for those damages they incur in excess of that threshold amount. A tipping basket is commonly understood to be more favorable to a buyer as compared to a deductible basket.

"Mini-Baskets" – Mini-baskets are used to determine what level of damages should be counted to apply against the overall basket. For example, if a mini-basket in a transaction is $1,000, then all damages for breaches of representations and warranties that are less than $1,000 would not apply toward the basket. Mini-baskets are often used in combination with tipping baskets so as to discourage a buyer from "loading" the basket with smaller items in order to trigger its tipping point back to the first dollar of damages.

"Caps" – Caps are used to apply an overall limitation of liability for any breaches of general representations and warranties, as opposed to "fundamental" representations and warranties mentioned earlier. While buyers and sellers understand that the seller must stand behind its representations and warranties, they acknowledge that the buyer still has purchased and will benefit from the overall business and, accordingly, it is appropriate to limit the seller's liability for breaches of most representations and warranties. Typical caps for indemnification are 15% or less of the total purchase price – with the median cap size over the last several years being 10%.

From a seller's perspective, a "cap" may sometimes be understood as being a purchase price reduction. You can bet that many buyers will do whatever they can, post-closing, to uncover as many seller liabilities that they can in order to reach that cap.

Just another dose of reality for the already-complex M&A game.

ABOUT THE AUTHOR

PETER Csathy is Founder & Chairman of CREATV Media, a leading media, entertainment and technology-focused business development, advisory and investment firm. Peter is a noted industry expert, futurist and "go to" resource. He is regularly featured on television and in *The Wall Street Journal, Los Angeles Times, The New York Times, TechCrunch, Variety, The Hollywood Reporter, CNBC, Bloomberg, Billboard, Digiday*, among others, and regularly speaks at major industry events. Peter is also a critically-acclaimed author, and has previously published two bestselling books, *Media 2.0 (18)* and *Media 2.0 (17). Fearless Media* is his third.

Peter's career spans both traditional and new media. He has led three media and technology companies that achieved successful exits (including music pioneer Musicmatch and video pioneer SightSpeed), and served as a senior executive and dealmaker at Universal Studios and New Line Cinema. A graduate of the Harvard Law School, Peter started his career as an entertainment attorney, representing clients that included N.W.A. and Madonna. Over the course of his career, he has structured and negotiated strategic partnerships, M&A, and joint ventures valued in excess of $3 billion. He is also a founding partner of SAM CREATV Ventures, a seed/early stage venture fund focused on innovative media and tech companies.

He works and lives with his family in Southern California, was born and raised in Minnesota, and apologizes for the Vikings constantly.

Printed in Great Britain
by Amazon